*Expanding Horizons
in Medical Social Work*

Expanding Horizons
in Medical Social Work

DORA GOLDSTINE

THE UNIVERSITY OF CHICAGO PRESS
Chicago & London

Library of Congress Catalog Number: 54–11423

THE UNIVERSITY OF CHICAGO PRESS, CHICAGO 60637
University of Chicago Press, Ltd., London, W.C. 1

5 / 20 / 76 ℳℴℴ𝓁ℯ 𝓉 𝒯𝓇𝒷𝓇 9. 80

Foreword

THIS volume completes the compilation of readings from the literature of medical social work, the purpose of which was to present articles illustrative of the full range of activities characteristic of practice in this field. It should be read in conjunction with the earlier volume,[1] which concentrates on the primary responsibility of medical social work to assist patients and their families with those social, environmental, economic, or psychological needs which may affect their ability to adjust to illness or their optimum use of medical care.

From this basic service medical social practice has expanded to include other activities less directly concerned with patient care but of fundamental importance in their effect on the functioning of medical and health programs. This volume presents articles illustrative of these additional areas of responsibility, as they relate to (1) the administration of medical social services within various medical and health agencies; (2) participation in community organization or planning; (3) contributing to professional education, both of social workers and of related professions; and (4) research.

In the literature of medical social work, as has already been noted,[2] major attention has been given to describing and analyzing services to individuals—an emphasis reflected both in the extent and in the depth of the writing devoted to this primary use of medical social service. Literature illustrative of the other areas of activity which engage the efforts of medical social workers is less extensive and also less fully developed in its analysis of the principles or concepts underlying the medical social worker's role. In selecting from such writings, one is guided, therefore, not only by such criteria as the interest and usefulness

---

1. *Readings in the Theory and Practice of Medical Social Work*, ed. Dora Goldstine (Chicago: University of Chicago Press, 1954).
2. Dora Goldstine, "The Literature of Medical Social Work: Review and Evaluation," *ibid.*, pp. 4–23.

of a particular article but, more significantly perhaps, by the expression of ideas provocative of further exploration and analysis or by the emergence of new ways of functioning, suggestive of trends for the future. It is from this standpoint that the articles in this volume should be read. Not only do they round out the picture of current medical social practice, but, more importantly, they exemplify developments whose significance for future practice is yet to be assessed.

Fortunately for the objective of better service to patients, neither practice nor the writings which describe it remain static. Even while the articles assembled for these two volumes were being selected, the horizons of both medicine and social work were continuing to expand; and recent literature reflects particularly a growing interest in analyzing the nature of the social worker's contribution to interdisciplinary teaching and interdisciplinary research, as well as to the services in which medicine and social work collaborate. The profound changes in medical education, including preparation for both clinical practice and the public health services, suggest that the view of "social medicine" is broadening to encompass areas of community life and responsibility that extend far beyond the immediate concerns of the individual and his family. The sights are widening also to include prevention as well as cure in many programs of health and medical care; and the results of new or modified methods of service in relation to a particular disease or a particular segment of the population can be studied for their fundamental applicability to other diseases or other groups. The articles selected here to sketch one or another aspect of these developments serve only momentarily to bound the expanding horizon. From their stimulus and from the growth and change always characteristic of services concerned with human life may emerge the substance of the future they foreshadow.

DORA GOLDSTINE

CHICAGO, ILLINOIS

Table of Contents

vii

SECTION II. THE PARTICIPATION OF MEDICAL SOCIAL WORKERS IN PROFESSIONAL EDUCATION

1. OF SOCIAL WORKERS

2. OF OTHER PROFESSIONAL WORKERS

APPENDIX

INDEXES

The Contributions of Medical Social Work to Medical Care

1. In Hospitals

The Medical Social Worker Sees
the Human Being First[1]

BY SIGMUND L. FRIEDMAN, M.D.

In the sufferer, let me see only the human being.—From the "Physician's Prayer," frequently ascribed to MAIMONIDES.

A GROUP of department heads had finished dinner and, over coffee and cigarets, was discussing hospital problems in general. One commented that some hospitals have, in addition to the customary meetings of department heads, a small committee composed of administrators and select department heads before which are brought questions of basic policy.

The next obvious question was asked immediately: "Of which department heads should such a committee be composed?" The list was accordingly drawn up: physician-in-chief, surgeon-in-chief, superintendent of nurses, director of social service, administrator of the outpatient department, and comptroller. The administration was to be represented by the director and his assistants.

The significant points to this story are the assumptions, implicit in the inclusion of the social service department on the list, that it is more than merely another department in the hospital, that the contribution which it can make to the formulation of major hospital policies is unique, and that its point of

1. Reprinted from *Modern Hospital*, May, 1947, with the permission of the Modern Hospital Publishing Co., Inc.

3

view must be considered before many major problems are decided on.

Important and interesting as are this attitude, these assumptions, and the conclusion so naturally drawn, they are no less interesting and no more significant than is the attitude of the physicians.

Until recently, physicians have only slightly, if at all, concerned themselves with medical social work, and, unfortunately, many still do not. This attitude was the result of many forces, only two of which were the prevalent fashion in medical practice and treatment and the state of medical social work itself before it became a profession and when it was still in the old-clothes business.

The fashion in medical practice about the turn of the present century divided the physicians into two opposing groups: the "clinicians" and the "laboratory men." It was not long before the "laboratory men" reigned supreme. The reasons for their victory were good, the results not so good, for the patient was divided and subdivided until he became like a bag in which the organs were separate not only from everything outside the body but also from one another.

These organs were not seen to belong to a patient with a past —and memories of that past—with a present, and a future based on the past and present. They were not seen as affected by domestic anxiety, by wars and the rumors of wars and stories of horrible mass destruction, by restless living, by a passion for the acquisition of wealth or by the lack of money, and by numerous modern industrial methods, with their tensions, monotony, and fatigue.

Disease meant a disease of an organ, not disease of a patient. This isolation of disease from the patient was purely a device of the intellect. The etiology, diagnosis, prognosis, and therapy became an abstraction.

This fashion has begun to change with increasing recognition that man's social environment affects his mental and physical health and well-being and that it will either produce disease of itself or alter other diseases. Many physicians now realize, and stress, the social aspect to almost every patient's every illness and its treatment. These are, of course, not new ideas, but old ones; but they became of the utmost consequence because of the emphasis now being placed on them.

Coincidentally with the realization of the importance of the patient's social milieu by a few physicians about forty years ago and antedating the new fashion, there came the demand for information about it and an insistence that something be done when necessary and when possible. The development of the modern social service department was an inevitable result.

However, the physicians have gone far since those early days. They have created departments of social medicine in a few medical schools. In others they are reorganizing or are planning to reorganize their entire teaching program so as to present disease as it is, not as a simple flat-surfaced picture, or as an intricately woven tapestry, but as something highly complex with almost innumerable facets. These extensive changes are being made lest this outlook on human disease, on human relations, and on the social environment of the human being prove sterile.

These changes are being made now in medical schools; they will be made very soon in university hospitals. But all hospitals are teaching institutions, formally or informally, by plan or by accident. All hospitals will, sooner or later, be affected by this "new" approach. For the hospital is a better medium than are the medical schools in which to teach the reciprocal relationships between social factors and the prevention, production, or aggravation of disease, on the one hand, and, on the other, the promotion of mental and physical health.

The creation of departments of social medicine in the medical schools and the possible formation of analogous departments in the hospital will not, however, replace the social service departments as they now exist. Rather will the latter enlarge in size, increase in importance, and, almost undoubtedly, undergo some change.

The social service department, like other living organisms, is always undergoing evolutionary changes. It has been by such a process that the social worker has been transformed in some hospitals from the assistant into the partner and even the teacher of the physician in the treatment of the patient in so far as his social and environmental aspects are concerned.

No longer should the physician tell the social worker, as he still does in some hospitals, that "the duodenal ulcer in the third bed on the left in the large ward—you know the one that's been in a couple of times in the last three years—says he can't go home tomorrow, and we need his bed badly. Find somewhere he can go for a while, will you? Thanks!"

Rather should he present the worker with the medical data (including diagnosis and prognosis for the immediate and ultimate future) necessary to give her a full picture of that side of the patient's illness, with such social information as he has (size of family, economic status and economic problems, living conditions, domestic difficulties, and emotional problems) and a statement of the specific problem in treatment which he faces.

In the hospital this information can be obtained by the house officer as a part of the routine history. The social worker, of course, seeks additional information, some of which she can extract from the physician, some of which she can obtain from other social agencies, but most of which she can get only from the patient and his family only after interviews and/or home visits.

Together, the physician and the social worker discuss the patient: his illness, the causative and aggravating factors in his environment at home and at work, the methods of alleviating that illness (medical, surgical, social; and it not infrequently happens that the medical and surgical plans are dependent upon social factors which may very well have been unknown to the doctor before the social worker entered on the scene).

Together, they plan for his immediate aftercare (chronic disease hospital, convalescent home, care at home—and here the social worker demonstrates her detailed knowledge of the community's resources) and for his subsequent care (return to follow-up clinic, transfer to outpatient department, transfer to home care, return to private physician).

Together, the physician and social worker discuss the plans

for the future with the patient, not going over the same ground repeatedly but approaching the discussion each from his own specialized point of view and each complementing the other.

Both attempt to teach the patient to adjust to his illness and environment, if that environment has been a factor in his illness and cannot be significantly altered. Both attempt to relieve him of his anxieties and fears. Both have thus helped the patient make plans for his medical and social rehabilitation.

Sometimes it happens that a patient cannot return to his former place in society because his illness precludes return to his former job. Vocational rehabilitation is then necessary, and, once again, the social worker is called on for her knowledge of, and her ability to summon, the available resources.

Parenthetically, the degree to which the social service department participates in and helps effectuate such a plan may be used as one index of its efficacy. Similarly, the ability, frequency, and wholeheartedness with which a medical service initiates and cooperates in such a plan are evidences of its realization that physicians must do more than merely attempt to prevent and cure illness, that they must exert every effort to maintain men as useful members of society and, when illness strikes, to return them early to their full usefulness.

But what constitutes "social information" is not part of the innate equipment of the house officer; he must be taught what it is and how important it is if he is to assess accurately the medical problem of his patient and wisely plan treatment. Until recently, few medical schools have done this. And most of these few have concerned themselves with the problem to the extent of leaving it almost wholly to the teachers on the hospital wards. In turn, these either have neglected it completely, as they have their social service departments, or have called on the medical social workers. The workers, by teaching medical students in more or less formal sessions, by making special rounds and holding special conferences with the house officers and residents, have in some hospitals educated a generation of physicians, and this education is continued by frequent consultations. The social workers have learned that such constant education pays, for the wisest use of their services occurs in hospitals in which there is a true appreciation of the role social factors play in illness.

As a matter of fact, such education by social workers must be carried on not only among physicians and physicians-to-be but among all the professional personnel in the hospital that deals directly with the patient. Not only must there be an adequate, though not necessarily extensive, understanding of the importance of the emotional and social factors in illness, but there must be developed the ability to spot difficulties in these spheres. It not infrequently happens that social workers first learn about a patient in difficulty from an admitting officer, a nurse, or a member of the administrative staff.

Such education must also be carried on for another reason. The medical social worker is probably more interested than anyone else in the hospital in maintaining the individuality of the patient and, like a missionary, she continues to preach her doctrine in an institution in which mass treatment has tended to rob every patient of his personal identity. Almost any department that the patient meets can be guilty of this mistreatment. (It must be pointed out that no attempt is made in what follows to relieve the administration of its final responsibility for the treatment of the patient as an individual human being by every one of its personnel.)

Admitting, for example. The number of times the admitting officer discusses individual patients with the social workers during a year is certainly high. It is through these discussions that she absorbs the philosophy of the social service department. That this philosophy coincides with the hospital's and is at the very root of its policy is made clear by the administrator not necessarily in a series of formal declarations but in his many day-by-day decisions.

It is surprising how few slips admitting officers make; but when they do make one, it is almost invariably of major importance to the patient and has serious repercussions for the hospital.

The most frequent error is to discuss with the patient his financial situation and ability to pay when that patient is emotionally unable to cope with this problem. The immediate results of such a discussion may well be serious: the hyperthyroidism aggravated; the pain of angina pectoris renewed; a status asthmaticus induced.

Should the patient out of fear or misunderstanding conceal his true financial status, the remoter consequences may be even more serious to the patient, his family, the community, and the hospital: the family all too frequently borrows to pay for the medical care which is its as a matter of right, particularly when it is beyond its resources; the patient, especially when he is a wage-earner, becomes harassed, and his illness is intensified and prolonged by worry over the possible inability of the family to meet the demands of the loan company; the budget for food and fuel all too often is cut dangerously so that financial obligations can be met.

Such an error is least likely to occur in those hospitals in which the admitting officer is a social worker or, if a lay person, is well indoctrinated with the philosophy of that department.

Ordinarily the only member of the accounting department whom the patient, or a member of his family, meets is the cashier, who, standing behind bronze bars, holds in her hand only a ledger card, never a medical and social record (nor should she ever have one!). And the surest way to depersonalize a human being is to discuss his ledger card on which, as a means of identification, appears an admission number. To learn to regard the person before her as a human being, sick or closely related to one who is sick, and frequently worried to distraction, is not easy. But, since it must be done, it can be done. Such instruction comes from the administrator.[2]

The social worker must seize every opportunity to present her side of the patient's story to the accounting department, for such opportunities do not come as frequently as in the admitting office. Nor are accountants generally as kindly disposed to social workers, for the notion that the social worker is but an indiscriminate dispenser of charity is all too common among them.

2. Ruskin: "Education does not mean teaching people to know what they do not know; it means teaching them to behave as they do not behave."

The damage that can be done by an accounting department can be unearthed in those hospitals which have overenthusiastic collection clerks or severe collection policies. Either has all too frequently forced a family to pay beyond its ability and at a cost out of all proportion to the amount the hospital might collect.

A hospital with a good social service department is unlikely to have a collection policy so exacting that there is no hint of indulgence. But even such a hospital can unwittingly employ a clerk who will attempt to impress his superiors by his genius at collecting old outstanding balances. In such a hospital, most of the dunned patients who are unable to pay will come not to the clerk whose name is signed to the letter, or to the chief accountant, but to the one employee who had been interested in them as individuals; they will head straight for their social workers. The social workers, knowing the patients as individuals, will see to it that each problem is handled on an individual basis by the administration.

Nurses, on the other hand, cannot regard patients as other than individuals; the care they render is too intimate to permit a metamorphosis of human beings into abstract figures. But most nursing students, like medical students, are graduated without ever having entered a patient's home, let alone cared for a patient there. They have thus lost one of the most valuable lessons in social medicine. This gap can be filled by formal lectures in the classrooms and, so that these lessons may assume greater reality, by case presentations and discussions in the hospital wards and outpatient department. The teaching can be done best at present under the supervision of the social service department.

A nurse so instructed will be a better nurse, for she will be an understanding as well as a skilful craftsman. And because she will appreciate what havoc emotions and environment can wreak, she will do more than passively watch the moods, idiosyncrasies, and interpersonal relations of her patients. She will actively observe them and then pass on her observations to the social worker. These observations may contain much that was unknown to either social worker or physician, for the nurse is with her patients more than is any other member of the professional staff.

It is, however, in the outpatient department that the patient is most likely to lose his personal identity the very moment he sets foot inside the door. Here he is not one of 6 or 10 or even 12 or 16 patients "in the large ward," he is one of several score attending a clinic that day; one of several hundred attending the outpatient department on a single day of the week. He is almost always but a number to everyone but the social service worker and the physician who sees him; and to the doctor he is usually only a chart and a localized area of the body about which there is a complaint and which may or may not be "diseased."

The social worker's interest in the patient as an individual person is, therefore, all the more important. Nevertheless, her work, as it relates to the physician at least, may be more difficult than in the hospital itself, for in many institutions the outpatient department medical staff is larger than the inpatient; younger and less experienced, less well supervised, and—calamitous but true—frequently of poorer quality.

In the outpatient department, too, the social worker, in working with a patient who is attending more than one clinic, helps the physicians co-operate with one another. Her knowledge of the patient, his illness and needs, makes such a role more or less inevitable. And when different members of the same family visit different clinics, she is frequently the only one aware of that fact because the usual outpatient department chart does not mention such "details." By calling the physicians' attention to this vital fact, she plays a pivotal role in modern medical practice, for a patient can no more be considered apart from his family and his social group than can a hand be considered as unrelated to the body of which it is a part.

In the outpatient department, also, the relationships which the social worker has with outside social agencies are seen in sharp focus. Not only does she carry on a continuous exchange of social information concerning her patients, but she interprets hospital policy to these agencies and the agencies to the hospital. Here she has a rare opportunity and a great responsibility, for her interpretations must be accurate and crystal clear or her patients will suffer.

Until quite recently, preventive medicine, when admitted as a function of the hospital, was regarded as properly belonging to the outpatient department. But the scope has been broadened so that it is more than the prevention of specific infectious diseases and the early diagnosis and treatment of such illnesses as carcinoma, diabetes mellitus, heart disease, and mental illness. It means now the "prevention of depreciation in health," the maintenance of health. With this, there has appeared a new definition of the public health problem: "Whenever a disease is so widespread in the population, so serious in its effects, so costly in its treatment that the individual cannot deal with it himself, it becomes a public health problem."

Until the emphasis of preventive medicine was placed on the individual, the hospital was little utilized as a public health center. With this shift, however, the hospital has become a major center. And the medical social worker in the hospital thus enters on her role in this field.

Another important function of the social service department is that of research. This work must be encouraged as a recognized part of every worker's activity and may be either individual or, what in the end may well prove more important, co-operative. Although it is becoming increasingly necessary for the various disciplines to collaborate and co-operate, they need not lose their identity by becoming hyphenated specialties. Social workers have already contributed to medical science by individual and co-operative research, and they should be expected to continue.

For one purpose, hospital employees may be divided into two groups: the healthy and the sick. The question has often arisen in connection with the healthy employee whether, when he has extra-hospital troubles, he should be referred to the social service department. Many departments regard such counseling as outside their province. The policy of such departments frequently is to permit the worker to listen to the employee's problem and refer him to that agency in the community best able to help him meet his specific difficulty.

Service to the sick employee is a different story, for "the basis of medical social service is the medical need of the patient"—and an employee who is a patient of the hospital receives the same services as any other patient.

Whatever the policy of the social service department, which should be determined by the administration together with the social service and personnel departments, it can be of invaluable assistance in the restoration to, and the maintenance of, the health of the sick employee, as well as in the improvement of the relationships between the hospital and its entire personnel.

Medical Social Service[1]

BY LEONORA B. RUBINOW

A HOSPITAL is probably as complex and intricate a piece of social machinery as has been devised, and hospital administrators are faced with a stupendous task in trying to keep this machinery well-oiled and running. But the goal of hospital administration, I take it, is not the maintenance of a smooth, efficient, and economical piece of machinery as an end in itself. Rather, it aims to provide the structural framework, the conditions, and facilities that best enable medical practitioners to apply, develop, and enrich both the art and the science of medicine in an institutional setting. In other words, it aims to provide necessary and appropriate care for the sick.

WHAT IS MEDICAL SOCIAL SERVICE?

There is a variety of ways of helping the sick. Medicine is one way; medical social work is another. The help a sick person requires depends on a number of things—the nature of the illness itself, the kind of person who is ill, the social setting of which he is a part, and the resources that are available to him. The needs of the sick are rarely simple; more often they are complex and require several kinds of help at the same time.

Traditionally, the physician has always had an interest in the social factors of the patient's illness, but his primary professional concern is the patient as a physical organism. In her approach to the patient, the medical social worker always starts with some understanding of the underlying medical problem, but her primary professional concern is the personal and social factors in the patient's situation, particularly those factors that have some bearing on the illness. The implications are that there is some-

1. Reprinted from *Hospitals*, March, 1943, with the permission of the American Hospital Association.

thing within the patient himself or within his environment that is contributory to his illness or that prevents him from traveling a smooth course from illness to physical recovery and from physical recovery to restoration to social functioning. Or there might be something in the nature of the illness itself that threatens serious and destructive consequences to the patient or to the pattern of living he has established for himself. Thus we see that if treatment of a medical problem is to be successful, in terms of the life-career of the patient, it must frequently include consideration and treatment of the social factors interwoven with it.

We might say, then, if we were asked to define what we mean by medical social work, that it is part of the individualized service which the physician gives his patient; that it attempts to understand the needs of and the circumstances surrounding the individual patient and the bearing these factors have on his illness. Through this understanding and through the application of social case work principles and techniques, it aims to help the patient utilize to the fullest capacity the medical care available to him and work out a pattern of life that is at the same time consistent with his physical limitations and satisfying to himself.

HOW DID MEDICAL SOCIAL SERVICE COME ABOUT?

I think hospital administrators know that it was not a matter of chance or accident that social service was first introduced into hospitals. It came in response to a need—a need that was felt by thoughtful physicians who were disturbed by the kind of medicine they were practicing in institutions. They recognized two standards of medical practice, the kind they practiced privately and the kind they practiced in institutions. The one was intensely personal, the other highly impersonal. They recognized gaps in their knowledge of clinic and hospital patients, gaps that baffled them in making a diagnosis and handicapped them in directing treatment. To bridge these gaps, these physicians proposed the introduction of social workers into the hospital for the contribution they could make to the understanding and care of the "whole" patient.

While there is definite evidence that at the turn of the century this general approach to the patient was developing simultaneously here and in England, it was not until 1905 that it was crystal-lized into an organized hospital service. Since that time the knowledge, skills, and areas of helpfulness of medical social work have deepened and expanded way beyond its modest beginnings, but the original premise still remains—the need to consider the "whole" patient.

In 1927, the eminent Dr. Francis Peabody, professor of medi-cine of the Harvard Medical School, lectured to his medical stu-dents as follows:

> Now the essence of the practice of medicine is that it is an intensely personal matter, and one of the chief differences between private practice and hospital practice is that the latter always tends to become impersonal. . . . When the general practitioner goes into the home of the patient, he may know the whole background of the family life from past experience; but even when he comes as a stranger he has every opportunity to find out what manner of man his patient is and what kind of circumstances make his life. . . . What is spoken of as a "clinical picture" is not just a photograph of a man sick in bed; it is an impressionistic painting of the patient surrounded by his home, his work, his relations, friends, his joys, sorrows, hopes and fears. Now, all of this background of sickness which bears so strongly on the symptomatology is liable to be lost sight of in the hospital. . . . When a patient enters a hospital, the first thing that commonly happens is that he loses his personal identity. . . . The trouble is that it leads, more or less directly, to the patient being treated as a case of mitral stenosis and not as a sick man.[2]

In this lecture Doctor Peabody is presenting what he calls the "larger view" of the medical profession.

Today we find a rebirth of this emphasis on the need to see the "whole" patient in the newer concept, still more popular in medi-cal discussions than in medical practice, of the psychosomatic ap-proach to medicine. Conditions existing in modern hospitals of today, particularly in the large, urban ones, do not make it easy for the physician to see the "whole" patient, even when he ac-cepts the validity of this concept. Sharing this responsibility with the medical social worker brings it closer to realization.

Out of all this, the facts important to our present discussion are that medical social service is still a relatively young service in the hospital field, that it was conceived by physicians for the express purpose of rendering their institutional practice more

2. Francis Peabody, *The Care of the Patient* (Cambridge: Harvard Univer-sity Press, 1928), p. 12.

effective, that it originated and grew up within the folds of clinical medicine, and that it is a dynamic force continuously moving ahead in keeping with developments in medicine itself.

WHAT ARE THE FUNCTIONS OF MEDICAL SOCIAL SERVICE?

As already implied, the central or major function of medical social service is social case work on behalf of the individual patient. In this capacity the medical social worker acts as part of the medical team, co-operating with the doctor, who is the leader of the team. Always in a medical social situation there are at least three elements—a doctor, a patient, and a social worker. There may be more, but there is never less than three.

The social worker sees the patient[3] not as a disease process but as a person who is ill and who reacts to illness in much the same way as he reacts to other difficulties in his life. She sees him in a specific episode of illness. She is not concerned with the name of the disease but rather with what it does to the patient, how he feels about it, and what his capacity may be for adjustment to it. She sees each patient as a unique entity presenting a unique situation. She recognizes the importance of having the patient participate in plans for his care and helps him accept responsibility for making important decisions in relation to it, for taking a difficult step, or for making a choice as between one possibility and another. In other words, she helps him see his situation realistically and do something about it in so far as he is able.

More consciously than other hospital personnel, the medical social worker refrains from passing judgment on the patient's behavior, knowing that illness with all its problems, real and fancied, creates conflicts within the person or intensifies already existing ones and causes him to act on the basis of motives that he himself does not understand. She sees his behavior as a symptom of underlying trouble, and she looks beneath the surface for its true meaning. Through this kind of acceptance and understanding, the so-called "difficult patient" ceases to be "difficult" and begins to co-operate with the doctor and the nurse in the medical care program.

3. For full discussion of this see Harriett M. Bartlett, *Some Aspects of Social Casework in a Medical Setting* (Chicago: American Association of Medical Social Workers, 1940), chap. 1.

The physician sees the patient isolated from his usual setting. The medical social worker sees the patient as an inseparable part of his surroundings, as a member of a family unit and of a wider community group. While her focus is on the patient, she must often extend her activity to include the family and others with whom he is associated. If the family does not understand the needs of the patient, it can ruin all that has been achieved for him within the hospital. It often becomes necessary for the social worker to draw the family into participation in the decisions to be made and the plans to be worked out.

Thus we see that the medical social worker is an important factor in assuring individualized consideration of the patient on the basis of his particular needs, in a setting which is highly impersonal, in which, for administrative purposes, the emphasis is on groups rather than on individuals, and where, in the rush of things, it is easy to lose sight of the individual.

Two examples illustrate what this process of individualization means in the treatment of the patient. They involve two house patients who presented similar situations to the doctor, in that they both made good recoveries following surgery, except for their inability to get out of bed and walk and their resistance to leaving the hospital. One was a young woman who had entered the hospital for gynecological surgery. During the operation it was found necessary to do a hysterectomy. The social worker learned that the patient and her husband had been professional dancers, traveling from city to city as members of a dance troup. After several years of married life, they left the stage in order to settle down, establish a permanent home, and raise a family. When the patient realized that she could not have children, she considered herself a total failure and disappointment to her husband, and brooded with a deep sense of personal guilt. She could not face him with this information and could not bear the thought of going home. When the social worker realized the basis of her difficulty, she suggested that the physician might discuss the situation with the husband, presenting it as a matter of medical reality rather than as a reflection of personal inadequacy. The patient grasped at this suggestion, a conference was held with the physician, the husband accepted the interpretation, the patient responded to this turn of events, was able to get up and walk, and left the hospital in a more cheerful frame of mind.

The other case was that of a middle-aged man who had ulcerative colitis. An ileostomy was performed. In spite of good postoperative results, this patient protested his inability to walk and found one reason after another for not feeling well enough to leave the hospital. The social worker learned that this patient had been "ailing" for many years and that he had long since relinquished to his wife the job of supporting the family while he puttered around the house. Illness had frightened him further. As a fundamentally dependent person, he clung to the security of the hospital bed. In this instance, treatment consisted of removing the patient to a small nursing home for a specified period of time, the expense to be shared by the family and social service. In this semiprofessional setting the patient received the security he needed, as there was a nurse in attendance, while at the same time he was provided with a more normal, homelike atmosphere than the hospital could offer. By the time the designated period was up, the patient had regained confidence, was walking about freely, and returned home cheerfully. Though not an economic asset to his family or community, he was prevented from becoming more invalided than he had been at the point of hospitalization.

In some instances the medical social worker must deal with the total situation of the patient, while in other instances her concern may be limited to a narrowly circumscribed area of it. For example, in planning adequate care for a child with a tuberculous hip, the social worker had to consider not only the various needs of the patient herself but also a childlike, overburdened mother with a pulmonary lesion, who could not adequately care for the child and yet would not release her to more competent hands and who would not accept medical care for herself; an irresponsible, shiftless father who occasionally deserted, never made an effort to support his family, and yet wanted to be respected as head of the household; two baby sisters who were being exposed to infection without any protection; a community that did not provide adequate sanatorium facilities and harbored a political situation that would do nothing about it; and a local ordinance providing for the isolation of tuberculous patients, with no teeth to enforce it. In this instance, the patient could not be treated apart from the total situation.

In the case of a woman with rheumatoid arthritis who felt she could not carry out the doctor's instructions for home physiotherapy because she lived in a rooming house, the social worker's only concern was with those aspects of her situation, real and subjective, which had to do with this specific problem. The patient felt she could not construct the necessary apparatus; she did not know where she would keep it if she had it; she was sure the people in whose home she lived would not permit it; she was afraid the electricity costs would be too high; she did not have a convenient outlet for the electric connection; etc. There were many unfavorable factors in this patient's total life-situation, but they had no direct bearing on the immediate problem and hence were not brought into consideration. It is the social worker's function to determine how much of the patient's total situation is pertinent to the problem at hand and accessible to treatment in much the same way as the physician must determine the direction and extent of medical treatment.

In addition to this primary function of case work, there are other activities in the hospital which a medical social worker is peculiarly well equipped to handle. These activities, while appropriate to medical social work, should not be confused with or substituted for its central function. They are largely administrative in nature, in that they involve the management of groups of patients, but they are wisely administered when they give consideration to individual differences within the group. Among such activities are admission of patients to clinic and hospital, setting of rates for medical care and appliances, follow-up of clinic patients and discharged hospital patients, etc. The social worker's knowledge of human behavior, her skill in interviewing, her ability to sift material, integrate various factors, and arrive at a fair and equitable decision make her particularly well suited to this kind of administrative activity.

When social workers engage in these administrative activities, it is desirable that there be a separate staff for this purpose. Such staff may be placed within the department of social service or may be part of administration. In large hospitals it is not difficult to plan separate staffs. In small institutions it may be necessary to combine these functions in one staff. Whenever this is done, however, the differentiation in function should be clearly understood by everyone concerned, as there is always the danger that hospital pressures will eventually push aside the primary function of case work before anyone becomes aware of what is happening.

There is still another group of functions with broader community implications. In the matter of communicable disease, the medical social worker may assume a public health function, as, for example, helping to keep the patient under treatment, planning with him for the examination of contacts, the source of infection, etc. She may participate in community planning for health and welfare; may teach social aspects of illness in allied fields, such as medicine, nursing, and dietetics; may supervise field-work training for students in medical social work; and may engage in medical social service study and research. These are legitimate functions of all medical social service departments.

HOW SHOULD A SOCIAL SERVICE DEPARTMENT BE ORGANIZED?[4]

The social service department should follow the same general pattern of organization as that used for other departments of the hospital. It should be an integral part of the institution. In some instances, social service has been established as a project of an outside organization. This is an undesirable practice, as it does not permit the establishment of sound interrelationships among the various hospital services, which is basic to effective care of the patient. There should be a professionally qualified director in charge of the department with direct lines of responsibility to the executive officer of the institution and through him to the governing board. The head of the department should have ready access to and frequent conferences with the executive officer for whatever consultation, guidance, exchange of information, and joint planning may be necessary. When a subexecutive acts as intermediary between the department head and the executive

4. For standards of organization see *A Statement of Standards To Be Met by Social Service Departments in Hospitals, Clinics, and Sanatoria* (Washington, D.C.: American Association of Medical Social Workers, 1949).

officer, the vitality of this relationship is lost and its effectiveness destroyed.

The director of the department should be expected to give leadership to the department through responsibility for program building and policy-making, through the establishment and maintenance of standards of service and of personnel, by developing good interrelationships, and by setting the professional tone of the department. In the matter of personnel, she should assume responsibility for writing job specifications and personnel qualifications, for recommending salary ranges and personnel practices, for recruiting staff, and for appointing and releasing staff members in keeping with the personnel policies of the institution. Likewise, the director should be expected to give leadership in relation to the professional growth of her staff: to provide adequate supervision as a means of sharpening the skills of the worker as well as a protection to the service, to enable staff participation in department policies and program, and to offer opportunity for job promotion in accordance with individual capacities. In a small hospital, direct supervision of staff will be given by the director. In a large institution, special supervisory personnel will be necessary.

The social service department should be financed through the hospital budget, as are all other departments, regardless of the sources of funds. After the budget is allocated, it should be controlled and administered by the director so that she may use it flexibly in meeting shifts in staff and other unexpected needs as they may arise.

The location of the department and the amount of floor space allotted to it are important considerations. In general, it may be said that the basement is not a desirable location, though failure to include social service in building plans has frequently made it a necessary one. Good standards require that the patient be afforded the same protection of privacy in his social interviews as he has in his physical examination. A comfortable, relaxed atmosphere, free from the irritation of interruption, will enable the patient to make the greatest possible use of the interview. Preferably, there should be a central office or reception room with individual offices that are accessible to both doctor and patient. In lieu of individual offices, scattered interviewing rooms will be found helpful. It is also desirable that the department have a conference room that may be used for staff meetings, for conferences with other social agencies, and for study committees of the staff.

Every social service department will find it helpful to have an advisory committee comprising members of the medical and nursing staffs, the administration, the governing board and other lay groups associated with the hospital. Such a committee can give the department a great deal of support within the institution and in the larger community by helping to maintain standards, to interpret functions, to bring about better understanding, and to further integration with other hospital services and other community agencies, thereby increasing the department's opportunities for helpful service. Preferably, such committee should be appointed by, responsible to, and represented on the governing board.

WHAT IS EDUCATION FOR MEDICAL SOCIAL WORK?

What do we mean by education for medical social work, and why is it necessary? All professions started their earliest training programs with the apprenticeship method. The embryo physician had his first lessons in medical diagnosis as he carried the bags of his mentor. The youthful aspirant to legal fame started out by reading lawbooks in the office of an established barrister. History records the magnificent achievements of individual doctors and lawyers who developed their skills under these crude methods. However, history has neglected to record the damage and destruction wrought by others who failed to learn in this manner.

In social work today, there is a body of knowledge, basic concepts, principles, and techniques that are known and can be transmitted by those who know them to those who want to learn them. Wanting to help is not enough and does not guarantee knowing how.[5] When a friend asks us for help or advice, we may give it either because we feel the friend needs it or because we cannot bear to refuse it. In either case, our "giving" is a personal reaction. The professional social worker does not help or advise on the basis of a personal reaction but only in relation to the function of her agency. She is aware of herself as a repre-

5. For fuller discussion see Dorothy B. Daly, *Case Work Practice in Public Assistance Administration* (Chicago: American Public Welfare Association, 1942).

sentative of an organization with a specific function to fulfil. While she is alert to the patient's reactions in a "helping situation," she is also aware of herself. "Psychology even more than charity should begin at home."[6] The worker is careful not to inject her own biases into the situation. She does not consider whether the patient is the kind of person she likes or of whom she approves. Her only concern is the patient's needs in relation to the ability of the organization to meet them.

Through professional education, the worker develops a "professional self" which makes it possible for her to function constructively in a "helping situation." A person who is terrorized at the thought of surgery cannot help the patient emerge from his panic and confusion and arrive at a decision to go ahead with the operation. A person who flinches at the mention of cancer cannot help the patient face months of torture ahead with calm and courage. A person who thinks of syphilis as an evidence of cardinal sin cannot be helpful to the patient who feels he has brought shame and disgrace to his family that he can never live down. Education for medical social work is a requisite for "helping" in situations of this kind.

Adequate preparation for medical social work requires graduation from a recognized university and the completion of two years of graduate study in an accredited school of social work. The first year is spent in basic preparation for social work, including its historical background and philosophical concepts, the major provisions for social welfare services, and the principles and techniques of methods of helping people with social difficulties. The student spends part of her time in a social agency, learning to practice under supervision. In the second year, in addition to advanced courses in principles and methods and a research project, the student specializing in medical social work also has a period of supervised practice in a medical social service department and the related courses in the theory of medical social work. The successful competion of the two-year program of study is attested by a Master's degree or certified by the school.

6. Lawrence Lunt, "Human Nature and Its Reaction to Suffering," in L. Eugene Emerson (ed.), *Physician and Patient* (Cambridge: Harvard University Press, 1929).

WHAT IS THE HOSPITAL ADMINISTRATOR'S RESPONSIBILITY FOR LEADERSHIP?

The hospital administrator is a very important factor in the establishment of effective social services within the institution. It is a matter of common observation that institutional personnel pattern themselves after the attitudes they see at "the top." Acceptance at "the top" is requisite to acceptance all the way down the line. This is particularly important in relation to members of the house staff, almost all of whom come out of medical schools with little awareness of the patient as a social being. In their zeal to apply what they have learned, they not infrequently become more interested in emptying a hospital bed than they are in what happens to the patient. The administrator can be helpful in presenting social service to them as having a rightful place in the hospital scheme and in giving them some knowledge of how to use it in the interests of their patients.

Administrators who appreciate the need for flexibility in the individualized care of the patient will not insist upon a routine, ritualistic carrying out of hospital rules and procedures. They will make it possible for the social worker to have considerable freedom in relation to the hospital structure. In this way they can be assured that the hospital's regulations are made to serve the interests of the patient and not to perpetuate rules for any virtue they may have in themselves.

Finally, hospital administrators would do well to draw social service into policy-making and program building as they relate to the patient group. Social service brings a new point of view—a different approach to administrative problems. By virtue of this difference it has a contribution to make. This should not mean a clash of opposing points of view but rather the injection of a healthy and enriching note into the whole fabric. The administrator plans for the management of a group of patients. Social service sees what happens at the patient level. In the final analysis, the acid test of a hospital policy is how it affects the individual patient. Social service, wisely used, can provide the testing ground for sound administration.

Problems in Administration of Medical
Social Work in Hospitals[1]

BY ETHEL COHEN

AN EXAMINATION of the topic—administration in practice of medical social service departments in hospitals—opens up a subject of real magnitude. There are many areas in this field which urgently need exploration and thoughtful study by our whole group as a profession. As a practitioner in administration, I look forward eagerly to the assistance which will accrue to us all from such organized study.

In this paper there will be no attempt even to enumerate the many problems of administration. Only a few of the major problems have been selected for discussion, such as, problems arising from (1) hospital and medical setting; (2) insufficient medical support; (3) function not clearly defined; (4) accepting and carrying responsibilities disproportionate to size of staff; and problems in relation to (5) staff workers; (6) organizational aspects; (7) hospital administrative policy; (8) other social agencies in the community; (9) administration as a special function.

Let us first examine the environment in which we carry on our activities. Hospital setting and medical setting were here mentioned separately very consciously. While they appear to be identical, they are in reality quite different phases of the total organization, and in certain given situations they even have opposing interests. The term "hospital setting" here connotes more than the areas of hospital administration. It includes the multiplicity of different departments, with their great numbers of personnel and the interaction of all of them upon each other.

Modern medical care has become increasingly intricate and expensive. A progressive hospital, to carry out its activities of

1. Reprinted from *Papers of the American Association of Medical Social Workers* (1941), with the permission of the association.

the care of sick people, of preventive medicine, public health, research, and education, has great financial burdens. The management of such enterprises requires business methods, which necessarily affect policies in relation to the patients, the community, and the hospital personnel.

The "medical setting," i.e., the area in which the physicians function, too, is complex, with its own form of organization. Most modern hospitals, particularly those affiliated with medical schools, have a medical policy-making board, a visiting staff, and a teaching staff of many ranks, as well as residents, interns, and medical students. All have their own particular responsibilities, standards, purposes, and outlooks. Their work is divided into medical and surgical general services, with many specialties, requiring highly developed, exact technical knowledge and skill. Teaching hospitals, also, have educational responsibilities to provide students with the broadest opportunities to diagnose and treat many acutely sick people with a wide variety of different diseases.

Care of sick people requires swift and skilful service. Doctors and nurses are trained to follow certain traditional and definite lines of action. Patients have their individual personal differences. The same illness may run different courses and precipitate different reactions. Hospitalization often represents crises for patients and families.

This, briefly described, is the environment in which the social service department of a hospital carries on its activities. The importance of the effect of this environment on the service cannot be too greatly emphasized, for the circumstances which give rise to the need of medical social work at the same time create some of the major difficulties in performing the service. The function of medical social work is help to sick people with problems arising from their illness or medical care. Its most characteristic feature is individualization of the patient, his particular needs, and his reactions to his illness, treatment, and his interpersonal relationships.

The activities involved in the medical social worker's efforts at resolving these problems bring her into close contact with the professional and often with many nonprofessional workers in the hospital, whose services in connection with a given patient do not and often cannot take into account this individual patient's needs, understanding, or desires. The medical social worker here has the problem of interpretation of this patient's need and of attempting to influence either directly or indirectly the activities of physician, administration, and others. To illustrate this concretely, let us consider the patient on the ward service of an acute general hospital, a young man who has had surgical treatment for active pulmonary tuberculosis. The surgeons consider him ready to be discharged to a tuberculosis sanatorium. The patient refuses to go. He had once been unhappy in a sanatorium, and, besides, Christmas is only two weeks off. He wants to be at home with his wife and two young children. The patient needs medical care and supervision, but not the type of service available in a general hospital. Beds in the hospital are in great demand for acutely sick patients. The surgeon, appreciating the danger to young children of exposure to open tuberculosis, believes the patient should not return to his congested and inadequate home. The patient's wife understands the situation, too, but fears the patient may suspect her of trying to get rid of him. The doctor's many unsuccessful efforts to modify the patient's attitude lead him to consider the patient unreasonable and unco-operative, and as a doctor, he believes he knows what is best for the patient, who should be sent to a sanatorium whether or not he wishes to go.

Here are the conflicting interests of patient, family, administration, physician, and the community. The postponement of the patient's discharge in the hope of modifying his attitude means more free care has to be provided the patient. This affects the hospital income. The continued occupancy of this bed excludes some other patient. Thus the service of the hospital to the community is reduced, and the opportunity of intern and medical student for maximum experience in study and treatment is diminished. The medical social worker in this case knew that, even were it possible to send this patient to a sanatorium, he would probably leave against advice before long; that his future medical care, his health, and his family would be jeopardized. She believed that his strong desire for Christmas at home could be accepted, with maximum safeguards to the family provided by public health nursing and others. By the continuing relationship with the patient and his family at home, the medical social worker by effective case work actually did lead the patient shortly after Christmas to go to a sanatorium willingly and to assist his wife to seek needed financial help for herself and children, which previously she had refused as rigidly as the patient had resisted sanatorium care.

This is not an uncommon hospital problem. It was included in this paper to demonstrate the many different interests involved. The management of this problem gave opportunity for the executive of the department to support the staff worker in her function, to influence hospital policy, and to broaden the viewpoint of the intern.

PROBLEMS ARISING FROM INSUFFICIENT MEDICAL SUPPORT

Medical social work, with its focus on the problems arising from or associated with the illness of individual patients, can function in hospitals only in relation to their medical care. The illness, its treatment, and their meaning for the particular patient must be properly understood by the social worker to enable her to gain sufficient insight into the social and emotional aspects as a basis for meeting the patient's needs. Her best source of information is the physician. The brevity of the average medical record, the usual absence of prognostic data and of evaluation concerning incapacity or disability or of specific recommendations for aftercare make the medical record useful only as a source of supplementary information. Close collaboration with the physician is of the utmost importance. Mutual understanding of each other's function and goals is required. Some physicians have always taken the social and emotional component of illness into consideration in the care of their patients. It is in service with these physicians that medical social workers have always been able to make their greatest contribution. Such understanding, unfortunately, has not yet been attained universally. Many factors contribute to this situation. Some physicians, absorbed by the so-called "scientific" aspects of medicine, are detached and less interested in the personal problems of individual patients.

Also, much of hospital work is carried on through the intern and resident staff. Few of them as undergraduates in medical school have had training in the interrelationship of social and emotional factors and illness. Ordinarily, they have not yet had the opportunity for experience in practice outside the hospital prior to their service as intern or resident. They are not accustomed to thinking of their patients in terms of their social needs. The knowledge of social and economic problems for many young physicians is derived only from undergraduate sociological study. In hospitals where the visiting staff or superior medical officers take little cognizance of the social or emotional aspects of illness, the intern, too, may question its significance and resist even spending the time needed to discuss the medical data adequately in relation to the individual patient.

The real integration of social work into the medical-care program of the hospital is a problem of greatest importance. While much depends on the influence upon the physician of convincing practice by the individual medical social staff worker on a case-by-case basis, the responsibility rests with the executive of the social service department for planning with the appropriate members of the medical and surgical staff the means by which such integration can be brought about. No one plan of work can be advocated for all hospitals. Any type of procedure that best fits the individual hospital setup should be put into operation. Official recognition by the hospital administrator and the medical administrative board is essential to give it status. Recognition alone, however, is insufficient. The active support of at least a small number of physicians and surgeons in positions of authority is imperative for the maintenance of any plan agreed upon.

The best plan in theory can deteriorate in practice without continuous observation and evaluation. Modifications are needed from time to time to improve and strengthen the execution of any procedure. This generalization has special significance in hospital work because of the constant stream of changing personnel. In teaching hospitals, interns and residents on a given ward or clinic may change every three to six months; staff men give their service for varying periods of time. This perpetually changing scene makes interpretation and education a never ending responsibility.

PROBLEMS ARISING FROM FUNCTION NOT CLEARLY DEFINED

Where the function of the social service department is not clearly defined, the hospital administration, physicians, and the community may request service of the department, which, though it may have some social element, does not involve trained social judgment. As new developments in medicine and hospital practice arose, they brought with them the need for new services. The traditional roles of doctors, nurses, and dietitians did not provide for these new services. The social worker, whose function had not yet become a tradition and who was the most recent addition to professional hospital personnel, was frequently expected to give these services, and she has done so willingly. The assumption of responsibility for such activities absorbs the time and energy of medical social workers, encroaches on their appropriate functions, and tends to keep performance on a superficial level. Many of these services, carried out obligingly as courtesies to medical staff, administration, and community agencies, have served as a boomerang to the social service department. Performance on this slight or superficial level gives the impression that that is the extent of the capacities of the medical social worker and of the quality of her service.

Similar adverse conditions are created in certain aspects of even appropriately accepted functions, if the medical social worker herself does not evaluate the situations clearly. For example, responsibility may be suitably taken for transportation of certain patients needing clinic supervision. This suitable function in a given clinic actually deteriorated to the proportions of a "traffic department" within a year by a worker who did not *constantly* apply the principle of individualizing each patient and his need. Partly this difficulty arose through her easygoing tendency to good-natured acquiescence to any request made of her. This is always easier and more agreeable than the refusal of a request for service.

PROBLEMS ARISING FROM ACCEPTING AND CARRYING RESPONSIBILITY DISPROPORTIONATE TO SIZE OF STAFF

The tendency already indicated in hospitals of placing more responsibilities on social workers has rarely taken into consideration (1) the size of the social work staff, (2) the extent of its capacity for service, and (3) the time involved in executing these services. Though hospital personnel know that social workers carry on their work outside the hospital and continue their interest in patients for considerable periods of time beyond discharge, their understanding of the time element is insufficient. The service of other hospital personnel does not extend beyond the hospital. Patients are served one after another while they are on the hospital premises. When a patient leaves, their responsibility for him ceases. The social worker's job often begins for certain patients just at the point of their discharge and may continue for long periods of time afterward. Moreover, she is simultaneously taking on problems of other patients who are just being admitted. Her case load grows in different proportions to that of physician, nurse, dietitian, and administrator. Her work does not always synchronize with their activities.

This element of time is an important factor, too, in the very nature of the social worker's service. For example, several hours may be required to discuss with patient and members of his family the need for medically supervised long-time chronic care. On the surface, this may seem to be a simple problem merely of transfer of the patient to another hospital. To the patient and family, however, this may raise a great number of problems; invalidism and physical dependency; radical change in the life of the whole family; inability to meet the cost of long-time care; separation from the patient at some distant or inaccessible hospital; or fear of death. The community may have the resource needed by the patient, but admission rules may bar the particular patient. Explanation to the patient and his family of the care needed; understanding of their reactions; helping them to overcome resistance; meeting their objections and swings in their decisions; mobilizing the resources to carry out the recommended plan; and strengthening the family situation concurrently to maintain the structure of the plan—all of this is tremendously time-consuming. Medical social workers have insufficiently interpreted to doctors and to administration the processes of helping and the time factor involved.

Medical social administrators have not always given adequate thought to the most productive use of the time at the disposal of a given size of staff. In their desire to serve patients with social problems, they have undertaken the 100 per cent review of (1) patients with given diagnoses or (2) specified economic level or (3) certain age groups or (4) all hospital admissions or (5) all hospital discharges. The service involved may be suitable and appropriate for social workers to perform. However, a small amount of service spread over a large area may leave little time to deal with the problems discovered. Unless the social service staff can be increased to carry an increasing load, it would seem reasonable not to undertake a requested function or to use a procedure which often results in inadequate service to the patient, frustration for the social workers, and insufficient opportunity to demonstrate the nature of sound professional medical social work. Unless there is convincing demonstration of qualitative service, there can be little opportunity for doctors to understand the kind of medical social work which can be an important part of the care of patients.

PROBLEMS OF ADMINISTRATION IN RELATION TO STAFF WORKERS

The administrator has the responsibility for the smooth functioning of the department and for its standard of practice, all of which is carried on by staff workers. The functions, both of administrator and of staff worker, make them interdependent. For effective work toward a common goal, there must exist a close understanding and harmonious relationship between the two functional elements. Anything which does not contribute to the development of the department as an integral whole should be discouraged.

In certain departments the medical social staff includes one or more supervisors, in addition to the administrative head of the department. The most characteristic setup, however, unfortunately lacks such a division of function. The executive who combines the administrative as well as case work supervisory and teaching function realizes the impossibility of serving adequately in all these roles.

Case work supervision requires uninterrupted attention to delicate problems of human relationships. An hour set aside each week as conference time for each worker is probably the minimum requirement for a continuous progressive learning experience for the staff worker. It serves also an as excellent medium for the supervisor to keep in close touch with the individual worker's progress and with the problems and activities of each service. For the young worker this weekly conference is a consciously directed teaching opportunity. For experienced workers it is rather a consultation service. In a department even of six staff workers, it is difficult for the executive to hold supervisory conferences away from her office or to make herself otherwise unavailable during these many hours. Unless she is able to do so, the constant interruption of the telephone, of requests for service from other equally important areas of the hospital, render supervisory conferences as unsatisfying to the executive as they are painful to the worker. The execution of both roles most effectively would seem to be by the separation of the administrative and policy-making function from the supervisory and teaching function. Certain elements which inhere in the executive role, such as seeing that policies are carried out, that the organization runs smoothly, that the various parts of the department are integrated into an effective whole, may interfere with the fostering of an ideal supervisor-worker relationship. The other side of this dilemma is that an executive who gives even a moderate amount of time to supervision may have difficulty in keeping closely enough in touch with other activities of the hospital. This, too, is essential to the promotion of an integrated service. Furthermore, the executive must have time to think, time to absorb the meaning of the happenings around her and to devise policies for dealing with them.

In all professions there is change or progress. Professional workers are all expected to continue their studies. Therefore, it is incumbent on the directors of departments, by reading and by participation in seminars, institutes, etc., to keep current with changing philosophy and techniques in the continuously developing professional field of social work. In addition to her own field of medical social work, she must keep informed of progress in medicine and in the allied fields of social work. Otherwise, she will be unable to contribute to her staff what they have a right to expect of supervision; and the department which she administers will not meet its full responsibilities to the hospital and the patients it serves.

In relation to the social service staff, the head of the department has a responsibility to stimulate their interest and desire for further professional development. There are many means for bringing this about: staff participation through program committees for staff meetings; special studies to contribute to policy-making; allowing time for attendance outside the hospital at social work seminars, institutes, conferences, and medical meetings; seminars or series of meetings within the department, with an invited leader or member of staff to discuss problems in relation to department practice; series of staff meetings with medical staff leadership discussing new developments in medicine, etc.

PERSONNEL PRACTICES

A major problem in the administration of a social service department in a hospital is the development of good personnel practices. The medical social worker belongs to two spheres of activity, i.e., social work and hospital or institutional work. As mentioned earlier in this paper, hospitals in general operate under heavy financial burdens. Most private or endowed hospitals have deficits, many of them staggering in proportion. Tax-supported hospitals usually have insufficient appropriations. Unfortunately, too frequently it has become a tradition that hospital personnel are poorly compensated and have personnel practices generally inferior to industry or other professions.

Provisions for vacations, sick leave, absence for study with pay, and many other aspects of practice have not yet been universally arranged in hospitals. Some hospital administrators find it very difficult to establish personnel practices for medical social workers on a level which will conform with practices in the general field of social work, because they are often higher than for other professional departments within the hospital. The subject of personnel practices, as a broad problem affecting the entire profession of medical social workers, transcends the limitations of individual hospitals. As such, it merits the attention of hospital administrators as a national organization. With their co-operation, the intensive study of the National Personnel Practices Committee of the American Association of Medical Social Workers should have far-reaching influence on local hospital practice.

The function of an administrator is to maintain an efficiently run organization which will render the service for which it was established and foster satisfactions among the staff directly giving the service. For the administrator, then, an understanding of human behavior is as essential as it is for the case worker in her work with individual clients. The administrator should know what is required of every functioning part of her organization. While she may not have had secretarial or accounting training or office management, she should know what is good practice in all these areas and the approximate length of time for executing these details of work. She should have a responsible person who can actually supervise the work, for an administrator carrying all details herself will be swamped and no longer be an administrator. The administrator's secretary might be that individual, or it might be an administrative aide, who understands the organizational structure, procedures, and forms. This worker would have no authority over staff but would consult with the administrator, keeping her informed of problems and advising her as to methods of improving management. As no other person in her organization, the administrator must have a greater sense of the department as a whole and be able objectively to view the whole, adjusting or eliminating parts whose function has become outworn or obsolete. No procedure should be used unless it has a distinct purpose in furthering the organization's efficiency. Departments cannot afford the waste of outworn, stereotyped routines which encourage casualness and ineptitude. Nothing contributes more to breakdown of organization than asking workers to carry out time-consuming details which are purposeless.

In broader problems of distribution of services to individual staff workers, there should be constant study of case loads in relation to the type of medical service and the problems peculiar to that service. For example, a worker on a teaching ward may be carrying a much heavier load of work, with a numerically smaller case load, than a worker in an outpatient clinic where the preponderance of problems involves prosthetic appliances. For various reasons, some medical services decline and others augment over a period of months or years. This will affect the distribution of work to the staff, and the administrator should be alert to such changes so that the work may be equitably divided among staff workers, and each worker may be assigned to the service where she can make the greatest contribution.

Problems of medical relief arise in hospitals which do not provide in their general budgets money for prosthetic appliances, taxi service, convalescent and nursing-home care. In many hospitals staff workers raise money for these needs through personal appeals to generous individuals in the community, to clubs and other nonprofessional organizations. This places an extra burden on staff workers, whose time and energy is being taken away from their primary function of case work. As far as possible, the administrator of the department should build up the funds to which staff workers may have access, centralization of control of the funds being placed with the director of the department. The best practice, however, seems to be for the hospital administration to include the necessary funds for such expenditures in the general hospital budget, with administrative responsibility by the director of the social service department for cases under care of that department.

PROBLEMS IN RELATION TO HOSPITAL ADMINISTRATIVE POLICY AND LAY BOARDS

It would be valuable for the director of the social service department to serve on an intra-hospital council or committee to present a social point of view in relation to the effect of certain hospital policies on patients and community agencies, as well as to interpret the needs of patients and community unmet through lack of hospital policy. Also, social workers often have to carry out certain hospital policies which are out of harmony with the general social goals of the hospital. If there existed some intra-hospital council, these problems could be brought up naturally and perhaps more effectively during the course of discussions of general hospital policies.

Representation also on lay boards of the hospital by all the professional departments would add to the layman's understanding of the various specialized functional problems and of the hospital organization as a whole. Members of the lay board would likewise have an opportunity to contribute directly by advice and active support to those aspects of the medical-care program which extend into the community. On such committees the social service administrator should represent her department, possibly with some staff participation.

PROBLEMS IN RELATION TO OTHER SOCIAL AGENCIES IN THE COMMUNITY

The hospital, and more particularly its social service department, serves the community as one of its social agencies. Some patients come of their own accord, and others are sent for study and care by public and private social agencies. Within the hospitals are many patients with social problems associated with their illness or with medical treatment, who need the assistance of nonmedical agencies in all the various fields of social activity. As different functioning parts of a whole social organism, all professional social work agencies have a responsibility to support and supplement the work of each other within the framework of their own particular function. Social work departments of hospitals are particularly handicapped if such co-operation is lacking, for large investments in medical care and hospital service may otherwise be wasted.

The great changes of the past decade in community organization, agency function, and techniques have brought about a certain degree of progress in community work. Simultaneously, however, limitation in agency function and scope of work have created large reservoirs of unmet needs. This is a problem which merits the serious consideration of public administrators, of community federations and councils of social agencies. In such councils the administrators of social service departments should have sufficient representation in order that the far-reaching social problems arising from illness and from conditions contributing to illness may be taken into account adequately in general community planning.

Provision for convalescent and chronic care following hospitalization is a major concern of medical social workers. Few communities have the resources, in either quantity or quality, to give this type of care effectively. In this area, too, the administrator of a department, through the cumulative experience of the whole staff, has the responsibility through interpretation and fact-finding to influence health programs.

ADMINISTRATION AS A SPECIAL FUNCTION

There are probably very few administrators of social service departments fortunate enough to have had training in preparation for their administrative positions. Most of us just had to find our way around on the job. While a certain amount of learning through trial and error is inevitable, it is, in general, exceedingly wasteful, both financially and from its potentially bad effect on practice. Unwise precedents or policies established through inexperience may have long-time and far-reaching consequences. Certain procedures and attitudes may become so crystallized as to defy necessary changes. While it is true that each hospital has its own individual personality, so to speak, with its own peculiar problems, it is also true that problems are not always unique to a certain given institution. There are general principles, a body of information, and certain techniques which can be learned. It is an anomalous situation that, as increasingly more training and expertness are being required of staff workers, no similar opportunities for training are available for the administrator, who is expected to exceed the staff worker in expertness and to have the competence and responsibility for the guidance and creative management of the whole department. As a professional group, medical social workers should encourage the establishment of institutes and postgraduate courses at schools of social work so that present administrators may have the opportunity to improve their practice and that future administrators may be prepared professionally for an exacting task that merits our highest capacities.

SUMMARY

In this paper have been discussed a few of the major problems of administration of medical social work within hospitals. Some problems arise naturally from the practice of medical social work itself; others grow out of the hospital and medical setting; still others are due to lack of clarity as to function on the part of some medical social workers themselves and of other professional groups. Some of the most perplexing problems result from the inadequacy in size of staff for the work performance expected.

With greater understanding of medical social function and active support by administrators, physicians, and other community agencies and with budgets increased to approximate the required number of personnel, many of the most time-consuming and pressing problems would disappear. Then social service administrators could devote their best energies to the study and management of problems arising from medical social practice.

Problems in Social Work Administration in Public Hospitals[1]

BY IRENE GRANT

THE public programs have the same fundamental administrative problems as the private agencies. They are (1) the continuous development and presentation of a program which warrants the supplying of funds by those who control them; (2) the co-ordination of social work with the functions of others; and (3) the securing of personnel and the development of increasing skill on their part.

A businessman would generalize these activities as control, direction, and supervision. He would say that control is based primarily on knowledge; direction on good sense; and supervision, or collaboration, on sensitivity to feelings. These are the same three qualities involved in the three steps in case work. In fact, skill in case work may well be carried over into administration. In administration, as in case work, there must first be knowledge, i.e., the assembling of the facts and identification of the problem and its tangible and intangible causes; second, good sense in determining the area in which activity can be undertaken, the goals that probably can be reached; and, third, sensitivity to the quality of the interpersonal relationships involved. In the administrative field these relationships are chiefly with superior authorities to whom there is responsibility; with colleagues in the same or other professions; and with the staff.

First, then, there must be knowledge of the legal framework within which the social work program operates. The limitations are usually more specific than in private hospitals. There must be literal compliance with the law, or the comptroller-general or a taxpayer may raise objection, and serious consequences will

1. Reprinted from *Papers of the American Association of Medical Social Workers* (1941), with the permission of the association.

ensue both to the organization and to the person responsible. But too great preoccupation with the limitations and bemoaning of them may prevent full activity up to the border line. The danger is that in the anxiety to keep within the law, not everything will be carried out that is permitted. This is often indicated by such expressions as, "We can't do this, we can't do that. Why try to do anything?" A vision of what is beyond the the legal limitations is necessary, or the full services which the law does permit and require will not be carried out.

Next, there must be knowledge of the functions of the many other types of employees within the public organization, in order to collaborate with them to the best advantage.

Medical social work is always practiced in association with the profession of medicine. The public department, however, must fit into a setting composed not only of physicians, but of executives, lawyers, authorities in charge of the budget, records, personnel, supplies, and so on. There may be an advisory committee or council, too. Often a piece of work such as the original contacts with personnel—a function of prime importance to social work standards—is handled largely by others. It is therefore important to know precisely what the functions of others in the organization are, to work well with others, and keep within one's own jurisdiction.

There must be an awareness of the weakest link in the program, whether it is in the extent or quality of services rendered or in the staff member. It is at the weak link that criticism arises. It is often easier and more interesting to focus upon the good work being done at a certain point and keep developing that, than to keep bolstering the inadequate department or individual. However, the program is judged by the unit or individual who is not functioning well, whereas the many places where the superior work is being done go unnoticed.

When criticism, or any problem does arise, it is always important, just as it is in case work, to know all the circumstances: the history of events that led up to it; the mental associations with it due to the past experience on the part of the individual involved; and the motivations, conscious or unconscious, of all concerned. It is important for the administrator of the program to have the reputation for always defending her personnel. By that is meant that an administrator should discipline herself to make a courageous demand that the full circumstances be learned before judgment is passed upon a member of her staff. The worker should always be assumed innocent until proved guilty. Such a stand, I believe, increases the respect from both outsiders and staff. When persons criticize or disagree on a policy, it is usually due to their having an entirely different set of facts or premises or goals. If they can be encouraged to elaborate on what they mean, the point where there is agreement can be established. There may be good reasons for their conclusions which, if brought into the open, give a clearer idea of the situation, which may indeed need correction.

In public work, too, one can expect an occasional investigation of the program by lay persons. Such investigations should be regarded as the right of the authority which allocates funds and which is responsible to the taxpayer. It is an opportunity to explain the program to persons unacquainted with social work or, if they are familiar with it, then as a chance to show what has been accomplished with the funds at hand, and the unmet needs for which resources should be provided. Further, the investigation or survey should be used as a chance to secure ideas from those outside persons as to how they would like to see social work function or how they believe the program can be improved. Investigations should therefore be met with a fearless open-minded attitude.

Finally, there is need for a continuously acute dissatisfaction with mediocrity and old-fashioned practices. There is a need to know not only what our professional association stands for, but what the most progressive individuals in it are accomplishing. Knowledge of the current literature in the field is important. An excellent practice, one taking only a moment, is to keep a card file of publications and jot down the names of authors and titles of books, journals, or articles, publishers, the dates and page numbers, filing the cards either by author or general subject, whichever is easier. When a staff member is developing a new project, this current record of the experience of others is invaluable. Not only social work literature but medical literature also need to be scanned with the idea not of learning how to recognize certain conditions or know the latest medical treatment for them, but to see where social factors are mentioned or may play a part in the cause of the situation or have bearing on its treatment.

Control in administration, therefore, requires, just as social casework does, the assembling of the immediate and the remote facts of the situation and the identification of the problem presented; in other words, knowledge.

For direction in administration, there is need, just as in case work, for determining the area in which action can be taken, in which one can move ahead. That action must be based on good sense. Two good rules in this connection were discovered a few days ago in an old book in a New England attic. It was called *The Economy of Human Life,* published in 1835 by John Tillinghast, at the Office of Zion's Friend. It purported to be a translation of a manuscript by an ancient Brahmin:

> As one that runneth in haste over a fence, may fall into a pit on the other side, which he does not see, so is the man that plungeth suddenly into any action, before he hath considered the consequences thereof.
> In all thy desires let reason go along with thee, and fix not thy hopes beyond the bounds of probability; so shall success attend thy undertakings, and thy heart shall not be vexed with disappointments.

Two things may be mentioned as fostering such success: interpretation and compromise.

The areas in which action can be taken sometimes remain restricted because of inadequate interpretation of the possibilities to the authorities in control of funds. Social workers are interpreting social work to everyone with whom they come in contact, whether they are conscious of it or not. As Miss Ora Maybelle Lewis, formerly of the Massachusetts General Hospital, used to say, "Thou knowest not what thine own life to thy neighbor's creed hath lent." There is no excuse for one who is trying to bring joy and enrichment to the lives of others to give an impression of a drab philosophy of life of her own. There is probably no instance where there is such complete identification of a profession with the person. The social worker herself modestly admits that her chief tools are her own knowledge, sense, and sensitivity. The layman can go into the kitchen or dining-room and eat the dietitian's food, pick up a good book in the library, or secure the librarian's help in finding references to a subject in which he is interested; he can see the nurse and occupational or physical therapist making the patient comfortable. The social worker can work only with no audience or onlookers.

Skeptics sometimes say the theory and objectives are fine, but they just do not believe the social work staff has either the time or ability to put them into effect. Undoubtedly, in the administration of a public program particularly, one should be in a position constantly to give vivid examples of both tangible and intangible services. It is best to begin at the point where a physician or layman is interested. If they are primarily interested in tangible environmental assistance to a patient, such as providing for adequate aftercare and making sure that insulin is available for the diabetic; or if they have little interest in psychosomatic medicine, it is a mistake to begin with a discussion of the emotional factors of disease. One should, of course, always be throwing in new ideas, since familiarity with them gradually brings greater acceptance. If the physician or layman sees a demonstration that is effective in the realm in which he is interested, he will become more open to ideas regarding new services.

As a means of interpretation and development of the program, the annual report constitutes a valuable resource, for both the social worker herself and the reader. It provides a chance to think through the trend in the objectives of the work over a certain period and a comparison of the present with the past, as well as a chance to identify the unmet, neglected problems and their causes.

In case work the spirit of compromise has now been carried to its utmost limits. Lois F. Meredith has said in her book, *Psychiatric Social Work:* "[There is] a growing realization of the greater effectiveness of a treatment plan initiated by the client rather than by the social worker." This is true to a large extent in administration also. Administration has possibly not fully accepted Miss Follet's thesis in her book, *Creative Experience,* that the result of good group conferring is always a better solution than the mere sum of the ideas held by individuals. Compromise, however, though it usually does not result immediately in the best possible plan, does usually result in the most workable plan in the long run, because all the persons involved feel that consideration was given their viewpoint, in part at least. They therefore stand more ready to collaborate in the future.

Not everything is equally vital or urgent. One may well go into a conference, having clearly in mind the things she would like to get and the things she will take. If one compromises in the less important things, there is a better chance that the spirit of fairness will permit the maintenance of the one or two points considered essential. Further, many persons who win out later have a slight sense of guilt, which tends to make them more compromising on the next occasion. This is not always true, of course, as there are some who must always feel they have won. One interviews all kinds of busy people, some who need to dominate, some who have so many responsibilities of their own that they prefer to place confidence in the good sense of the social worker, if she can build up a reputation for this. They want her to state her recommendations immediately and give her clear, concise reasons. No one wants to be a rubber stamp, however, and the social worker should always remember that the other person, even a layman, who is not so deeply involved in the problem can often contribute new and valuable perspectives on it or put in motion a new set of associations which have not occurred to the social worker.

A mistake sometimes made is to force or permit a decision or a plan before the other person has had a chance to see the situation clearly. It is helpful to present several alternative courses to the person interviewed. Perhaps nothing is so irritating as an indirect, evasive reply. Candid admission of a mistake or weakness in a program is often disarming, because it indicates the question is not a surprise and that it is a problem thought of as the next area of activity. Incidentally, it is good practice now and then to write up in detail an interview that turned out badly and try to see what was wrong. But to return to the subject of compromise. It is not necessary for the social worker to feel that she alone has the one and only solution to the problem or that there is terrific urgency to solve every single one immediately. Prompt action is, of course, important on an urgent matter, but time itself solves some problems by bringing in new ideas and associations or by bringing along some difficulty that is so much greater that the first one suddenly looks small in comparison, and no longer holds the relatively gigantic position involving many emotions on the part of all concerned. In contemplation of the new problem, the old one may almost solve itself. Many things work themselves out eventually, if the machinery is kept in motion and patience is maintained.

Good sense in determining the area of activity which is regarded as the second step in both case work and administration requires, therefore, recognition that every step taken interprets social work favorably or unfavorably in the eyes of others; and the eternal spirit of compromise.

But it is the third aspect of administration, namely, supervision or collaboration, which most closely resembles case work, mainly because of similar dependence upon the establishment of a certain quality in the interpersonal relationships, whether with doctors, volunteers, staff, or students. When a social worker admits that she constantly uses her case work technique with her collaborators and friends, some of these persons, without identifying those occasions, immediately reject the idea in the fear that they may be "case worked," which to them suddenly becomes synonymous with being patronized and managed. Why this objection? What would be thought of a doctor who said he would not think of receiving medical treatment, or a nurse who disapproves of nursing care, or a dietitian who would not eat her own food? Is it that there is believed to be a wide chasm between the theory of case work and its practice? Harold Laski says[2] a theory is not sound unless it works well in practice. Is not the fear of being the recipient of case work expressed because in actual practice it is often carried out under a different theory from the one we profess to use? Is it not because elements of management and superiority do still creep into the actual practice of case work? It is not that the administrator undertakes

2. "Bureaucracy," *Encyclopaedia of the Social Sciences* (1930), III, 70.

deep therapy with those with whom she works, nor is it meant that all administrators can or should use exactly the same methods. One has to use an approach that is part of herself, one in which she feels at ease. There are, however, two basic necessities, namely, the acquiring of a sense of security on the part of the social worker herself and the conscious purpose of developing security on the part of others.

First in regard to herself. How does one develop and maintain a sense of security? The little book from the attic says: "In all thy undertakings, let a reasonable assurance animate thy endeavor. If thou despairest of success, thou shalt not succeed. Terrify not thy soul with vain fears, neither let thy heart sink within thee from the phantoms of imagination."

We may well look within ourselves to see just what it is we fear, just what the things are we most need to give us peace of mind. One may well scrutinize one's thinking and behavior for signs of insecurity. One of the first signs—and it is not confined to public departments—is the tendency to seek safety through bureaucracy, which someone has defined as "a passion for routine in administration, the sacrifice of flexibility to rule, delay in making decisions, or a refusal to embark on a new experiment." As Justice Cardozo once said, "Beware of that insularity of mind which perceives in every encroachment upon habit, catastrophic revolution." Other signs of insecurity are the tendency to go on the defensive the minute any opposing ideas or action is offered; the need to win out on every occasion; feelings of resentment of criticism, irritability, anger, and the habit of placing the blame entirely upon the other person as "just not socially minded." These are all danger signals. "If thou bearest slight provocations with patience, it shall be imputed under thee for wisdom and if thou wipest them from thy remembrance thy heart shall feel rest and thy mind shall not reproach thee."

It is probably also unnecessary to go to the defense of every cause in which one believes every time that it is challenged. One should try to decide whether one's major cause, social work, will be hurt more by so doing than the other cause will be promoted. Sometimes we are insecure because we do not have enough knowledge of the facts of the situation or what good standards demand, or how others have attacked this problem. Perhaps we have not acquired quite the sense of abandon and habit of looking upon challenges as new adventures. Sometimes executives are afraid of staff members who have all the latest jargon at their command, whereas it should be the executives' pride to encourage the maximum specialized skill on the part of each of her staff. One should avoid decisions that give one a sense of guilt. It promotes peace of mind to endeavor to carry out a fair course toward everyone on the staff and to practice analyzing the reasons for any prejudice of which one suddenly becomes aware—a prejudice sometimes based on the most superficial associations with someone else.

One should remember, too, that one's ability fluctuates from time to time. Few people can stay on the same level of accomplishment month after month. A downward curve should not frighten us. A secure person can endure a failure now and then. If we cannot afford even a modified form of psychoanalysis, it is sometimes possible to develop security through a variety of minor supplementary interests. It is not necessary or even desirable to devote every minute to one's major interest of social work. Cherished friendships probably top the list as sources of security. Religion, music, the theater, art, and hobbies help dilute the intensity of the burden of responsibility and that tired feeling which, by lessening self-assurance, is the greatest enemy of good administration. An article in the February *Social Work Today*[3] questions the necessity for attending quite so many meetings and luncheons and dinners, and the motivations involved. I wonder if many executives do not have so many engagements, professional and social, that they become overfatigued and tense. The administrator owes it to her staff to observe her own reactions and try to keep fresh and sound her own inner security.

The administrator also must develop security in others, whether they are her superior authorities, physicians, or colleagues on the social work staff. No matter how lowly or how high the other person's position, their words or behavior often represent an appeal for acceptance and the desire for a sense of

3. Mary K. Simkhovitch, "Keeping Up with the Jones'," *Social Work Today*, February, 1941.

safety. The effectiveness of the interrelationship with that person and the results to be obtained for the social work program often depend on the ability to meet that appeal. Most people in these war days are carrying increasingly heavy and new responsibility which they sincerely feel quite unequal to meeting and which they can scarcely see their way through. The social worker should never add to their sense of insecurity. It is her duty to encourage a sense of adequacy as a part of the general morale of the country.

The secret of morale, about which so much is being said today, is the presence of this sense of security. The social work program advances when the social worker is regarded with the same feeling as that recently expressed by a hospital superintendent regarding the social worker in charge in a state hospital program near here, "Doesn't it do one good to see her coming?" The other person's security is increased when he feels that the social worker is interested in promoting his purposes, his successes, and not merely her own. If he shows the least indication that he wants to express his hopes and plans, the social worker must encourage him to do this so that she can see how her plans can best fit in with his in a way that will be favorable to his interests as well as her own.

Sometimes a person's security is thwarted by the serious urgency with which the social worker approaches a problem. A much better relationship is usually established when the social worker indicates that she herself is not too disturbed by the size of the problem; that she is not determined to have her own way and will not feel injured at all if the decision is not in her favor. Sometimes apparent resistance or apathy with which a proposal is greeted is due to that person's disliking to face issues which seem too big or untimely. Sometimes they are satisfied with the status quo and want to maintain it. They themselves have lost the desire to struggle for a cause and feel that a sin of omission will be less severely criticized than one of commission. Sometimes they are uncomfortable because the social worker is always bearing witness to some distressing fact for which they can see no solution and which almost frightens them.

When resistance is encountered, one must listen carefully to what the other person is saying and try to gather its significance. When Miss McMahon used to say to us in 1919, "Know the psychology of your doctor," one had to depend chiefly on intuition. In recent years a great volume of literature has arisen which helps us grasp more easily the meaning behind the other person's words, attitudes, and behavior. Here I should like to mention the great mistake, even impoliteness, of using technical, particularly psychoanalytical, language with a physician who is not interested in psychiatry, to say nothing of psychoanalysis. We should consider what our own purpose is in using these words and concepts. Do we use them merely to practice and reassure ourselves? Is there a superiority element involved, or really an inferiority, because of inability to translate such terms into everyday words? It is probably a mistake always to be pointing out the unconscious meaning of the behavior or words of the person being interviewed, or to carry on an interview in a language with which he is not familiar. Just as case workers have found out, it is inadvisable and unnecessary to go into a verbal exposition of the other's conscious and unconscious. This is a temptation from which many seem to get unholy satisfaction. Most people are not so introspective as social workers, and they resist such interpretations and at the same time the person who gives it and her program.

Public agencies often have more or less to do with politicians who have been asked by their constituents to secure some favor. On that politician to a certain extent the future income of the hospital may depend at the time appropriations are made. It is therefore important to realize what his predicament is with his constituents and look ahead to a point where the social worker's interest and his purposes meet in a common goal, that is, the welfare of the hospital in which both are interested. It is important to come to an agreement which will supply him material that he can use effectively in his reply to the constituent, one that will help him maintain his relationships with that person. Frankness and helping him in finding a way that he can handle his situation, if the favor cannot be granted, add to the security of all concerned.

The same general rule holds true for relationships with the

staff. Their morale depends on the inner sense of security they feel. It is promoted by their feeling that fairness and justice are always applied to them. Hostilities, rivalries, jealousies, dependencies on the part of the individual staff members, are signs of insecurity. Today a great deal is being said of the importance of encouraging people to express their hostilities and grievances. Their outpouring should be received not with a counterattack, nor with the irritating silence and apathy, which wrongly have been associated with the idea of passive treatment. The interpersonal relationships that build security on the part of the staff member demand warmth and kindliness and some indication of the understanding and sympathy, together with a sense of ease, which show no resentment and no intention of punishing the person for his revelation. The full expression of a grievance, when thus received, has a good administrative effect.

The security of the staff is enhanced by the sense of interdependency between the administrator and the staff and their knowledge that she realizes that the program requires joint participation and collaboration. Further, they like to have presented to them a challenge or responsibility that is just big enough to intrigue them without "flooring" them or embarrassing them before others. They want to see themselves progressing. The fostering of their skill requires that they be taught from the point where they are and that new ideas be related to the ones they already have, so they are led to come to conclusions themselves, rather than feel ideas are imposed upon them. As Alexander Pope said:

> Men must be taught as though one taught them not,
> And things unknown proposed as things forgot.

This does not mean disingenuousness, but avoidance of the superior-inferior relationship.

In conclusion it may be said that administration, which consists of control, direction, and supervision, is very closely allied to the three steps in case work, namely, knowledge of the situation, with understanding of its causes; the sensible determination of the area in which activity can proceed; and the establishment of interpersonal relationships based on sensitivity to the emotions and motivations of the persons involved.

2. In Health and Welfare Services

The Philosophy of Medical Social Work under Public Auspices[1]

BY EDITH M. BAKER

ALL social work today has to be considered in the light of a changing world. Many of the social advances that have come and others not yet accomplished have been foreshadowed by leaders striving for democratic ideals on behalf of the physical and social welfare of the people. Twenty years ago, in her presidential address entitled "Child Welfare Standards: A Test of Democracy," Julia C. Lathrop said to the 1919 National Conference of Social Work:

> Infant mortality can be largely prevented and the lives of mothers safeguarded to this end. And a federal measure is proposed which will be costly in money but economical in life. In large areas of our country, where local taxes are raised with difficulty although the tax rates are high, we are confronted by poverty and by isolation. These are areas far removed from doctors, where the visiting nurse is unknown, where hospitals are inaccessible, where hygiene is not taught, and in these regions mothers and babies suffer and die unattended. There are industrial areas, too, where mothers and children are treated with fatalistic neglect. These mothers and these children need public health nurses, hospitals and medical attention, above all homely lessons in hygiene and how to keep well. These things should be provided as the public schools are provided, to be used by all with dignity and self-respect.[2]

In discussing the importance of child-welfare standards, Miss Lathrop continued:

1. Reprinted from *Papers of the American Association of Medical Social Workers* (1939), with the permission of the association.
2. *Proceedings of the National Conference of Social Work at the Forty-sixth Annual Session Held in Atlantic City, New Jersey, June 1-8, 1919* (Chicago: Rogers & Hall Co., for the National Conference of Social Work, 1920).

The whole question of putting such standards into operation is this: Are we willing to spend the money? Can we make ourselves spend the money? Will we steadily push forward the new legislation, State and Federal, which is needed to give them effect? And let us not forget that the universality of their application is a stern test of our democracy. Without universality the standards are sounding brass.

Miss Lathrop questioned our willingness to spend large sums for social betterment and our readiness to bring pressure for social action in regard to the enactment of our social philosophy and pointed out the necessity for eliminating the inequalities of service for certain areas. Similar notes were struck 10 years later in the presidential address, "Social Work: Cause and Function," by Porter R. Lee at the 1929 National Conference of Social Work. Mr. Lee said:

> What about the costs of social work? How much social welfare can we afford? There are several quick answers to this question. The chests talk about "the saturation point." The professional money raisers tell us that there is no limit provided the cause is legitimate and the campaign properly organized. Some of us believe that, wherever our resources, we cannot afford to stop our efforts to rid the world of evil, no matter what expenditures for luxuries need to be curtailed or what new methods of money raising need to be devised in order to find the ways and means. . . .
>
> I believe this question to be inportant for social workers because I think we have never faced the cost of the logical extension of our demonstration programs to all those persons in American communities who might benefit by them. Some of these services, like vaccination, are relatively inexpensive. . . . In between and outside and all around are services and potential benefits in health, in economic security, in education, in cultural opportunity, representing all degrees of costliness. Can civilization afford all of the benefits which it knows how to create? I incline, temperamentally at least, to believe that it cannot afford to do without them.[3]

Mr. Lee's address preceded by a few months the economic crash of autumn, 1929. It was given at a time when private philanthropy bore much of the cost of welfare activities. During the ensuing years the prolonged and widespread depression made it clear that the expense of the care of the unemployed could not be carried by privately supported charitable endeavor. Recognition ultimately had to be given, although at first grudgingly, that the victims of unemployment had certain rights as citizens

3. *Proceedings of the National Conference of Social Work at the Fifty-sixth Annual Session Held in San Francisco, California, June 26–July 3, 1929* (Chicago: University of Chicago Press, for the National Conference of Social Work, 1930).

and that the staggering cost of expanding relief services might be met through taxation. Bertha C. Reynolds has given a vivid account of the struggle that took place between the forces that opposed democracy and the movements for democracy in her articles on "Re-thinking Social Case Work."[4]

A profound effect on the philosophy of social work resulted when the democratic principle largely supplanted the philanthropic principle in assistance to the needy. Gradually there has come an extension of governmental responsibility for meeting certain needs of the people on a nation-wide scale. Some measures, such as that establishing the F.E.R.A., have been of a temporary nature, and others, such as the Social Security Act, the National Labor Relations Act, the U.S. Housing Act of 1937, the Fair Labor Standards Act of 1938, represent more permanent and fundamental attempts to attack economic and social inequalities. During this period the principle was finally established that certain types of insecurity that individuals are powerless to cope with alone must be met through public action, that human conservation is an obligation of government.

Last summer, almost a decade after Mr. Lee's address, a conference was called in Washington to consider the unmet health needs of the people and to discuss the tentative proposals for a national health program. Still included among the unmet health needs were the lack of medical attention and hospital facilities for mothers and children mentioned twenty years previously by Miss Lathrop. The conference was presided over by Josephine Roche, chairman of the Interdepartmental Committee To Coordinate Health and Welfare Activities. In her opening remarks Miss Roche stated:

Fifty million Americans are in families receiving less than $1,000 income a year; illness and death increase their toll as income goes down; medical care decreases sharply as need for it mounts.

This staggering aggregate of suffering and death can and must be lightened. But putting aside for the moment the human aspect of the problem, let us look straight at the economic waste to the Nation of these unmet needs.

On an average day of the year, 4 million or more persons in the United States are disabled by illness. Every year, 70 million sick persons lose more than 1 billion days from work. The total cost of illness and premature death

4. *Social Work Today*, April, May, and June, 1938.

in this country is approximately 10 billion dollars a year. This estimate includes only those factors which can be expressed in dollar values—the
cost of health services and medical care, the loss of wages through unemployment resulting from disability, and the loss of potential future earnings through death.

We cannot attack successfully with small change a 10-billion-dollar
problem. To carry forward a long-time program of health services and
medical care commensurate with need will cost the Government millions,
but save the Nation billions. It must be a program which not only safeguards but advances the quality of medical care.[5]

The conference was attended not only by representatives of
the professional groups concerned with the provision of medical
care but also by representatives of the consumer groups. The
evidence concerning untreated illness and preventable morbidity
and mortality that was presented was impressive and convincing.
There was general agreement concerning the need of the people
for help against sickness and disability. The problem that remained was to develop the measures to ameliorate these defects
and to insure a wider distribution of medical services. Recommendations for an adequate, comprehensive health program were
submitted by the Technical Committee on Medical Care.

A few months later, on January 23, 1939, President Roosevelt,
in his message to Congress in respect to the report and recommendations on national health of the Interdepartmental Committee To Co-ordinate Health and Welfare Activities, wrote as
follows:

The objective of a national health program is to make available in all
parts of our country and for all groups of our people the scientific knowledge and skill at our command to prevent and care for sickness and disability; to safeguard mothers, infants, and children; and to offset through
social insurance the loss of earnings among workers who are temporarily
or permanently disabled.

The committee does not propose a great expansion of Federal health
services. It recommends that plans be worked out and administered by
States and localities with the assistance of Federal grants-in-aid. The aim
is a flexible program. The committee points out that while the eventual
costs of the proposed program would be considerable, they represent a
sound investment which can be expected to wipe out, in the long run,
certain costs now borne in the form of relief.

5. *Proceedings of the National Health Conference, July 18–20, 1938, Interdepartmental Committee To Co-ordinate Health and Welfare Activities* (Washington: Government Printing Office, 1938).

These excerpts from various papers are given in order that we may trace through them something of the social philosophy that has developed with reference to social inequalities, the obligation for social action, and the implications of financial support for health and welfare programs through governmental sources. They have significance for the social thinking of the present, just as the social thinking of the present has implications for the future. Today many social workers, as members of a profession that is an integral part of the social scheme, realize that they have a continuing responsibility for the assumption of constructive leadership in the development of a social order guaranteeing the essentials of life to all the people. Charlotte Towle in a recent article, "The Individual in Relation to Social Change," points out that

the contribution of those social leaders and educators in the field of professional social work, who saw beyond the times and who long ago exerted strong leadership in striving for democratic ideals in social work through emphasizing the need for reform of the poor laws rather than for their abolishment, cannot be overestimated. They not only laid the groundwork to be utilized in more receptive times, but they also set a pattern for social workers to function as leaders rather than as followers in the process of social change.[6]

Perhaps we can consider that the philosophy of the profession of social work has contributed to the broadening concepts of public health and welfare and to the expanding principle of governmental responsibility for social welfare. Perhaps also we may consider that the profession has shared with others in effecting social change. However, history will reveal more clearly than we can determine today the various forces that have shaped social progress.

Thomas Mann in *The Coming Victory of Democracy* relates that the French philosopher Bergson sent to a philosophical congress which recently met in Paris a message in which he set up this imperative: "Act as men of thought, think as men of action." Then Mr. Mann comments: "That is a thoroughly democratic slogan. No intellectual of the pre-democratic era ever thought of action, nor of what kind of action would result if his thinking

6. *Social Service Review*, March, 1939.

were put into practice."[7] These ideas have a meaning for social workers, who sometimes are so immersed in their own particular day-by-day practice that they neglect to turn their attention to the issues of wider significance. However, the increasing interest in questions of social value, the developing philosophy in regard to social action, and the sense of loyalty to the deepening democratic process in this country on the part of many social workers today constitute the chief hope for the effectiveness of social work leadership and practice in the future.

Medical social workers have shared with other social workers the responsibility for thought and action in regard to the social changes taking place in recent years. They recognize that these changes have many implications for medical social work. They know something of the extent of illness; they know the consumers of medical care intimately; they know many of the gaps in medical services and facilities; and they know at first hand the meaning of these lacks in terms of human suffering. They are peculiarly prepared, because of their experience, to offer convincing evidence of the need for adequate medical and hospital care as part of a national health program. Hence medical social workers have a major philosophical interest in all that pertains to the extension of social security to the vital field of health.

With the coming of government into the field of social work, medical social workers have been drawn into public medical-care programs. Previously they have served mainly in voluntary or public medical institutions and infrequently in state or local departments of health. Following the adoption of Rules and Regulations No. 7 on June 23, 1933, setting up a program of medical care under the F.E.R.A., and the passage of the Social Security Act in 1935, medical social workers have been included in many extramural programs of medical services, federal, state, and local. On the state or local level these medical-care programs have usually been developed in departments of health or welfare. In one state, California, medical social positions have been created in the medical program sponsored by the Farm Security Administration. In one national agency, the National Society for the Prevention of Blindness, a medical social worker has been added

7. *The Coming Victory of Democracy* (New York: Alfred A. Knopf, 1938)

to the staff. One of the activities of this agency has been the development of medical social service in eye clinics, both public and private. There are other instances of the extension of medical social work under governmental auspices, but these examples will serve as illustration of the trend in recent years.

Naturally we ask ourselves why this has happened. What are the medical social implications in a medical-care program under governmental auspices? What particular services can medical social workers render in these medical programs designed to care for certain categories or groups or to provide for the medical needs of those on relief? What roles do medical social workers play, and what activities do they perform? Where in the whole range of services, from the diagnostic processes through active medical treatment and aftercare, can they be most helpful? The current study that is being made by the American Association of Medical Social Workers in co-operation with the American Public Welfare Association will do much to advance our knowledge of the content and method of medical social work in public programs, under health and welfare auspices, in several states. In the meantime, certain observations in regard to medical social work in the crippled children's program may be pertinent. This program and the policy-making that shaped it reflect the general trend in social thinking concerning public medical-care programs.

The comments that I have to make at this time are based mainly on my experience with the program of services for crippled children developed through federal-state co-operation in the 48 states, Alaska, Hawaii, and the District of Columbia. This appears to me to offer a valid basis, since the crippled children's program is primarily a program of medical care which involves the correlation of many diversified services in the interest of the sick person. The crippled children's program has served as a laboratory in which to test the effectiveness of policies and procedures in making medical care available and medical treatment effective for one specific group. This program has many similarities to the other public medical-care programs in which medical social workers are functioning, and the social thinking in regard to it is applicable to such programs.

The essence of the program is federal-state co-operation. Administration and control of activities carried on in the states remain in the hands of state and local authorities. The function of the federal government is to provide financial assistance under certain regulations and to furnish consultation services. Subject to necessary basic requirements, each state is at liberty to set up a plan of its own formulation geared to its own needs and facilities. A new philosophy of federal and state agencies has emerged. It has been necessary to establish clear-cut channels of relationship through which supervisory and advisory services can flow, in order that there may be participation with the states in the mutual development of policies and standards. The field consultant service, medical, public health nursing, and medical social, affords the chief means of disseminating information, interpreting general objectives, promoting desirable administrative practice, and stimulating the development and maintenance of a broad-gauge program of services.

In the crippled children's program, medical social workers are functioning on the federal, state, and district levels. Some states have no medical social workers, other states have only one worker, and a few states have workers assigned on a district basis. Although certain functions may not be performed by all the workers and the amount of time devoted to certain activities may vary, there appears to be enough uniformity of service to make it unnecessary to distinguish between the different levels of service in this discussion of medical social work in the crippled children's program.

It seems to me that the medical social worker has a point of view that brings into focus those phases of the program where consideration of each patient as an individual is needed in order that the feelings of the patient about his illness and the recommendations for treatment and his ability to use and profit by medical care may be understood; in order that any adjustment may be made that will facilitate the continuity of medical care; and in order that the patient's social and environmental needs may be met as they affect satisfactory medical care, aftercare, and rehabilitation. I believe that the medical social worker can be aware of the way in which each policy and procedure of the program operates to further or to block the patient's participation

in the medical plan. She brings an understanding of the relationship of psychic and environmental factors to the development
and recurrence of disease and to its treatment—that is, the social
component of medical care. Perhaps her peculiar contribution to
program planning is her point of view in regard to the patient—
her consistent emphasis on the fact that each patient reacts, always individually, to his illness and to each step in medical treatment—and her ability to integrate the medical and social factors.

The nature and character of medical social work is inevitably
influenced by the setting within which it is practiced. For it is
the setting which to a great extent determines the nature of the
philosophic concepts developed. The purpose and the function
as defined by statute and the administrative structure of the agency are important in their influence. As previously indicated, the
setting in which medical social workers usually function in these
newer programs differs from the setting in which they have
generally functioned in the past. The agency is extramural rather
than intramural. The program must extend throughout the state.
Services must be planned with this purpose in mind, and local
activities must be effectively related to the whole program. The
special emphasis on services for rural areas makes it important
for medical social workers to acquire the knowledge and skills
essential to function effectively in such surroundings where lack
of certain resources must be minimized, available resources must
be used most effectively, and new ones must be created. It is
necessary to understand the customs and the attitudes of rural
groups, and the various forces operating in a rural area. It is also
necessary to learn how to work satisfactorily with the local physician under conditions that differ from the usual ones within
the medical institution. Implicit in the purpose of the agency is
the responsibility for furnishing service for all patients coming
within the scope of the program. This implies acceptance of the
philosophy that the persons for whom service is established under
governmental authorization have an inalienable right to use that
service, as Miss Lathrop has said, with dignity and self-respect.
All these factors and many others influence the method in medical social practice in public programs. Although the setting of
the public organization within which medical social work is

practiced may be different, consideration of the individual and the meaning to him of the illness and each step in its treatment are the essential threads running through medical social service provided under any auspices. Fern Lowry has pointed out that a philosophy of setting is a primary requisite for the case work practitioner and that it is necessary for him to have an awareness of and relatedness to the setting within which he is practicing. Without such a philosophy, case workers are in danger of becoming isolated from, sometimes insulated against, the community and the program of which they are a part.

If the progress of a sick person could be followed from the time the public agency first hears of him through the successive steps of diagnosis, treatment, convalescence, aftercare, and rehabilitation, there would be found certain points where the effectiveness of the care is vitally influenced by social factors. The points of special significance to the medical social worker are the points of intake or acceptance for public medical services, hospitalization, convalescence, and aftercare.

At the point of intake it is necessary to understand the patient's attitude toward his condition and his readiness to use medical services. It is important that the patient be helped to see his situation clearly enough that he has the basis for making an intelligent decision concerning his acceptance of medical recommendations and his participation in medical treatment. Due recognition should be given to the right of the patient to use or to refuse medical services, and no pressure should be imposed upon him unless the protection of others is involved. This means that it is not satisfactory merely to provide facilities for meeting medical needs but that policies must be initiated to insure that advantage can be taken of these opportunities in so far as possible. The sick person must be encouraged to seek medical care at the earliest possible moment. Too rigid application of restrictions may discourage the full use of medical resources and so thwart the purpose for which they are intended. Although I believe that the medical care provided by a public agency should be available for all persons who wish to avail themselves of it, there is inevitably an interim period during which funds and facilities are limited. This necessitates some selection among the applicants for medical services. Selection involves a decision concerning eligibility based on medical and social factors. In order to secure the information required for an understanding of medical need, diagnostic services should be freely available to everyone. The medical data must be related to the social data regarding resources and obligations when the decision concerning acceptance for care is made. Flexible policies are necessary so that emergencies may be cared for promptly. When a selection of applicants on a categorical or other basis is made, there will inevitably be certain persons ineligible for care to whom adequate assistance should be given in developing an alternative plan of care or to whom advice should be given in regard to appropriate resources where they may seek assistance.

Preceding the admitting process some public programs, notably the crippled children's program, are obligated to locate the persons for whom the services are designed. The intent of these programs is to seek for and provide services to all people of a given category, whereas other public programs of medical care deal primarily with those who apply for medical attention or with sick persons on relief rolls. This responsibility for case location implies the development of a case-finding technique that continuously utilizes all available resources in a community. Experience in the crippled children's program has shown that when rural areas know about the services included in the state program and understand the steps to be undertaken in referring a child for care, crippled children are more readily and systematically located and provided with medical treatment.

It is unnecessary to point out to medical social workers the social factors that affect medical care, whether it is provided in clinics, in hospitals, or in convalescent facilities. Emphasis has been placed on the understanding and treatment of the whole person in relation to his particular situation. Attention has been drawn to the importance of giving consideration to the feelings of the patient about his illness and the recommendations made for treatment and of recognizing that the patient's reactions determine the efforts which he makes to use medical care and to participate in the medical plan. The waste of highly skilled medical service is apparent when the patient's willingness to carry out the recommendations raises obstacles to its completion. In clinics, where pressure and tension are prevalent, and in hospitals, where the setup is impersonal and complex, the patient has special need to be accepted by someone who looks upon him as an individual with his own unique personality and his own particular environment. Many of these patients are from rural areas, where people enter hospitals infrequently and usually only for extremely serious conditions. Such patients need the opportunity to express any doubts or fears and to secure answers for any questions they wish to ask. Unless they have such an opportunity, they may refuse to follow the medical regime. In these instances they may be "discharged against advice" and classified as "unco-operative"! When clinic services are too hurried to allow for a full explanation of the doctor's recommendations to be made and home visits to interpret the medical plan are delayed, similar reactions may be anticipated. These examples of ways in which medical care may break down are given to illustrate some of the problems that arise at the points or areas of service under consideration. It is well known that patients can be more satisfactorily and permanently restored to health when medical study and treatment take into consideration the social, psychic, and environmental factors and when help can be offered to patients in working through their worries, fears, feelings of insecurity, and sources of tension; in making any needed adjustment in their environment; or in making use of the services of community resources.

It seems to me that the attitude of medical social workers toward questions of national health and well-being and the social thinking underlying their activities in public programs of medical care indicate trends in the developing philosophy of medical social work under public auspices. I believe that changes in our philosophy have occurred because of our actual experience through the years. From action and policy-making emerges the general thinking of the period. I should like to suggest the five points that appear to me to epitomize medical social philosophy of today:

1. Assumption of responsibility for sharing with others in social action leading to health security.
2. Conviction that public medical services should be available for those

who need them and that the utilization of such services should not bear the stigma of charity.

3. Concern for reaching and extending service to all persons coming within legislative provisions of the program.

4. Belief in the freedom of the individual to accept or reject medical treatment in whole or in part when the lives of others are not endangered.

5. Emphasis upon the necessity of individualization of the sick person in a program designed to serve large numbers of people—the case method versus the mass method.

Does it seem to you that these things have a part in aiding men to achieve justice, equality, freedom, and the happiness that comes from social security and health?

The Functions of Medical Social Work in Departments of Health and Welfare[1]

BY LUCILLE MARTIN SMITH

SIGNIFICANT trends in professional practice are more easily identified and better understood when presented in relation to the historical development of the movements that have affected the origin and evolution of that profession. In order to evaluate properly the functions of medical social workers in departments of health and welfare, it would, therefore, be necessary to review the history of hospitals, of medicine, of public health, and of private and public welfare. Obviously, time does not permit of any such exposition. We can, however, point out that in its brief history of thirty-five years in the United States, medical social work has gone through three easily identified periods, in each of which the scope and method of practice have been modified substantially to meet the changing requirements of the social institutions from which the need for medical social work emanates.

The first period was originally described in the writings of Dr. Cabot, who presented so vividly the need felt by physicians for an additional member of the medical team to bring to the physician interpretations of social and psychological factors which affect the patient's health and to assist the patient in his efforts to bring about changes in his social situation in order that medical recommendations may be effectively carried out. In the first period, medical social work was practiced exclusively in hospitals and clinics. In a sense this period, of course, extends to the present, for medical social work in hospitals and clinics has had a steady, continuous, and progressive growth.

The second period can be said to date from 1918, when Minnesota established medical social work as part of the department

1. Unpublished paper presented at the New York State Conference of Social Welfare, October 10, 1940. Reprinted with the permission of the author.

66

of health. Possibly in some other states this was done at an earlier date, although no references can be found which antedate the Minnesota experience. Massachusetts appointed a medical social worker to its department of health in 1924; Los Angeles County, in 1927; and subsequently many state and local health departments have incorporated medical social services as an integral part of health administration. In the early stages of this period we find the first attempts to apply to the problem of mass control of communicable disease the philosophy and method of medical social case practice as developed in hospitals and clinics.

The third period is that of the present, beginning about 1933, when the auspices under which medical social work was practiced were further extended to include departments of public welfare. In some instances, as in New York City, functions previously discharged by health departments were transferred to welfare and integrated with the related functions of the assistance program. In other communities, both state and local, medical social workers were employed to assist in the organization and administration of new developments in public assistance which had to do with providing health services to recipients. The impetus given by the Federal Emergency Relief Administration to the employment of medical social work under extramural auspices was increased after the passage of the Social Security Act, when federal money was made available to state agencies for expansion in the maternal and child-welfare services, public health services, crippled children's services, and for federal participation in state and local funds used for assistance to the needy aged, the needy blind, and dependent children. In this period a few private agencies, such as health education organizations, community chests, hospital councils, and the like, also employed medical social workers for duties other than medical-social case work.

It is the purpose of this paper to contrast the practices of medical social workers in departments of health and welfare with the practices of medical social workers in hospitals and clinics. Unfortunately, at the present time no comprehensive figures are available on the number and distribution of medical social workers in departments of health and welfare; nor has much been written about their duties. We do know, however, that as of June 1, 1940, 59 medical social workers were employed in 29 state crippled children's programs. We know also that medical social workers are in state welfare agencies in Massachusetts, Rhode Island, New York, Louisiana, Minnesota, Oregon, and Washington. In city departments of public welfare we find medical social workers in Boston, New York City, Rochester, Chicago, New Orleans, Los Angeles, Portland, and San Francisco. There are probably other places where medical social workers have been employed in such organizations.

In reviewing what these medical social workers do, one is impressed by the striking applicability to this type of practice of the standards recommended by the American Association of Medical Social Workers[2] for practice in hospitals and clinics. The methods by which medical social workers achieve the ends described in this statement of standards necessarily differ in accordance with the purpose for which each agency was established, the size of the group for whom the agency is responsible for providing care, the adequacy of funds and of staff and other factors. But the similarities are as significant as are the differences. For our discussion today I am dividing the activities of medical social workers in public agencies into four groups: administration, in the broad sense of the word; consultation; case work; and education.

ADMINISTRATION

In contrasting practices in departments of health and welfare with practices in hospitals and clinics, an outstanding characteristic appears to be greater emphasis on administrative duties in the former than has been true in hospitals and clinics. Directors of divisions of medical services in welfare departments and directors or supervisors of medical social services in health and welfare are engaged primarily in administrative duties.

In the last ten years the administration of departments of health and welfare has changed substantially as to both scope and method. In the welfare departments we have seen the number of

2. American Association of Medical Social Workers, *A Statement of Standards To Be Met by Medical Social Service Departments in Hospitals and Clinics: A Report of the Committee on Standards*. Adopted May, 1936.

persons eligible for assistance multiplied many fold. We have seen legislation establishing categories of assistance, eligibility for which may be dependent upon health considerations, as, for instance, incapacity of the parent in the aid to dependent children program and blindness in the aid to the blind program. In the health departments we have seen the scope of the program greatly extended by the shift in emphasis to more personal services to individuals than were formerly performed by such departments.

Although in both health and welfare we find medical social work executives having wide administrative responsibilities, this is particularly true in the latter type of agency. Welfare administrators usually are equipped neither by education nor by experience for discharging many health responsibilities that have been either delegated to them by law or assumed by them because of the lack of an organized health program to meet the needs of recipients of assistance.

The great expansion in public welfare, accompanied as it has been by frequent shifts in legislation, by extension of responsibility, and by diverse authorities for different methods of care to various groups in the population, has required considerable specialization. As has been pointed out by Mr. Urwick, an outstanding British authority on administration:

> The application of scientific discovery to economic life in the course of the last century has increased enormously the volume and variety of specialized knowledge available to contribute to the conduct of enterprises of all kinds. This knowledge must be used, and used effectively, if the enterprise is to be conducted with reasonable efficiency. On the other hand it is impossible and unreasonable to expect every individual in a position of responsibility to be fully acquainted with, and to maintain his knowledge of, all the specialized sciences and skills which he must use in the course of his work.[3]

It is natural that administrators in the welfare agencies should have found it expedient to employ, as part of the technical staff, persons whose education has a generic base common to that of other employees of the welfare agency. The training of the medical social workers has the same common background as that of the administrator himself, if he has had social work education,

3. L. Urwick, "Executive Decentralization with Functional Coordination," *Management Review* (American Management Association, 20 Vessey Street, New York City); XXIV, No. 12 (December, 1935), 361.

and of the social work staff who assist him in the development of administrative policy. As a rule, however, none of these persons has sufficient knowledge of the relationship of health and economic status, of the symptoms of various diseases which indicate the need for medical services, of the reasonable costs of such services, of the resources in the community best equipped to give care, of the relationships of social and medical factors in treatment, and of other considerations that vitally affect the way in which the welfare agency meets the needs of the persons whom it is designed to serve. The wise administrator of departments of health and welfare expects his medical social workers to contribute to policy-making.

The most recent trend which is discernible in the administrative duties of medical social workers in departments of welfare is typified by differences in the jobs of medical social workers in general relief programs and those in the categorical assistance programs. In the former, medical social workers are concerned almost exclusively with that part of the agency responsibility which has to do with making medical services available to recipients of assistance and with strengthening the policies and procedures of the agency in such a way as to make it possible for the medical care to be effective. In the categorical programs other equally important duties are seen.

Let us examine the aid to dependent children program as a case in point. As has been said earlier, one of the conditions of eligibility for assistance under the aid to dependent children program is the incapacity of a parent. In order to determine whether or not this condition is met, the agency must establish policies and procedures which will provide evidence that the parent is incapacitated. Such a statement oversimplifies the process. All of us would admit that incapacity is difficult to establish. Judgment in regard to physical or mental incapacity is not always obvious, nor is it always easy to establish. More is involved than organic findings, since the reaction of individuals with identical physical findings will vary widely. More may be involved than inability to support. Decisions in regard to incapacity rest upon social and medical judgments into which subjective elements inevitably enter. Public opinion in many communities militates against decisions which, while safeguarding the future of children, may appear to relieve parents of responsibility. The assistance agency, therefore, must establish policies and procedures that are sufficiently specific and technically sound to safeguard the agency from making rigid and harsh decisions or, equally important, from making decisions that arouse criticism in the community that persons are accepted irrespective of disability. Medical social work has much to contribute to the promulgation of the agency's practices in this regard.

Where medical social workers, as in Boston, Louisiana, and Oregon, have participated in this part of the agency's program, they have pointed out several basic considerations which affect the administration of the program: first, that the agency is responsible for making the decision in regard to eligibility for assistance and, therefore, may not, as has been done in many places, place upon physicians the entire responsibility for determining incapacity. A report from a physician in regard to the patient's diagnosis and prognosis is, of course, part of the evidence which the assistance agency needs in determining eligibility for assistance. What is wanted from the physician, however, is a diagnosis and recommendation for medical care, not a decision in regard to eligibility for assistance. Likewise, it is important that the agency clearly recognize that the medical report, although very significant, is only one part of the evidence and that such reports must be evaluated by the agency staff in relation to the economic, environmental, and psychological factors that are also involved.

In addition to pointing out to the administrator the responsibilities of the assistance agency in such situations, the medical social worker will usually be helpful in advising the agency on further details of policy regarding who shall make the medical or psychiatric examination. She will realize that the agency's needs will be best served if physicians qualified by training and experience are designated for this purpose. She will be helpful in determining what facts the medical report should contain. She will advise the agency about various possibilities by which the medical report may be reviewed by a competent medical authority to insure that the medical examination has been adequate and that a reasonable diagnosis has been established. She will undoubtedly influence the assistance agency in seeing the medical report not only as evidence of incapacity but also as evidence of services which the incapacitated person needs in order that his health may be conserved or restored. Similarly, she will see in the medical report indications that point to services to other members of the family who may need medical services as a protection against the same health hazard which caused the parent's incapacity.

The influence of medical social work concepts in drafting procedures for implementing the agency's policies in regard to determining eligibility for assistance is particularly important. The practices of the agency in securing medical information necessary to establish incapacity as a factor in eligibility must be interpreted to the staff as measures designed not only to prescribe who shall be eligible but also to indicate what services are required, to reduce to a minimum both the degree of incapacity and its duration. In this connection it should be pointed out that some of the case work concepts in regard to assuring the applicant's participation in establishing eligibility, desirable as they are in theory, may result in undesirable practices unless based on full appreciation of what such participation involves. In explaining to the applicant the procedures for establishing the eligibility of his children to aid, on the basis of his incapacity, what is implied? Does he seek medical examination to learn what his disability is and how it can be improved; or does he seek medical opinion for the express purpose of establishing his disability and the consequent eligibility of his children for assistance? Does he see himself in the eyes of his wife and children as one whose disability has denied him his usual role in the family group? In demonstrating his incapacity to the agency, does he become so discouraged as to interfere with treatment and recovery or so diverted by the requirements of the agency that he forgets his own requirements and ultimate objective?

The staff's appreciation of the temporary, partial, and changing nature of many disabilities, of evidences of the part that the agency may play in assisting the applicant to meet and adjust to the handicap imposed by illness, will determine to a large degree the extent to which the incapacitated parent participates in the establishment of eligibility. The staff's understanding will also affect the applicant's attitude toward re-establishing his health so that assistance may no longer be needed.

Medical social philosophy and method have equally important influences in the policies and practices of the agency in regard to continuing eligibility for assistance. In order to insure the most effective response to treatment during illness and convalescence and to foster the greatest possible maintenance of health that has been restored, the worries and anxieties of incapacitated parents must be relieved wherever possible. Fears built around the certainty that assistance to his family will be discontinued on the day of his discharge from an institution may seriously delay recovery. The difficulties encountered by the family in adjusting to the economic disruption that accompanies summary discontinuance of assistance when need continues to exist, although incapacity has ceased to exist, jeopardize the maintenance of health to which the parent has been restored. Medical social workers will emphasize the wisdom of policies which stress the potentialities of the aid to dependent children program for rehabilitating incapacitated parents instead of policies permitting the perpetuation of incapacity.

As has been indicated, many of the medical social worker's efforts to influence the medical social aspects of the program will be directed toward the agency's own staff. She will also have liaison duties with other agencies. Medical social workers in departments of health and welfare are responsible for conducting a liaison between the agency which the worker represents and other public and private agencies responsible for health and welfare services. In the welfare agency the medical social worker has liaison responsibilities with hospitals and clinics and with other persons in the medical community. In the health department she has liaison responsibilities between the health department and between other medical agencies and departments of welfare. The importance of these relationships cannot be overstressed. Without a satisfactory liaison, much medical care is wasted. With a good liaison, the facilities of the community may be much more effectively mobilized for the use of sick persons.

The second major grouping of activities, and probably that

of second importance in departments of health and welfare, is consultation and guidance. These are equally important in departments of health and welfare and of considerably more importance than such duties in hospitals and clinics. These activities may be described as of three types: (1) consultation with the director of the service and the department heads of other divisions in relation to policy and methods of carrying out the work; (2) consultation with the representatives of other agencies, both public and voluntary; and (3) consultation and guidance to the social workers, public health nurses, and others who come into direct contact with patients.

As has been indicated in the section on administration, consultation with the director of the service and the department heads of other divisions offers the medical social worker an opportunity to influence the entire program, as well as the scope, quality, and the cost of medical services made available to persons eligible for medical care. Consultation is equally important when it involves relationships with the social work staff, public health nurses, and others who come in direct contact with patients.

In the welfare agencies this duty is a major function of the medical social work staff, that is, of the medical social personnel responsible for consultation and case work rather than for executive duties. The difference between a patient's complaint, the worker's observation, and a diagnosis made by the physician is not always understood by staffs of welfare agencies. Many times the importance of differentiating between the three is not appreciated. Symptoms that suggest the need for medical care are not recognized. The staff needs help in appreciating the significance of social, economic, and psychological factors in illness; in acquiring familiarity with the resources for medical care; and in a variety of other facts that contribute to making medical care effective. A continuous job of staff education is performed by the medical social workers through formal educational programs, group conferences, through individual conferences with case workers about specific situations, and through other means.

In the health departments medical social workers endeavor to give to nurses and others a better understanding of the interrelationship of social and medical needs. Consultation with representatives of other agencies will also be an important duty. Since only a few welfare departments have medical social personnel, the medical social worker in health departments spends a great deal of time interpreting to the welfare departments the type of information that the agency would expect from its own medical social consultant if it had one.

CASE WORK

Although examples are to be found where medical social workers do considerable case work in departments of social welfare, such situations are unusual. In many health departments, however, medical social workers do medical social case work in much the same way as is done in hospitals and clinics. One of the reasons for this differentiation lies in the fact that in the welfare departments health services are usually not administered directly by the department but are purchased from established medical institutions and from professional practitioners. In the health departments, however, where medical services are actually provided, the medical social consultant interviews patients, relatives, and others, employing the same concepts and techniques usually utilized by medical social workers in clinics.

EDUCATION

In discussing the educational activities of medical social workers, there is necessarily some overlapping with the functions described under consultation, as consultation is one of the very important methods of staff education. Most medical social workers in departments of health and welfare participate formally or informally in the training of new members of the staff. In some instances the agency has an affiliation with a school of social work, so that students are assigned for certain services; or the agency's association with schools of social work or universities may provide for special lectures by the medical social director, supervisor, or consultant to students of social work, public health nursing, or senior medical students. Similarly, education in the community is an important duty which is discharged by the release of written statements, annual reports, and the like, by participation in local, state, and regional conferences, and by other methods of developing community understanding of the services provided by the agency.

In summarizing this discussion, it is well to realize that the period during which the scope of medical social work has been extended to include the functions described in this paper has been so short that the expansion must be considered as still in the experimental stage. It is obvious, however, that the activities of medical social work in departments of health and welfare do not differ substantially from the five activities in which, according to the association's *Statement of Standards*, social service departments in hospitals may appropriately engage:

1. Practice of medical social case work.
2. Development of the medical social program within the medical institution.
3. Participation in the development of social and health programs in the community.
4. Participation in the educational program for professional personnel.
5. Medical social research.

The outstanding differences appear to be these:

1. The practice of medical social case work in departments of welfare is much more limited than in hospitals and clinics. It is somewhat more limited in departments of health than in hospitals and clinics. The practice of medical social case work in departments of health, however, is much more extensive than in departments of welfare.

2. The development of the medical social program within departments of health coincides entirely with similar functions discharged by medical social workers in hospitals and clinics. In departments of welfare this function is modified to include also the impact of medical social concepts on the development of the entire assistance program.

3. It would appear that medical social workers in departments of health and welfare participate in the development of social and health programs in the community considerably more than do medical social workers in the hospitals and clinics. Several publications of the American Public Welfare Association point

out the confusion, division, duplication, and overlapping of responsibilities for medical care and indicate the great need for correlation among the various services. Medical social workers both in hospitals and clinics and in departments of health and welfare hold important posts for the much needed correlation of services. While thus far the duties of medical social workers in health and welfare agencies appear to emphasize this function more than is done in hospitals and clinics, this will probably not continue to be true.

4. As has been pointed out, medical social workers in departments of health and welfare participate in a wide variety of educational activities. In departments of welfare their educational activities until now have been directed largely toward the nonmedical and nonmedical social personnel of the agency—the executive and case work staff. In departments of health the medical social workers' educational duties usually relate to the executive and nursing staff of the agency and, to a greater extent than in welfare, to the staffs of other health and welfare agencies.

It is to be hoped that in the near future the educational activities of medical social workers in both health and welfare will be further extended to include participation in the education of medical social personnel for work in the public services.

5. The fifth and last activity included in the association's statement of standards is medical social research. Very little has been done in this area in departments of health and welfare. The same can be said of medical social research in hospitals and clinics. The need for further research in both types of practices is self-evident.

To quote again from Mr. Urwick:

Where new relationships which develop in the evolution of organization give rise to new duties and a new form of authority, a final and satisfactory solution is never reached, until the duties involved are isolated, analyzed, and defined. They have then to be grouped in suitable positions, the relations of those positions to others analyzed and regulated, and the positions filled by individuals, properly selected and suitably trained.[4]

We need very much to analyze the adaptations in medical social practice that are to be found in health and welfare departments. We need research to establish suitable methods for

4. *Op. cit.*, p. 366.

compiling statistics in regard to services and costs. We need studies of the administrative procedures that have been developed, to learn, for instance, whether better service results to the patient when he calls the doctor direct, without the so-called "red tape" of government, or whether the "red tape" of requiring authorization of medical service offers the doctor and the social worker an opportunity for correlating medical and social treatment that contributes significantly to the quality of service to the patient. We need to study the relationships of medical social workers to the other personnel with whom they are intimately associated—the medical director, the public health nurse, the other specialists on the staff.

The list of much needed research could extend indefinitely, which is as it should be in a new field in which patterns are in a fluid stage and in which the practitioners concerned have the inquiring attitude that foreshadows sound development of professional theory and practice.

A Medical Social Worker in a
Public Assistance Agency[1]

BY EVELYN GROSS COHEN

IN FEBRUARY, 1942, the St. Louis Social Security Commission, which administers general relief, aid to dependent children, and old age assistance, added to its staff a medical social worker, for the purpose of demonstrating the value of intensive case work with ill clients.

The adminstrative heads of the agency, as well as members of the staff, were aware that there were many individuals in relief families who for various reasons were not getting the medical care they required and that there were others who, although their physical condition could not be improved, could be helped to make a better social or vocational adjustment in spite of their illnesses. Also, it was known that there were many cases in which the visitors, because of lack of time or skill or lack of co-operation from the medical agencies, had inadequate medical information; this hampered them in planning with the client and in some instances affected the determination of eligibility for assistance.

The medical social worker was engaged for the purpose of demonstrating the need in the agency for a program that would insure greater attention to the medical needs of the clients and would eventually raise the health standards of the client group.

It was recognized that there were many families in which there were medical problems requiring attention. However, one worker could not effectively handle such a large number of cases. It was decided, therefore, that the medical social worker would limit her attention to families dependent because of illness of the wage-earner, in which there was an apparent possibility of re-

1. Reprinted from *The Family*, March, 1944, with permission of the Family Service Association of America.

storing the wage-earner to employment. It was felt that the greatest number of individuals would benefit if attention were directed primarily toward the goal of restoring as many families as possible to an independent status.

At the time the experiment was started, production for war had gained considerable momentum and jobs were plentiful in the St. Louis area. The number of families receiving general relief had been reduced, leaving only those who were unable to work because of physical handicaps or those who were unable to find their places in industry because of some type of mental or emotional incapacity. Because of limited funds for relief, which necessitated careful expenditure of money to insure assistance to those most in need, and the availability of a job for everyone able to work, the agency would not assist any family that had an "employable" member, except on a temporary emergency basis. In order to prove eligibility for assistance, the head of a family had to present a doctor's note giving diagnosis and a statement that the man was unable to work. Thus the problem of illness, in some form, was present in every general relief family. In addition, a large percentage of the families receiving aid to dependent children had been certified for this type of aid because the fathers were considered physically unemployable.

Although no statistical study had been made of the illnesses in the families of these two categories, it was generally known by the workers and supervisors that many of the diagnoses given in the doctors' statements did not indicate total disability. Some men had chronic ailments, only partially disabling for some jobs and not at all disabling for many types of work. Obviously, some of the men who considered themselves "unemployable" were for some reason ignoring their own potentialities. The commission reasoned that if these men could be helped to realize their assets, some of them would become self-supporting. A much smaller number of men were considered unemployable on the basis of acute illnesses. In many of these cases, the doctors' statements were months old. These men should have recovered in a short time and returned to employment. Apparently they had either failed to receive the medical or surgical care necessary to insure recovery, or they had failed to recover from the idea that they were ill or from the dependent attitudes accompanying illness. It seemed that a worker with an understanding of illnesses and their emotional concomitants would be able to help these men obtain and accept medical care or, if they had recovered physically, to help them assume again the role of a well person.

Many of the families that were receiving assistance on the basis of the types of illness described above had been receiving relief a year or longer, and it was reasonable to assume that they were unable to hoist themselves to an independent status if left entirely to their own energies. The visitors had large case loads and at most were able to visit each family only three or four times a year. Apparently these families would continue to receive assistance for an indefinite period unless they were helped to realize whatever potentialities they had. Since the rehabilitation of even four or five of these families in a year's time would more than pay a medical social worker's salary for a year, it appeared that the commission had little to lose by the experiment. Actually, the results of the project showed that the agency had much to gain by offering this type of service.

The St. Louis Social Security Commission is organized into five case-carrying districts, all centrally located, with each district responsible for the cases in a designated geographical area. It was decided that if the medical social worker were to carry cases on an intensive basis, she must have total responsibility for the cases she accepted for care. Since all cases carried over a long period must be accounted for statistically by one of the districts, the medical social worker was assigned to one of them, and was supervised by the head of that district. She accepted cases from any visitor in the agency, but, once a case had been accepted by her for care, it was transferred to her statistically and counted by her district.

Referrals were the responsibility of the individual visitors, who, after deciding with their supervisors that a family had possibilities for rehabilitation, would lend the record to the medical social worker for reading. After study of the case and discussion with her supervisor, the medical social worker conferred with the visitor and supervisor who had referred the case, in order to clarify reasons for rejection or acceptance. When the case had been carried to a successful conclusion or when the medical social worker decided that she could not help the family any further, the case was closed or transferred back to the district in which it was geographically located. At that time the medical social worker discussed the work done with the visitor and supervisor who had referred the case.

These discussions with the visitors and their supervisors at the time of referral and again at termination of the medical social worker's service did a great deal to publicize the project to the agency and to explain the medical social worker's function. Other methods were used to bring the program to the attention of the staff and to describe its purpose, so that the staff could use the service to the fullest extent. In the early days of the experiment, a guiding committee was formed, consisting of the director and case work supervisor of the agency, as well as the heads of districts. This committee was appointed mainly to direct the project, but it was also very useful, in that its members were in a position to explain the program to the staffs of their respective districts. The medical social worker wrote two bulletins in the course of the eight months' experiment, the first defining her function and explaining the method of referral, the second describing results. These were sent to all the district heads for circulation to their staffs. In addition, the medical social worker met at least once with the staffs of each district in order to discuss the program and to answer any questions the visitors might have.

The number of referrals was small in relation to the total agency case load; but this was to be expected in view of the residual nature of the load and the narrow scope of the experiment. In spite of this, enough promising material was brought to light to provide a continuing full case load. During the first five months of the experiment, from February 1 to June 30, a total of 50 cases was referred. Twenty-nine of these cases were accepted for care, and the case load continued at approximately that figure. This load entailed about 70 office interviews and visits a month. The interviews were usually long, and the families were scattered over the city. This case load, together with the reading of referred cases, committee meetings, staff meetings, case conferences, and bulletin writing, was large enough to put some pressure on the worker, but in all probability can be considered a reasonable number of cases for that type of worker to carry.

In the first weeks of the experiment it became apparent that most of the cases were "tough" and that only a very few of them would show final results in a short time. In most situations the unemployment was due to complex, interrelated factors of illness and dependent attitudes. Most of these families had been transferred from private agencies in 1933 and had shuttled back and forth between relief and WPA since that time. Several had come to St. Louis from rural areas a few years before and had never had a private-industry job in the city. These families required various kinds of service, mainly directed toward helping them see their situation realistically, reinforcing and stimulating their drives to become independent, and showing them their strengths and potentialities in relation to what the community had to offer them. This had to be done differently in each situation, in accordance with the nature of the illness, the client's environmental needs, and his attitudes. Of the first twenty-nine cases, there were possibly four or five instances in which the individual's will to get well and to get a job dominated any emotional drive to remain dependent. Of these, it was found that three of the clients had long-term illnesses, one had a permanent handicap, and only one had a condition quickly remedied by operation.

In spite of all these seeming difficulties, the results accomplished left no doubt as to the usefulness of the type of service given. Of the first twenty-nine cases accepted for care between February 1 and June 30, most had shown some progress, and seven were entirely self-supporting by October 1. Six of these families had been receiving assistance for a year or more, and it seemed a foregone conclusion that these families would have continued to need relief indefinitely if they had not been given special attention. About $350 monthly was saved by the rehabilitation of these families. The total amount saved can hardly be calculated, as there is no way of knowing how long these families would have continued to receive assistance. However, the

value in money saved is small compared with the benefits derived by every individual in the families restored to financial
independence, and the benefit derived by the community in
gaining additional productive members at a time when manpower was sorely needed.

The above discussion undoubtedly raises many questions as to
the medical social worker's methods, the types of cases that were
carried, and the specific results that were obtained. These questions can best be answered by a presentation, necessarily tele-
scopic, of some of the cases carried during the course of the
experiment.

Two of the cases were "easy" in point of simplicity of the immediate problem. They required only three or four interviews
to set the client in the right direction.

The T family consisted of the husband, 29, and the wife, 21, who was
pregnant. Mr. T had arrested pulmonary tuberculosis and had never held
a steady job of any kind. He had been hospitalized twice for periods of a
year and more, and in between had eked out an existence by peddling
notions and doing odd jobs. The couple applied for relief when Mrs. T
had to give up work because of pregnancy. Separate interviews with the
man and woman showed strong family cohesion and drive on the part of
both to be financially independent. Mr. T said he had lived with various
relatives and friends during childhood and adolescence and that he had
never received any vocational direction. A brother-in-law in whose home
he had lived for a time was a mechanic, and he expressed interest in learning a mechanical trade. Since information from the clinic indicated that
Mr. T was able to do light work, he was referred to the Vocational Rehabilitation Service. Arrangements were made for him to take a course
in airplane welding, and he attended classes regularly. The worker thought
that Mr. T might be having some difficulties in adjusting to this new
activity and he was asked to come to the office for an interview.

At this time Mr. T expressed fear that he would not be able to carry
through the course; he complained of pains in his arms, and of becoming
tired easily. In view of his previous diagnosis, there was some possibility
that his fears had a real basis, and the worker did not attempt to give him
any reassurance at this time but suggested that he return to the clinic and
discuss his symptoms with the doctor. Mr. T did so, and the report we received from the clinic stated that he was physically able to do a full-time
job at airplane welding, and that his symptoms were due to the unaccus-
tomed activity. The worker again interviewed Mr. T in the office and discussed his symptoms with him in accordance with the medical information received. Mr. T's fears regarding his physical inadequacy were to a
great extent released, and he was able to function to his full capacities.
Shortly after completion of the course, he obtained employment at a local
airplane factory.

The second family consisted of Mr. V, 52, and Mrs. V, and four children. Mr. V had applied for General Relief for the first time a year before. During the year that the family had been receiving assistance, they had been visited twice but the man's diagnosis had not been discussed. In the first interview with the medical social worker, Mr. V stated that he was unable to hold a full-time job of any kind because of a severe case of hemorrhoids. He had not been treated for this condition for over seven years, and had never received medical treatment since the family's arrival in St. Louis from a small eastern community in 1938. During the interview, several factors were revealed as having prevented Mr. V from obtaining treatment. He thought that there was no treatment other than operation; he was afraid of an operation; he thought he was too old; he thought he had a bad heart; doctors like to experiment; he did not know his way around the city and did not know where to apply for medical care.

Mr. V's various fears and uncertainties were discussed with him in detail, so that he was able to take the first step of obtaining an examination at the clinic. It was explained to him that operation is not the only treatment, and that he was not in any case committed to an operation by attending a clinic for examination. Further, the doctors would not recommend an operation if he were not in condition to withstand surgery. Mr. V was asked how he knew that he had a bad heart. In attempting to explain this, Mr. V came to realize that he had no definite facts upon which to base this belief. The worker told Mr. V that he would be eligible for care at one of the university hospital clinics. He had already heard of this hospital and readily accepted the worker's assurance that he would receive the best quality of care there. The worker offered to make a definite clinic appointment for him, and Mr. V said he was willing to go. He was given definite directions for getting to the clinic. Mr. V kept the appointment which was later made, and an operation was recommended. After another interview with the worker, in which he was able to express and resolve some of his fears regarding operation, and assurance was given that his family would be taken care of while he was in the hospital, Mr. V underwent surgery. He recovered speedily and obtained a job as a maintenance man shortly after.

These two cases had each been carried over a year by the regular visitors, and in each the basic problems had remained unmentioned and untreated. This may have been due to lack of time or lack of training. However, it is possible that some of the visitors were themselves giving the type of service described above, while only the more difficult cases requiring a longer period of service were referred to the medical social worker.

The situation characterized by long-term illness to which the individual needs continual help in adjusting is typified in the following case.

In the D family were the father, aged 29, the mother, 23, and five children, the oldest aged 7. The family applied for assistance for the first time in February, 1942, because of the man's illness. Diagnosis was rheumatic fever, and it was recommended that Mr. D have complete rest for several months. However, Mr. D could not accept his dependency on the agency, and several weeks after applying for assistance took a job doing carpentry, his regular trade. He became severely ill after two days' work, and was forced to stop work and apply again for assistance. The family was soon referred by their visitor to the medical social worker. It was found that Mr. D had a great deal of anxiety about the situation, that he could not accept his dependent role, and that in order to avoid facing the fact that he would have to be dependent for a long time, he was insisting that he was not very ill and that he was able to do some kind of work.

The medical social worker visited the home about twice a week, gave Mr. and Mrs. D an opportunity to talk out their feelings about being on relief, gave assurance in various ways of their social acceptability, assured them that their needs would be met, interpreted to them the nature of Mr. D's illness and the necessity for carrying out medical recommendations. In addition to this, various services were secured, such as volunteer motor service to the clinic, occupational therapy in the home, and referral to an agency where glasses could be secured. As time went on, Mr. D became noticeably less agitated in manner, and appeared to be accepting the situation with less protest. He attended the clinic regularly and avoided strenuous activities. Several times he telephoned the worker to ask whether he should undertake certain activities.

Nevertheless Mr. D's underlying need to be independent persisted and eventually expressed itself in action. One morning about three months after the worker's first contact, Mrs. D telephoned the worker that Mr. D had gone to work at a carpentry job that day. She was worried about it and was afraid of the consequences. She was asked whether she thought Mr. D would be willing to go to the clinic the next day to discuss his employment with the doctor. She was sure that he would do so, and the worker arranged for a clinic appointment the next day, enlisted the help of the clinic social worker in obtaining recommendations from the doctor. Mr. D did attend the clinic and upon the physician's recommendation quit the job. Six weeks later, Mr. D was told by the doctor that he could return to his regular employment, and he was back at his old job the next day.

Although Mr. D was not able to assume a dependent role completely, the medical social worker helped him accept his situation to a sufficient degree to enable him to carry out medical recommendations well enough to insure recovery. The importance of the worker's close relationship with the family was dramatically illustrated when Mr. D went back to work for the second time. If Mrs. D had not had enough confidence in the worker to inform her of Mr. D's move, and if Mr. D had not understood the importance of discussing his employment with the doctor, the results might have been disastrous. If this family had been carried in a regular case load, it is very likely that Mr. D would have tried working again long before he did, and that he would have continued working until he actually felt very ill, and perhaps long enough for his heart to become involved. While this family required a considerable amount of the worker's time, thus entailing a great deal of expense to an agency whose funds were very limited, probably very much more expense would have been entailed to the agency and the community at large if the family had been left to grope its own way during this crisis, with the certainty that the man would not carry out medical recommendations and the danger that he would become permanently incapacitated.

The cases characterized by interrelated factors of illness and dependency were quite varied, and the degree of dependency ranged from a nearly immovable, quiescent passivity to a passivity that expressed itself in an active and hostile resistance to change. The degree of illness ranged from no physical illness at all to complicated illnesses requiring long-term treatment. For the most part some change in attitude was noticeable in those clients who were seen over a number of months. Some actually secured private employment and did not require further assistance.

The M family, consisting of Mr. M, 35, Mrs. M, and five children, had been known to the agency since 1933. Mr. M was an armature winder by trade and had been employed in private industry off and on. The case had been open a year and a half when referred to the medical social worker. Mr. M had been operated on for perinephritic abscess in City Hospital a year before and it was noted in the record that Mr. M still complained of not feeling well. A statement from City Hospital eight months old gave a diagnosis of "boils" and said that Mr. M was able to do light work. Mr. M told the medical social worker that the skin eruptions had disappeared. However, he still had a number of vague complaints which he associated with his operation. He was making little effort to find work, as he was afraid he was not well enough to keep a job.

The worker received the impression that Mr. M is a passive individual who does not have strong drives toward independence and is not seriously disturbed by "not having," and that he was further inactivated by fears regarding his physical condition. Mr. M was encouraged to return to the clinic to discuss his complaints with the doctor. He did so, and reported to the worker that the doctor told him that his symptoms were indeed a result of the operation, but that they did not indicate any danger, and that he was able to return to his regular occupation. The worker had regular office interviews with Mr. M thereafter, in which his job-hunting efforts were discussed. The worker emphasized Mr. M's ability to hold a job and pointed out various opportunities to him. Mr. M was told that he could find better employment than WPA, and he finally obtained a job at his trade through the United States Employment Service. He informed the worker of his employment immediately, with a "thank you for all that has been done." Three months after this case was closed, the family had not reapplied for assistance.

In another case the worker was able to show the man that physical illness did not exist at all and that he was using illness as an escape from his real problems. As a result, the man obtained a job and the worker was able to refer the family to an agency that was equipped to help them with their actual difficulties.

The B family was made up of Mr. B, 45, and Mrs. B, and seven children, aged 12 and under. Mr. B had not had private employment at least as far back as 1933, had alternated between WPA and General Relief. He was invariably relieved of his WPA job because he stated he was ill, and it was noted at several points in the case history that Mr. B's excuse for various shortcomings was "illness." At the time of referral to the medical social worker, Mr. B had given illness as a reason for not reporting to a new WPA assignment. He had obtained a statement from a private physician which listed a number of complaints and recommended hospitalization for complete checkup.

In several interviews, in which the worker helped Mr. B analyze his symptoms, he was able to express the feeling that they were mostly due to worry over the financial situation. However, he insisted that he was nevertheless unable to do heavy work, as he had arteriosclerosis. He was induced to go to City Hospital clinic, and after the doctor had written a statement that he was able to do any kind of work, Mr. B relinquished his defense completely and said that he would be willing to take a WPA job. Within a few days he obtained a private industry job. There was a brief anticlimax when Mrs. B reapplied for assistance, because Mr. B had lost his job and left the home. During this period the worker interviewed both Mr. B and Mrs. B. Mr. B ascribed his inability to keep a job to Mrs. B's exceptionally slovenly housekeeping, and Mrs. B ascribed her slovenliness to Mr. B's habits of drinking and inability to keep a job. After six weeks Mr. B obtained another private industry job and returned to the home. In the meantime, the medical social worker had attempted to interpret Mr. and Mrs. B's respective points of view to each other, and referred them to a private agency for further help in working out their problems. Neither said anything about illness, which had been Mr. B's excuse for his shortcomings for many years.

The agency had been helping this family off and on since 1933, on the basis of the man's illness, when actually illness was not the problem at all. The outer layer of deception which Mr. B had been using to escape facing his problems was cleared away, and the family was helped to face and to try to work out its problems. If the family applies again for assistance, the agency will have a basis for analyzing the situation, and will be in a position to help the family in accordance with its real needs.

The cases sketched above, while they do not constitute the total accomplishment of the experiment, do demonstrate that some assistance recipients who are considered "unemployable" may be restored to useful employment if they are given understanding assistance with their problems. And "understanding assistance" to ill persons requires a case worker who understands the limitation implied by a diagnosis and who knows what reactions the individual is likely to have to his specific illness and limitations. It requires, as well, a case worker with a small enough case load to insure that all the attention necessary can be given to the families under her care.

The project was carried through at a time when every worker's capacities could be used to the fullest extent in production. Whether this type of service would show results under conditions wherein the obtaining and keeping of a job is a highly competitive undertaking is open to question, and we shall not attempt to consider that here. However, the labor shortage still exists, and we are being told that after the war production for peace needs will insure full employment for some time to come. Under such conditions there is no compromising with the fact that unused manpower is wasted manpower; and the public assistance agency is obligated to give whatever service is available to insure that every relief recipient who is a potential wage-earner becomes an actual wage-earner.

The Role of Medical Social Service in the Public Health Program[1]

BY BEATRICE HALL

THE establishment and development of medical social work over the last forty years has come about because of recognition by physicians of the significance of the social and emotional aspects of health and medical care. A broad concept of medical care has never been limited to treatment of the organic impairment but has combined treatment of the physical illness or handicap and treatment of unfavorable social factors that influence the effectiveness of medical care and contribute to the degree and duration of the disability.

Increasing consideration of environmental and emotional influences upon illness is noted in medical literature in recent years. During the same period the practice of medicine has become increasingly complicated. The treatment of illness today involves the utilization of a variety of scientific techniques and specialized resources. In the course of a single illness a patient may require the services of several specialists; he may receive care through a number of related institutions.

In medical-care programs carried on by health departments medical services may be provided by a large number of physicians, hospitals, clinics, and convalescent homes. Social services are available through a variety of official and nonofficial agencies. The development of these programs has resulted in increased need for liaison and co-ordinative services by medical social workers on the staffs of health departments in order to further the integration of medical, nursing, and social treatment.

In the treatment of venereal disease and cancer, consideration

1. Paper given at the Eighteenth Annual Conference of Health Workers of Western Massachusetts, Westfield State Sanatorium, Westfield, June 8, 1944. Reprinted from *The Child*, February, 1945, with the permission of the U.S. Children's Bureau, Federal Security Agency.

of social and emotional aspects in the patient's situation is vitally important to the successful carrying-out of the physician's recommendations. Anxiety about family affairs, fears related to the diagnosis, and apprehension about the future frequently prevent these patients from obtaining maximum benefits from the treatment services that are available to them. Staff workers in tuberculosis hospitals have known many situations in which patients failed to carry through the recommended regime because of family or occupational responsibilities.

There are important social aspects in all phases of the treatment of crippled children under social security programs, which in 29 of the 52 states and territories are a responsibility of health departments. Early location of a crippled child and early acceptance of care by his parents may have a direct bearing upon the degree of improvement that will result. Refusal of care or failure to co-operate in carrying out recommendations is frequently based on attitudes of members of the family group, which, if understood, can be modified. Social, educational, and recreational services must frequently be provided for a crippled child, if he is to obtain the best results from his medical care.

The responsibilities of health departments in relation to maternity and pediatric care have been very greatly increased during the past year and a half through the administration of the emergency maternity and infant-care program for wives and infants of enlisted men in the lowest four pay grades. This program is now in operation in all the states and in Alaska, Hawaii, the District of Columbia, and Puerto Rico.

As a basis for discussion of the role of the medical social worker in the public health program, the social needs among patients receiving services through the crippled children's and the maternal and child-health services will be considered here.

SERVICES FOR CRIPPLED CHILDREN

The objective of present-day programs for crippled children is not only to enable the crippled child to attain the best physical condition that is possible for him but at the same time to enable him to develop all his potentialities as fully as possible within the limitations of his handicap.

Unfavorable emotional factors are inherent when there is an obvious handicap which sets a child apart from his fellows and limits his activity. A case described in a report of the New York City Commission for the Study of Crippled Children is an example of this:

A mother reported her child, who seemed well adjusted when at school or playing with friends, was found several times in front of the mirror talking to his crippled arm, exclaiming, "I'll kill you, I'll kill you."

Problems in the home frequently interfere with carrying out physicians' recommendations:

A teen-age girl with rheumatic fever was reported by a visiting-nurse association as not being at bed rest, although this had been ordered. The mother had refused to allow the girl to go to a convalescent home because her services were needed to take care of the younger children while the mother went out to work.

There are implications of social difficulties in a plan for medical treatment that necessitates periods of care in a hospital or a convalescent home at some distance from the child's home or that entails prolonged nursing care at home, placing a heavy burden upon an already overworked mother. Unless the interrelationship of medical and social factors is recognized and is given consideration in making plans for a crippled child, he cannot be helped toward the useful and satisfying life which is the ultimate objective. This objective can be achieved only if the medical treatment and nursing care of the child are integrated with his growth and his development in social adjustment, education, and vocational training:

Ruth was a 15-year-old high-school girl who came to the crippled children's clinic for treatment of her right leg and hand, which had been partially paralyzed since birth. Her home situation was particularly difficult in many respects, and this, combined with her handicap, resulted in lack of acceptance by her schoolmates. Ruth was unable to concentrate on her school work or co-operate in the plan for her medical care. The orthopedic consultant planned a series of operations designed to improve the functions and the appearance of her arm and leg. This treatment extended over a period of years, during which plans were also made for her education and training, so that by the time her physical handicaps were removed, she would be ready to be a self-supporting member of her community.

Through the guardianship of one of the protective agencies, Ruth went to live with an elderly couple whose companionship, sincere interest, and affection gave her a feeling of security for the first time. She attended a school for crippled children, and soon found a place for herself in spite of her handicaps. She made many friends. The medical treatment was carried out as planned, with consequent improvement in her physical appearance and in the functioning of her leg and arm.

Later, she found an opportunity to work and live in a supervised boarding home for girls. For the first time she became aware of her earning capacity and soon accumulated a savings account of almost $100. Today she is happy, has become independent, and has learned to make decisions for herself and to plan for her future. With the co-operation of local social and health agencies and the division of vocational rehabilitation of the department of education, it has been possible to instill in Ruth a feeling of self-confidence and of assurance that she can maintain herself in a constructive position in the community.[2]

MATERNAL AND CHILD-HEALTH SERVICES

All of us who have been concerned in any way with the emergency maternity and infant-care program see frequent evidences among this group of patients of the stresses and strains inherent in the war situation. We have all been impressed with the youth of the wives and mothers who are receiving care through this program and with the problems arising from the absence of the husband and father from the home. One hospital social worker has known several young wives who asked about giving their babies away because they felt completely helpless to make any plans for themselves and their children. In the absence of their husbands some girls were becoming overdependent upon their own mothers and tended to throw upon them the entire burden of planning. In some instances this responsibility was accepted so readily by the young mother's parent that one fears its eventual influence upon the girl's future and that of her baby. Other cases revealed conflict, disturbing to the baby's routines and habits.

Some months ago a visiting nurse association reviewed its experience in providing maternity nursing services to a group of 40 servicemen's wives. Half of these wives were seventeen to twenty-one years of age, and more than half the husbands were under twenty-five. Thirty-nine of the babies were first babies. Excerpts from the nurses' notes reveal typical problems:

2. Edward G. Huber, "Services for Crippled Children," *Bulletin of the Massachusetts Department of Public Health*, Vol. II, No. 3 (April, 1944).

Husband not contributing to support of wife and baby. Wife living with her family. Family antagonistic toward husband. Mrs. A very immature and will take no responsibility for care of the baby. Her mother has taken over completely.

Nov. 4: Patient in rooming house. Not sufficient food, and housing inadequate. Red Cross gave relief at request of nurse. Nov. 9: Bewildered and unable to follow nurse's instructions. Baby not having adequate care. Nov. 24: Mrs. X wants to join husband. Relatives discourage her. Family did not approve of the marriage.

These women and girls have had little time or opportunity to prepare themselves for the responsibilities that are being thrust upon them. Their husbands are young, too, and in many instances equally unprepared to assume the responsibilities of family life. They are anxious and worried about their wives and are at the same time facing a hazardous future and the necessity of adjusting themselves to a new way of life and to military discipline. The resulting insecurity of these husbands and wives expresses itself in a variety of ways. They question policies and procedures, they write long letters to those in authority, the women break appointments and fail to follow medical recommendations, they change doctors frequently, they delay in making preparations for care.

Sometimes these patients and their husbands have been characterized as "demanding," "unreasonable," "unco-operative," and so forth, and frequently attempts are made to deal with the manifestations without sufficient recognition of the motivating force. Increased understanding of the total problems these women are facing makes it possible to give greater help to the patients and also contributes to an easier and more effective administration of the program.

In preventive health services, such as child-health conferences, many social needs come to the attention of the staff. The effectiveness of these health services is greatly increased when the staff is alert to indications of social needs, understands how to obtain social services through community agencies, and accepts responsibility for helping families to make use of available resources. Increased understanding of home situations helps the conference staff to have a keener appreciation of the value of flexibility and individuality in health instruction. It facilitates recognition of parental attitudes and early manifestations of behavior patterns in children which may lead to serious problems in family and social relationships if skilled service is not promptly made available. On the other hand, community agencies providing social services frequently need help toward a better understanding of health problems, in order that they may respond promptly and effectively to requests for services from the health agency.

CONSULTATIVE AND CO-ORDINATING ROLE

OF MEDICAL SOCIAL WORKERS

Many of the medical social workers employed on the staffs of state and district health departments are called "consultants," a term which seems truly descriptive of their primary function. The medical social worker on a state or district staff does not duplicate the services of social workers in state or local welfare departments, of hospital social workers, or of public health nurses and other personnel on the health department staff. As a specialist in social problems related to health and medical care, she provides consultant services to all these workers on individual and community problems that interfere with the effectiveness of health services. Through her liaison activities with hospital social service departments and social agencies, she strengthens the integration of health and welfare services. She interviews patients and parents in the health department clinics, in order to discover and evaluate social aspects in individual situations. She plans for meeting problems in co-operation with other members of the health department staff and with local social workers.

In communities where no social agency is able to provide the service which the patient needs, the medical social worker in the health department may provide services herself, as a temporary measure, to supplement the services provided by the community. In some rural areas the need for these supplementary services is considerable at the present time. The extent of the services that may appropriately be provided by the medical social worker and the way in which she operates in any community depend upon local needs and the availability and adequacy of local services. The necessity to provide direct service decreases with the development of local welfare departments, expansion of child-welfare services, and increased provision for social services by hospitals and convalescent homes. Local responsibility for health and welfare services to individuals is generally accepted, and we know that local participation and local responsibility are essential in the development of stable, permanent services. State and district medical social workers are looking forward to the time when local communities can take responsibility for providing services, with medical social consultation service available through the health department.

The medical social worker helps to speed the day when this will be possible, by participating in community efforts to improve and expand local social services. As a member of the health department staff, she is in a strategic position to know the extent of unmet social needs and the often tragic end-results of a community's failure to take steps to meet them. She can also act as an impartial observer in instances of overlapping or duplication in the services of social agencies and can help communities in working toward more effective and economical use of available facilities. Individual situations illustrating such problems can be used most effectively in discussions with social agencies directed toward extension of services or modification of rigid policies and procedures which present barriers to effective utilization of available services.

Because medical social workers are social workers, they approach community and individual welfare problems with a deeper appreciation of the welfare agency's point of view and can often bring about a better understanding between a health agency or hospital and a social agency. The parents' acceptance of recommendations made in a child-health conference or through the school health programs is not enough in itself, if they are unable to obtain medical care through their own resources. In some communities they must seek help in obtaining care from other agencies. The agencies to which they turn for necessary assistance must also have understanding and acceptance of the recommendations. Medical social workers have made headway with such problems through participating in conferences between public health nurses and welfare departments and through discussion with staff and supervisory workers in the welfare departments. In some states they have participated in the inservice training programs of the welfare departments. This works both ways; welfare workers can contribute to the programs of health departments. Such an exchange gives the staff of each agency a better understanding of the other's programs and paves the way for more effective joint effort.

The medical social worker in the health department can also be of assistance in strengthening the working relationships between hospitals and local health and welfare agencies. In small hospitals where no medical social worker is employed, plans have been worked out for prompt exchange of medical and social information and joint planning between the hospital and community agencies in the interest of certain groups of patients. Several workers in state crippled children's programs have helped hospital administrators establish social service departments or have been instrumental in bringing about extension and improvement of these services.

The activity of the medical social worker in the health department clinics in discovering and evaluating social aspects in individual situations has been referred to earlier in this article. Responsibility for recognizing and considering these factors is shared by all members of the health department staff and by all persons who come in touch with the patient. The social component in illness cannot be filtered out and handed over to any one person as a sole responsibility—be it physician, nurse, medical social worker, or welfare worker. The medical social worker has primary responsibility in this respect, however, and her training has been concentrated upon understanding the social and emotional aspects of human behavior, particularly as related to illness and medical care. She can therefore give help to other staff members by increasing their understanding of social factors that affect the medical, nursing, or other care which is their primary concern. The effectiveness of the public health instruction given by physicians, public health nurses, nutritionists, and so forth, is dependent to a great extent upon the approach to and the receptiveness of the mother or child on the receiving end, so to speak. All professional groups have some training and experience along this line, but opportunity for consultation with the "specialist" may reduce the number of situations sometimes called "failures to co-operate" and lessen the time necessary for follow-up.

The medical social worker is available for such consultation, and her services are being utilized increasingly, particularly by state and local public health nursing staffs through group discussions and individual conferences. In certain instances a medical social worker may be asked by the public health nurse to visit a family, in order that she may secure a more complete understanding of the social problems before giving consultation. After this, the medical social worker and the nurse decide upon the next step. In some situations the nurse continues to carry responsibilities for helping the patient to meet his problem, either alone or in co-operation with a local social agency. In other instances it may be decided that the medical social worker is to assist the nurse further, through consultation or by provision of certain services directly to the patient. It goes without saying that whenever two or more members of the medical team, such as doctor, public health nurse, and medical social worker, are concerned with the social situation in the same case, they must agree among themselves, by occasional conferences, what responsibility each will carry. The medical social worker can participate successfully in such joint activity because she, also, has been trained to recognize and encourage the patient's relationship to all members of the medical team.

SUMMARY

The medical social worker brings to the public health program an emphasis upon the social aspects of health and medical care, aspects that are of concern to all the members of the medical team. She has primary responsibility for the discovery and fulfilment of social needs that prevent individuals and groups from being able to make effective use of health services. Her chief activities are in the fields of consultation and co-ordination, although she may provide services herself in the absence of other facilities for meeting needs. Her consultation services are available to other members of the health department staff and to local

health and welfare workers on individual and community problems. In her liaison capacity she brings to welfare and social agencies continuing explanation of health department programs and
policies and to the health department increased understanding of
what services are available through these agencies and how their
services may be utilized most effectively in the promotion of
positive health for the community.

The Road to Rehabilitation[1]

BY HELEN J. ALMY

PHYSICIAN, medical social worker, public health nurse, physical therapist, teacher, rehabilitation agent—each of these contributes professional skill in helping the crippled child to become a healthy, self-supporting adult. If these skilled workers can begin to help the child early enough, their teamwork may obviate the need for formal rehabilitation measures.

The children whose stories are given here benefited from what might be called "prehabilitation" services, which help to prevent crippling conditions and crippling emotional attitudes. The care was provided through Services for Crippled Children, Massachusetts Department of Health, in co-operation with workers on the staffs of community agencies.

CASE HISTORIES

Case 1.—A baby with clubfoot needs to be taken by his parents to the doctor at once. If they accept the instructions that are given them and co-operate with the doctor, the nurse, and the physical therapist in carrying out the treatment prescribed, the condition can usually be corrected so that no handicap results.

Johnnie, a baby born with two clubfeet, was not so easily helped. His parents were poor and ignorant. Their home was crowded, and a new baby was born almost yearly. The family lived in a small town. Johnnie's clubfeet were noticed by the doctor and the nurse at a general clinic where the mother had taken him on account of an eye condition. The clinic doctor told her to take him to the crippled children's diagnostic clinic nearest their home for further examination. When she failed to take him there, the medical social worker at the general clinic communicated with the medical social worker in the district health office. This worker and the local public health nurse persuaded the parents to take Johnnie to the crippled children's clinic. The orthopedic surgeon recommended that Johnnie's feet be operated on.

Then it was the task of the various workers to persuade Johnnie's father and mother to let him be taken to a hospital 50 miles away. The

1. Reprinted from *The Child*, February, 1945, with the permission of the U.S. Children's Bureau, Federal Security Agency.

orthopedic surgeon, the clinic medical social worker, and the public health nurse explained the situation to the baby's parents, who finally agreed to have the two operations performed at the distant hospital.

The next problem was how to get proper follow-up care for Johnnie after each of the operations. Both the medical social worker and the public health nurse felt that good care in the baby's own home would be impossible and that an arrangement should be made for convalescent care in a foster-home near the hospital. Again the nurse who had helped the parents to agree to the operations was called upon. She discussed with the parents the plan for a foster-home, and she was successful in getting them to consent. The medical social worker then enlisted the co-operation of a child-placing agency in making the plans for foster-home care.

After each of the operations Johnnie stayed at the foster-home under the close supervision of a nurse and a physical therapist. All the time he was away from home the medical social worker, the public health nurse, and the worker for the child-placing agency co-operated in working with the family to make sure that Johnnie's place as a member of the family was not jeopardized.

Johnnie is now expected to grow up without a crippling condition. His experience shows that not only medical and surgical care, nursing, and physical therapy were needed for his physical restoration but also social planning. In spite of the excellent medical and surgical facilities that existed, Johnnie would not have had the benefit of them without the joint work of all the members of the medical team. The home factors would have been too great an obstacle to success.

Case 2.—Sometimes the child's crippling is not so serious a problem as the behavior accompanying it, and any successful plan for helping him must include not only orthopedic care but also recognition and treatment of the causes of his behavior.

Peter, 12 years old, had a conspicuous deformity. From birth one leg had been very much shorter than the other. He wore an orthopedic brace, and got around well. Peter was receiving clinic supervision, with the possibility of surgical treatment at some future time.

The public health nurse in the community where Peter lived learned that his behavior was causing serious difficulty at home and at school. He was defying relatives and teachers, and he was lying and stealing.

The nurse knew that Peter did not have either his father or his mother living with him and suspected that his troublesome behavior was related to his lack of a real family as well as to his crippling. She asked the medical social worker to look into the situation.

The medical social worker learned from the local physician and the nurse that Peter's mother had deserted the boy and his father when Peter was 3 years old, and that his father had boarded him with relatives and had gone to live in another town. Peter's behavior difficulties had begun about the time when his father had stopped paying board for him and visiting him and had even stopped writing to him. Peter obviously felt that he had lost status, both at home, where he heard his relatives blaming his father, and at school, where he needed to be able to talk about his dad like the other boys.

It was obvious that someone must help Peter revive the bond with his father and in other ways build up his sense of security so as to get over his difficulties. With the co-operation of a children's agency, the worker arranged to have Peter go to a child guidance clinic, where he was encouraged to express some of his feelings and to realize that, in spite of his handicap, he could hold his own at school.

The father was given a better understanding of Peter's needs and was helped to realize how much he could do to benefit his boy. It was impossible for the father to make a home for Peter, but he did begin to write to him, to pay board for him, and to send him occasional presents.

Peter's attitude at home and at school improved. His stealing and lying stopped. Moreover, during his attendance at the child guidance clinic it was discovered that he was unusually bright and gifted. In a few years he could be expected to make use of vocational rehabilitation services with marked success.

It is impossible to know how much of Peter's behavior trouble resulted from his crippling condition and how much was connected with his father's desertion and would have been present, handicap or no handicap. His physical handicap no doubt was partly responsible for his feeling that he was not wanted. And the idea that he was not wanted, along with the fact that he was different from other children, had dominated his attitude at home and at school.

Case 3.—Sometimes the feeling of being unwanted or different dominates the patient's mind out of all proportion to the severity of the handicap.

Margaret, at 17, had a slight curvature of the spine, which was hardly noticeable when she was dressed. Yet she believed that everyone was staring at her "deformity."

Margaret's extreme timidity and unwillingness to make social contacts attracted the attention of the medical social worker at a crippled children's clinic. The medical social worker felt that Margaret's attitude indicated deep-seated problems that needed psychiatric attention. The clinic physician agreed and advised referral to a psychiatrist.

It then became the job of the medical social worker to get Margaret to understand the need for this kind of help and to want it. But when the social worker first suggested to the girl that she go to a new doctor, who, as the worker phrased it, "might help her to understand better her feeling about her back," Margaret's response was, "If he will make my back straight I will go to him."

After a number of talks with the worker, however, the girl began to feel that it might be good to talk with this new kind of doctor who would help her to understand herself better. She kept her appointment with the psychiatrist and was able to benefit from his treatment. Gradually she showed more courage and willingness to join in social activity.

In preparing the way for Margaret's acceptance of the special services of the psychiatrist, the medical social worker provided a service that is frequently necessary when the real problem is not so much the crippling condition as the patient's feeling about it.

It often happens that a patient does not understand the need for the physician's recommendation. Such a patient does not follow the recommendation merely because it has been made or because an appointment has been obtained. He may need much explanation from the medical social worker and an opportunity to discuss his feelings, before he can make good use of the service recommended.

All the members of the medical team share responsibility for recognizing and considering social factors, and all contribute to an understanding of the individual patient. It is the medical social worker, however, who is expected to take the primary responsibility with regard to the patient's social needs and to initiate planning for them. Her training has been especially concentrated upon understanding the social and emotional factors related to illness and physical handicap.

The problems of the child or young adolescent in relation to physical restoration and later rehabilitation often involve the problems of his father and mother. The attitudes of the child's parents frequently play an important part in his adjustment to a handicap. Parents who are overanxious may stimulate the child to do too much, and those who are oversolicitous may allow, or cultivate in him, an attitude of overdependence. Other parents take little interest in their child and neglect him.

If the mother is overburdened, sometimes social resources in the community can be utilized to get financial assistance or housekeeping service, or to place the child under temporary foster-home care, as was done for Johnnie, the baby with clubfeet.

Sometimes, however, an oversolicitous attitude in the mother or her lack of interest in the child may be symptoms of real problems within herself. She may have a feeling of guilt, thinking perhaps it is her fault that the child is crippled. Or she may be full of self-pity because of the restrictions and deprivations that the care of the crippled child has imposed upon her. Or there may be marital difficulties or other family friction.

In such cases an agreement is sometimes made by the nurse or the physical therapist and the medical social worker for co-operative work. Under this arrangement the nurse or physical therapist works primarily with the child, while the medical social worker may center her attention on the mother or on the other members of the family. Such co-operative service can be very successful if the workers plan and work closely together.

If the mother finds in the medical social worker a person who is especially interested in her, someone with whom she can talk about her problems, she is likely to be released from some of her tensions and be able to take a more relaxed and wholesome attitude toward the child. As a result, the child will have a better chance to grow up psychologically, to become emotionally independent, and to be able to use rehabilitation services when the time comes.

Thus far stories of what might be called "prehabilitation" have been discussed. Two stories will now be presented in which the early steps are followed by successful rehabilitation in the more technical sense of the word. For each of these stories a patient with severe structural scoliosis has been chosen—patients for whom long and repeated periods of hospital care were necessary.

Case 4.—Mike was 16 when he was referred to a crippled children's clinic. He had a severely deformed back, and he was extremely sensitive about it.

His father and mother were foreign-born and had difficulty both in understanding and in speaking English. They had a good deal of Old World fear and suspicion of hospitals, and they would not hear of having the spinal operation performed that the orthopedic surgeon at the clinic recommended. The first job of the clinic workers, therefore, was to persuade the parents to consent to the operation. This was a difficult task. After some time they said they would consent if the doctor would guarantee a cure. This was a step forward, but it was clear that many additional steps were needed.

The clinic doctor patiently gave the boy and his parents explanations of how much and how little an operation might do. And the physical therapist and the nurse did their part with continued and detailed explanations. Questions and more questions were asked and answered. The medical social worker, fortunately able to talk with the parents in their own language, had many interviews with them and also with Mike. Sometimes she went to their home in the evening so as to be sure to see the father.

All this took almost two years, for the parents, ignorant and fearful, had great difficulty in coming to a decision. At last Mike himself was won over, and after a while his father and mother also agreed to having the operation performed.

At the time Mike was admitted to the hospital, the clinic medical social worker sent a social summary of his case to the hospital social worker, to help her make the circumstances of the case clear to the physicians and others responsible for his hospital care. The sharing of information between the diagnostic clinic and the hospital can materially help the patient's adjustment to the hospital, especially when there has been resistance to hospitalization.

Mike's hospital career was a great success. The physician saw to it that he was placed near a boy who had already had the type of operation that Mike was to have, and this boy's experience greatly reassured him.

Mike made friends among the hospital personnel. A teacher assigned by the local public schools to the hospital gave him lessons.

After a successful operation Mike went home and made a good adjustment there. A home teacher continued his lessons until he was able to return to school. His good adjustment at home was undoubtedly contributed to by the social experience at the hospital—the contacts there with the friendly nurses, doctors, and teacher.

Mike's straight back is a miracle for him and for his family. He tried for the Navy, showing that he felt he was no longer handicapped. He was rejected, to be sure, but he continued to think of himself as a whole man, and he longed to do war work.

Now, a year and a half after his operation, he has a job in the Navy Yard as apprentice electrician. It is the nearest thing to his ambition—being in the Navy. He seems truly rehabilitated.

Case 5.—Another patient with a severely deformed back, whom the state crippled children's agency saw through to successful rehabilitation, was a girl named Helen, who did not come to the attention of the diagnostic clinic until she was 18 years old—almost too late. At that time she was a very lame, crooked little person, with an alert, attractive face and a friendly manner. The orthopedic surgeon at the clinic predicted that unless treatment was provided promptly her legs might become paralyzed.

Conditions in her home were bad. Her mother was dead, and her father was alcoholic and was irregularly employed. She had four younger brothers. Helen was trying to keep house for this family with only casual help and supervision from an aunt living near by. In spite of all these difficulties, there was a strong family affection.

Helen and her family accepted the doctor's recommendation that an operation should be performed, and she was brought to one of the Boston hospitals.

From the medical social worker's report the physician realized that proper supervision and follow-up care could not be given Helen in her own home, and therefore convalescent care was arranged in a home in Boston.

While Helen was at the hospital and the convalescent home, the public health nurse received reports on her progress from the medical social worker and kept the family informed.

After going home Helen resumed her heavy home duties too soon, whereupon the medical social worker made arrangements for her to live for a while away from home at a special school. In her absence the aunt looked after the younger children, and the public health nurse continued to visit the home for general oversight.

Helen had expressed a desire to become a beauty-shop operator, and so the worker referred her to the district representative of the state vocational rehabilitation services, who arranged for the training. Thus the young girl learned that she could support herself.

Temporarily Helen took a job in a plant producing war materials, but she expects to return to the beauty-shop work for which she has been specifically trained.

To carry out the various steps of medical care, convalescence, schooling, vocational rehabilitation for Mike and Helen, many professional people contributed. First, of course, was the physician. But the other clinic personnel, the health and welfare workers in the local communities, the hospital and convalescent-home personnel, and the rehabilitation workers all played important parts. The chief role of the medical social worker in the crippled children's agency was to mobilize and co-ordinate these services so that there was continuity in the medical and social plan and consistent guidance toward the ultimate goal of successful rehabilitation and placement in a job.

Sometimes a medical social worker in a crippled children's program is asked to define the social problems that she believes should be referred to her. It is difficult to make such a definition, for a problem that calls for the medical social worker's services is not basically the problem of the crippling condition. It is the reaction of the individual to his condition, and this reaction depends on the resources at his disposal—within himself, in his family, and in his community.

To be sure, a crippling condition probably always creates a problem. Many an individual, however—astonishingly many—finds strength within himself through which he meets his problem and can use the services and facilities in his community to become, within the limits of medical science, physically restored and in every way rehabilitated. Such a person, if given the information regarding the necessary resources—orthopedic nursing, physical therapy, educational, rehabilitation—is in a position financially and emotionally to take advantage of them. Other persons, however, because of unfavorable conditions in the community, in the family, or in themselves, need special help in taking one or more of the steps along the road toward rehabilitation. If they do not get this help, the medical care they receive will not be effective, and the possibilities of rehabilitation will not be utilized. Betsey Barton in her recent book, *And Now To Live Again*, has described the task that confronts persons to whom a severe crippling handicap has come. She speaks of the agonizingly slow mental adjustment that must be made to reach the victorious state of mind so necessary in coping with a new and terrifying world.

SUMMARY

Successful rehabilitation of the physically handicapped individual includes (1) the optimum of physical restoration, (2) personal and emotional adjustment to handicap, (3) vocational guidance and training for those who can benefit from them. But the social problems related to disability must be treated as well as the organic impairment if either medical care or rehabilitation is to be effective.

The program must meet the needs of the individual. Each patient comes from a different background and presents a condition and attitude peculiar to himself.

All the members of the medical team have a responsibility for recognizing and considering social factors affecting the individual. The role of the medical social consultant in a state crippled children's program is threefold: To mobilize and help to co-ordinate services of the social and health agencies, to act as consultant in the area where medical and social factors come together, and in certain cases to give direct service to the patient. The aim of all is rehabilitation. Any program that fails to plan for the social, as well as the medical, rehabilitation of the crippled person and his eventual placement in the niche where he can best function falls short of its real objective.

The Role of the Medical Social Worker in Securing Provisions for Medical Care[1]

BY ZDENKA BUBEN

O<small>N THE</small> American scene today, we stand on the threshold of a new era in medical economics, an era which will ultimately produce a national health program dedicated to the principle that health promotion, disease prevention, and adequate medical care shall be available to all the people. Much progress has been made in recent years in diagnosing the reasons for the gap between the knowledge and skills of medicine and the utilization thereof by the people. Much progress has been made in achieving general understanding as to why the existing pattern of economic and social organization of medicine is unsuited to the present social order of which we are a part. In an address before the American Urological Association on June 21, 1944, Wendell Berge, assistant attorney-general of the United States, presented one of the finest analyses of the situation I have had the privilege to read. He said:

First, the art of medicine has refused to stand still. . . . Second, the community which the physician must serve has changed with the times. In the good old days the parson, the squire, and the doctor each held sway over his flock. Allegiance to the family doctor was a tie so firmly rooted that it took a crisis to break it. But our world no longer invites so durable, so personal, so exclusive a relationship. The machine, the corporation, and the pecuniary calculus have made over our work, our lives, our personal relationships. Our society has become urban, industrial, gregarious. We have become a new sort of wanderers—a race of modern nomads operating a material culture.

For most of us a job has come to replace an equity in the old homestead. For most of us livings, no longer taken directly from the farm, are pent in between the wages we receive and the prices we must pay. As individuals,

1. Paper presented at meeting of American Association of Medical Social Workers, National Conference of Social Work, April, 1947, San Francisco. Reprinted from the *Bulletin of the American Association of Medical Social Workers,* November, 1947, with the permission of the association.

we are as stubborn as ever our ancestors were. But we act far less on our own, and far more as managers, agents, or employees. Our industry is operated by corporations, our farmers band themselves into cooperatives, our workers, skilled and unskilled, gather into unions, even the great mass of our scientists make their discoveries while working for others. In our culture, the group has come to be the regular thing.

Against such forces, our minds cannot stand firm. Profound changes in habit, interest, and value have come in their wake. The standard of living has moved to a place of primacy among our everyday concerns. It makes the costs of medical service an inescapable problem. The care of the sick no longer can be absorbed by the family; it becomes an item of expense in the budget. If it is a wage-earner who is ill, there is a double cost; absence from work means loss of earnings and bills are there to be paid. So, medical service becomes a sheer economic necessity, for unless a man's capacity to work is maintained, he ceases to earn. Health thus becomes an aspect of the operation of the national economy.[2]

Through the recruitment process of the war just ended, we learned that about 40 per cent of 22,000,000 men of military age were unfit for general military duty.[3] This fact alone seems sufficient to bring home the realization that as good a job as is possible has not been done with respect to the distribution and utilization of medical care. The citizenry of our nation has awakened to the significance of this circumstance, and is doing something about it. Congress has been most interested and active in the past year or more, as evidenced by the enactment of the National Mental Hygiene Act, the Hospital Survey and Construction Act, and the increased appropriations for maternal and child health services.

President Truman in his State of the Union message to Congress last January 6 commented: "Of all our national resources none is of more basic value than the health of the people. . . . I urge this Congress to complete the work begun last year, and enact the most important recommendation of the program, to provide adequate medical care to all who need it, not as charity but on the basis of payments made by the beneficiaries of the program."[4]

2. "Justice and the Future of Medicine" (Reprint No. 2595), *U.S. Public Health Reports*, LX, No. 1 (January 5, 1945), 6, 7.
3. Hon. Claude Pepper, speech before Senate of the United States on July 25, 1945, on Maternal and Child Welfare Act of 1945, p. 3.
4. "Health and General Welfare," *New York Times*, XCVI (January 7, 1947), 16.

Everywhere we look about us, on the federal level, in the states, in public programs, and within the private practice of medicine, we see attempts of one kind or another to answer the problem, attempts to affect reorganization of medicine so that the people, all of the people, may have the full benefits of the knowledge and skills of medicine. We witness attempts at national legislation, such as the Wagner-Murray-Dingell Bill, or the more immediate National Health Act of 1947, or state legislation such as the Governor's Health Insurance Bill pending in the 1947 California legislature, all proposing the application of the principle of insurance on a mandatory basis rather than leaving it to the individual judgment of employed persons to protect themselves and their dependents.

Contrasted to this approach, we have witnessed during the last fifteen or more years the development of many voluntary health insurance plans protecting the individual and his dependents against high costs of hospitalization, or medical care usually related to so-called "catastrophic" illness, all founded on the principle that, given a good voluntary plan, the majority of people will avail themselves of the opportunity, as they protect themselves against fire, theft, loss of life, and other hazards. Conflicting as these approaches are, we must agree that all groups concerned are fully aware that a problem exists which is regarded as national in scope and character, and are earnestly working toward a solution.

In California, those of us who have been closely identified with community planning for health have been extremely interested in observing the development of public opinion with regard to the health field. Progress in public health in California has been closely tied up with an evolution in social thinking. The citizenry is formulating its own ideas as to the kind of public health it wants. Increasingly, it is showing concern for the total health of the individual and is no longer satisfied with the concept that public health programs shall be limited to communicable disease control and control of the environment.

As medical social workers functioning in programs of medical care, particularly in programs offering free or part-pay medical care, witnessing, as so often we do, the cause and effect of medical neglect, we may well ask ourselves what role we play in securing provisions for medical care so that patients are served according to need and not on the basis of criteria such as race, legal residence in a given community, or ability to pay for service. To the conscientious medical social worker, eager to serve the patient well, the application of some of these limitations to economically and socially disadvantaged people is the very antithesis of the fundamental purpose for which she was introduced into medical-care programs, namely, to alleviate or remove obstacles to medical care. Frustration takes hold when she witnesses, for example, the application of the legal residence requirement as a condition of securing adequate medical care, knowing that since the seventeenth century it has been applied without success as a means of punishing the individual who left his home community and then expected service away from home.

As an approach to understanding the medical social worker's role in securing provisions for medical care, let us consider the nature of her practice through which she may make a contribution.

The medical social worker is usually an integral part of an organized medical-care program. Her principal contribution to furthering adequate care for the patient is made through dealing with unfavorable social factors which influence the effectiveness of medical care and contribute to the degree and duration of disability. These factors are inherent within the patient's personality or his environment, or both. Accordingly, the medical social worker in her day-by-day practice is constantly studying and analyzing the social component of the patient's situation and dealing with factors that need alleviation or resolving before the patient can be expected to respond fully to treatment.

At times, these factors are primarily emotional responses to the given circumstance, such as negative attitudes toward the diagnosis, toward prescribed recommendations for care, toward leaving home for hospitalization, toward institutional care itself, toward circumstances within the treatment situation, such as fear of surgery, unhappiness about being separated from family, dislike for the type of food being served, impatience with chronicity and its attending limitations, discouragement because improvement is slow, anxiety related to giving up the status of wage-earner in the family, fear of the future vocationally, and many others.

Then there is a whole group of situations causing concern, fear, and even anxiety prompted by economic problems related to needed medical care, such as estimated costs of care far beyond family income, indebtedness for medical care, possible loss of equity in the family home, loss of furniture being purchased on the instalment plan, need for supplementary aid for the family when the wage-earner is the patient, need for financial assistance during the long convalescent period, and others.

Then there are the environmental situations, such as inadequate housing or home conditions, need for a housekeeper or foster-home care for the children if the mother is the patient, inadequate occupational therapy, inadequate recreation, unsuitable vocational placement. All these are typical of the type of situations with which the medical social worker deals in her daily practice.

Considering the areas of practice of the medical social worker, these may include medical social case work; consultation service on medical social problems; participation in community planning for health; participation in research concerned with understanding the economic, social, and emotional factors related to ill health; participation in in-service or staff orientation programs; and participation in professional education for students in medicine, public health, nursing, and social work.

Directly, or indirectly, the medical social worker can contribute to securing provisions for medical care through any of these areas of practice. It is from medical social case work practice that the profession's contribution toward securing provisions for medical care stems. Medical social case records are full of evidence reflecting economic pressure on family life, unmet health needs, and unhappiness related to ill health. It is not uncommon for the medical social case worker to experience the full impact of complaints of patients related to what the patient or family regard as exorbitant costs of medical care; to observe the incongruous relationship at times between estimated costs of care and family income; to observe an equally incongruous relationship between the amounts of bills for medical care and hospitalization and the particular family income; to learn of family indebtedness for medical care prohibitive to other family plans, such as sending the young son or daughter to college; to listen to the stories of patients whose recurrent illness implies that they resumed the responsibilities of "wage-earner" sooner than was medically wise, for the reason that they could not feel comfortable about accepting a prolonged convalescent period while others in the family were the providers; to hear endless stories reflecting emotional discomfort related to the whole problem of medical-care economics.

Furthermore, it is from medical social case work practice for low-income groups that gaps in community health service are revealed, lacks such as psychiatric service, dental service for children, beds for adult hospitalization, beds for convalescent care. Through her efforts to utilize community facilities in behalf of patients, the social case worker can soon learn which ones are available, which are lacking, and which have certain limitations imposed as a condition at intake, so that all patients who apply are not accepted for care. For illustration, she knows of existing prejudices against racial or religious groups. She knows of the unhappy experiences of patients who lack legal settlement in the community and accordingly are allowed care only for emergency conditions. She knows of the punitive measures that are applied at times with the hope that depriving such patients of adequate medical care may induce them to return to their community of legal residence. She hears the stories of patients of why they refuse to return for purposes of medical care. She has a wealth of source material from the experiences of patients seeking help to arrange medical care. These data are available. The question is, Are they being utilized effectively to reflect the health needs of patients? What more can medical social workers do to call such data to the attention of appropriate administrators or groups where it will count?

The twentieth century marks the beginning of a national philosophy emphasizing that the health and welfare of the nation is the deep concern of the people as expressed through their government. If we compare conditions throughout the states today with what they were ten or more years ago, we note a marked growth and development toward minimum adequate standards of health and welfare that is good for the nation. This has been possible because of joint planning and joint financing between federal, state, and local jurisdictions of government. It implies that no longer are the people satisfied with the standards we had before the depression, when in too many localities throughout the nation people had to be severely ill or grossly poor and dependent before public health and welfare were available to them. The modern trend emphasizes community organization, which applies preventive medicine and preventive social welfare, and community planning, which meets needs early in ill health, or in the scale of dependency due to social disadvantage. With focus on prevention, appropriate community planning for health and welfare increases in significance, and again we, as medical social workers, need ask ourselves what contribution our field may make, in co-ordinating our effort with that of others toward serving our community accordingly.

It is from her "grass-roots" experience that the medical social worker brings her evidence to the community-planning area of service. On the basis of existing conditions among the people she serves in day-by-day practice or the conditions revealed through the service of her staff if she happens to be the supervisor or administrator, the medical social worker participating in community planning is offered an opportunity to reflect the medical social needs of people. There are a number of settings through which her contribution is possible. If her district of the American Association of Medical Social Workers is active in community planning, she may participate through her district. If she practices in an urban area, such as one of the larger metropolitan centers, she may wish to participate through one of the larger co-ordinating social or health agencies concerned with broad community planning for the health field, such as the Health Division of the Welfare Council of the Community Chest, or a health organization such as the Tuberculosis and Health Association, the Mental Hygiene Society, the Heart Association, the Crippled Children's Society, and countless others representing a special health interest. If she practices in a rural or semirural area, she will usually find at least the nucleus of community planning through some smaller group of citizens who meet regularly and who, if not already engaged in some phase of community-wide planning for health and welfare, can be readily interested in a project if the need is clearly demonstrated. At times the group through which the medical social worker will gain support will be one of the service clubs, or a church group, or a community co-ordinating council such as we have throughout the rural areas of California. At times, when the usual patterns of community organization are not available or are for some reason not appropriate, a special committee for a given project may be organized. In general, though, it is well to affiliate with regularly constituted agencies or established structures rather than set up just one more isolated group, unrelated to the life-stream of the community.

Unless she is affiliated with a group composed entirely of medical social workers, organized to explore some phase of medical social practice, the medical social worker interested in community planning will usually participate as one member of a cross-section group, representing the health field and including members such as physicians, nurses, hospital administrators, and other allies of the health field, together with a sufficient number of lay members presumably representing the consumer or possible beneficiaries of service.

For illustration as to how the medical social worker may participate in community planning for health, may I cite the experience with which I am most familiar. In our community we have a Welfare Council within which there is a Health Division. Composed of delegates representing all the health agencies within membership of the division, the delegates each year elect a Committee on Health Services to represent the health interest throughout the year. The relationship of the Committee on Health Services to the delegate body is similar to that of a board of directors to the general membership of a large organization.

At the beginning of each council year, the Committee on Health Services reviews unfinished business from the previous year, takes stock of current thinking as to what new program should be initiated, and outlines a program for the year mutually satisfactory to all concerned. Because the health interest has many and diversified interests, there are usually more ideas than there is personnel or time to execute them. Accordingly, it is well to agree on priorities for the given year and gear the balance of the program to available staff and time. At the moment our priorities include mental health and dental health, though services to crippled children, adult hospitalization, and a number of smaller projects are receiving their due share of attention by the Committee on Health Services. Subcommittees usually are appointed per project undertaken. They devote all of their time to study and the development of a report to the Committee on Health Services which meets regularly every month. After the Committee on Health Services passes favorably on the report of a subcommittee, the report passes on to the Executive Committee of the Welfare Council for consideration and approval. Approval implies that social action will be initiated in following through on a recommended and indorsed program in the community.

The role of the medical social worker on such a community-planning body for health is to integrate medical social thinking into the group process. The other members of the committee have a comparable opportunity for the special profession or interest they represent. The effect of bringing together the various interests concerned for joint thinking and joint community planning for health results in effective integration of the various interests concerned. Medical social workers share on an equal basis with other professional groups in bringing to the experience source material reflecting needs of patients, interpreting the needs and the gaps in community service, and suggesting ways and means for social action to improve medical and social services.

In our community for the last twenty years, medical social workers have participated in community planning for health, for the most part, in relation to programs furthering service to socially disadvantaged groups. Such programs have included mental health, dental health, convalescent care, hospitalization, crippled children's services, visiting nursing service, development of medical social service, and others. Furthermore, they have participated in budgeting for health agencies of the Community Chest. They have served on the Welfare Council committees concerned with health legislation as well as on the council's over-all legislative committee concerned with all phases of health and welfare legislation. They have been members of the Executive Board of the Welfare Council. In the Los Angeles County Health Department, at this time, one medical social worker is attempting to achieve adequate dental service for school children in a desert community located about seventy-five miles from metropolitan Los Angeles, and not for children whose parents are financially disadvantaged, but rather, for children whose parents are well able to pay for private dental practice. There are but two dentists in the community. For lack of private-care facilities and in defense against having to travel great distances for dental service, parents have applied to the public health department for dental service, though care is restricted to patients unable to pay private-practice rates.

Another medical social worker, in appreciation for her part in a community planning project which resulted in achieving a visiting nursing program for the local community, was made an honorary member of the local district of the California Nurse's Association.

The effectiveness of the medical social worker in community planning for health will depend on a number of factors, all within her control; factors such as how clear she is regarding medical social function as compared to other professional skills; how well she is grounded in the problem under consideration; how well she is prepared to substantiate her point of view with factual information as reflected through field practice; how effectively she interprets, so that she is readily understood not only by the members of her own profession but by other professional groups and lay people; and on how willingly she applies herself to the project until its completion or termination, even though at times it implies years of application.

It is in the field of community planning for health and welfare that the medical social worker, if she chooses, is offered her best opportunity to share with others in moving on from the service of interpreting medical-care needs to social action for procuring medical-care facilities. At times the social action implied concerns only the local community. For example, if mental health services are the urgent need in a given locality, the program of interpretation leads into a consideration of ways and means for expanding existing mental health services or initiating new facilities, usually through local community interest and fund-raising. On the other hand, if the program for needed medical care relates to the state-wide or even the nation-wide community, social action with respect to legislation is indicated. The extent to which a given community planning group, of which the medical social worker is a part, will participate in promoting legislation will vary with the group. Most effective groups today feel that their responsibility to the public implies that they take a position with regard to specific legislation promoting programs of public health and medical care and are doing so. We recognize that there are varying points of view as to the appropriateness of a professional group participating in legislative programs. There are those who hold that the sole responsibility is limited to interpretation and education. There are others who hold, Why stop at interpretation and education without following through into social action? The answer lies, it seems to me, in the pattern already operating in the community of today.

Medical social workers must take their place side by side with other professional groups in securing provisions for medical care, including not only adequate service to patients during acute illness but preventive health services, appropriate care during convalescence, supplemented by financial assistance as a right and a corollary to medical care, so that the convalescing patient will not feel economic pressure prompting him to return to the status of wage-earner sooner than is medically advisable, and adequate care during chronicity and disability. Let us ask ourselves, Are we making medical social studies and research available where it will count? Are we interpreting the unmet needs of patients and reflecting community gaps in health service as effectively as possible? Are we participating in community planning for health to the best of our ability?

Recently, I had the opportunity of discussing the subject of this paper with one of my colleagues, a medical social worker well qualified by professional education and experience, who happens for the time being to be employed in a family service setting. When I asked what she saw as the possible role of the medical social worker in securing medical care for people, her instant reply was: "I wish we could go farther back than the medical-care setting, and consider what might be done to increase awareness, understanding, and responsible participation of social case workers in nonmedical social agencies in the application of preventive medicine and medical care." The ensuing discussion was interesting, focusing on questions such as: "How well is preventive medicine and medical care integrated into the total service for the client of a social agency? To what extent does the social case worker accept responsibility for helping the client initiate desirable health service through her own understanding of health resources in the community and intake policies that pertain? If a physical examination is indicated or if the client gives a history of having been advised to have certain care, surgery for instance, or an orthopedic appliance—a recommendation which he completely rejects—to what extent does the social case worker assume responsibility for studying the underlying reasons for the blocking and help the client resolve his problem so he can move ahead in accepting medical care? Does she help him recognize and evaluate the meaning of his symptoms to him, and why he prefers holding on to them? In other words, to what extent does she help the client toward an understanding of how he is using illness or disability to meet some emotional need? To what extent is the social case worker of the nonmedical social agency sharing responsibility with the medical social case worker in the hospital or clinic in furthering a prescribed program for medical care?

There are large public welfare departments that employ medical social workers to serve as consultants to the staff social case workers. Most social agencies, however, do not have medical social consultants, so that whatever health program is inherent to an agency is largely dependent upon the degree to which the individual social case worker, her supervisor, and her administrator are health-conscious.

What role can the medical social workers of a given community play in furthering good health programs in social agencies? Can we do anything to help the social agency take stock of health conditions among its clients? Do we initiate interagency

programs to stimulate the utilization of available preventive medicine services, such as immunization against smallpox and diphtheria, well-baby conferences, and prenatal care for the expectant mother to which most clients of a public welfare department
or voluntary social agency would be eligible? Can we stimulate
the social case workers to take stock of their individual case load
to know whether or not their particular clients are immunized;
to know whether infants and children of preschool age are under
active supervision, and whether expectant mothers are under
supervision? Can we stimulate periodic health examinations of
well children, particularly children deprived of parental supervision, for purposes of verifying that the child's health is satisfactory; and do social case workers encourage the early correction of defects discovered and actually follow through? If we
find we cannot spare the time for such a program of health interpretation to social agencies ourselves, can we steer the directors of such departments to others in the health field, particularly health officers and public health nurses, who might be helpful? What can we do to co-ordinate health and medical-care
services of public health departments, schools, and social agencies in behalf of children who are socially disadvantaged, and
for whom the social agency social worker becomes the parent-
substitute? This whole area of service is still another contribution that medical social workers may wish to study further in
the interests of providing medical care to socially disadvantaged
groups, especially children under social agency supervision.

Our last consideration is to evaluate the possible contribution
of medical social "teaching" to securing provisions for medical
care. The objective of such teaching is to achieve the best possible medical care of the patient. The focus of such teaching is
invariably on the social aspects of medicine. The hope of such
teaching is to develop an awareness of the social component in
each patient's situation, to study the patient in all his significant
social relationships as these affect his illness and response to treatment, and ultimately to achieve such understanding of the interrelationship between the medical and social factors that no practitioner of the future who has participated in such a teaching
experience would wish to consider the one without the other in

the interests of good medical care. While teaching the social aspects of medical care may, at first glance, seem more remote to procuring adequate medical care for people than do some of the other possible contributions of the medical social worker, actually the effect of such teaching on the whole outlook and approach of the doctor, nurse, or social worker toward serving the patient achieves in the end a high standard of service for the patient.

For illustration, at one time in our department the staff orientation program for new staff nurses and medical social workers was not as well developed as it is today. Today new staff medical social workers have the opportunity of the same orientation program as do the nurses, and the administration of medical social service is desirous of having each new staff medical social worker understand not only the Medical Social Service Bureau, how it functions, and how it relates itself to other services of the department and the community, but to have an understanding of the function of other services in the department, and especially public health nursing, with which we work as closely as we do with clinicians. Similarly, the administration of the Bureau of Public Health Nursing is desirous of having each new staff nurse joining the department understand the functions of Medical Social Service, and how public health nurse and medical social worker may utilize one another's skills in behalf of good service to the patient. The orientation program of new staff nurses, under the auspices of the Bureau of Public Health Nursing, includes eight hours of class work devoted to medical social service, supplemented by a supervised field experience in which the medical social case worker participates.

The method employed is the usual one, of utilizing actual clinical material as a basis for the teaching process. The new staff nurse is under the supervision of a teacher-nurse for the public health nursing component of her field work, while the medical social worker is responsible for helping the new staff nurse with the social aspects of the cases she carries. The medical social worker's role is to help the nurse develop greater sensitivity to the social component of her cases and, as a second step, to help her evaluate whether it is best that an inherent social problem be referred to the medical social case worker, who, of course, is a member of the medical team in the Los Angeles County Health Department; whether she herself should assume responsibility for the social aspects of the case, utilizing the medical social worker as consultant for the service; or whether it is a mutual problem case on which each should participate in serving the patient. Together they decide in which of the following categories the situation belongs:

a) When the health problem is paramount, the public health nurse should carry the major responsibility, and the medical social worker should serve only as needed in a consultant relationship for the social aspects of service.

b) When the case is a mutual problem case calling for the special skills of both public health nurse and medical social worker, the case should be carried co-operatively.

c) When the social situation assumes major proportions, responsibility for social study and treatment should be assigned to the medical social worker.

Indirect a service as the area of teaching the medical social aspects may seem to securing provisions for medical care, experience clearly suggests that, when the student fully realizes the interdependence of medical care per se and the social services, his whole future practice is colored by an ideology demanding better medical care for people.

In closing may I say that I realize full well how skeleton-like this presentation may seem in view of all that should be said to cover the subject adequately. If, on the other hand, the medical social worker is prompted to participate in medical social studies and research arising out of her social case work practice or consultation services; if she is prompted to participate more fully in community planning for health and manifests a willingness to move on into social action with regard to legislation if necessary; and if she can realize the possible influence of the teaching role as it promotes good medical care, then this brief presentation will have served its purpose.

3. Emerging Trends

Family Sessions: *A New Co-operative Step in a Medical Setting*[1]

BY MINNA FIELD

For many years past, medical social workers have concentrated on developing a teamwork relationship with the doctors. They argued, and rightly so, that the very nature of their job made it necessary for them to work closely with the doctors, in order to have an authoritative medical interpretation of the patient's condition and to share with the doctor their knowledge of the patient's social situation.

At Montefiore Hospital, where an attempt is made to practice total medicine, there has been a constantly growing effort to integrate the medical and social aspects of the patient's treatment. Medical social rounds, entries in medical charts, ward rounds, participation in medical conferences—all these devices were utilized in the process. Each device in turn increased the freedom of give-and-take and demonstrated to both members of the team the real value to the patient inherent in such an integrated approach.

The process was further helped by the increasing awareness on the part of the medical profession of the interaction between the emotional and social components in illness, the influence of physiological phenomena on the mind, and of psychological phenomena on the body. With acceptance of the fact that "patients are people" and that "patients have families," recognition inevi-

1. Reprinted from *Journal of Social Casework*, December, 1949, with permission of the Family Service Association of America.

tably followed that "family members are people" and that they have a right to participate in planning for the patient.

Until recently, however, family members were excluded from direct participation in the doctor–social worker–patient relationship. It is true that the medical social worker maintained a close relationship with members of the family and attempted to integrate the work with the patient, on the one hand, and the work with the family, on the other, the doctor being called in difficult situations. The routine doctor-family relationship, however, as in so many other hospitals, was confined to the doctors' being available to family members during regular ward visiting hours.

The inadequacies of this arrangement have been evident to all concerned for some time. Relatives frequently complained that visits were unsatisfactory because their attention was divided between the patient and attempts to "catch the doctor." When they were able to find the doctor, lack of privacy and pressure of time meant that frequently many questions of primary concern to the family remained unasked. In other instances, the doctor familiar with the patient was called away by an emergency, and the substitute, knowing the patient only slightly, if at all, was unable to give the family members the kind of information that would help to allay their anxieties and fears.

The doctors, too, were conscious of limitation of time, lack of privacy, pressure of other duties, all of which meant inadequate service to families and a resulting feeling of frustration and dissatisfaction.

To eliminate some of these difficulties, arrangements were made to set aside a special hour, immediately preceding the Tuesday night ward visiting hour, during which the entire medical staff was to be available to interview family members and answer whatever questions they might have. Soon after the sessions were instituted, it became apparent to the doctors that many of the problems brought to them were of a medical social rather than a purely medical nature. Accustomed to having such problems handled by the social workers on the ward, the doctors requested social service participation in these Tuesday night sessions.

THE PLAN IN OPERATION

Thus the joint sessions inaugurated on August 18, 1948—which include doctors, social workers, and family members—represent a natural evolution in co-operative relationship and medical social integration, stemming as they do from the already established and integrated work on the wards.

The sessions are held in the large hospital auditorium. The doctor and social worker representing their respective wards are located in specifically assigned parts of the room, sufficiently separated to insure privacy, the visitors being guided to the proper sections by volunteers. The very openness of the hall lends itself to calm, quiet discussion, and the sight of so many other relatives talking freely with the doctors reassures the more timid among them.

As was to be expected, the problems brought by these relatives differ with the nature of the patient's illness; the social, economic, familial, and emotional problems the illness creates; and the amount of anxiety and guilt the illness provokes. All these are in turn influenced by the nature of previously existing familial relationships and the patient's place in the family group. While the greatest number of problems falls into three main categories—those dealing with interpretation of medical information, problems in planning for the patient's discharge, and problems in relation to the patient's adjustment to the hospital—the intricate pattern of intrafamilial relationships is apparent throughout.

In frequency, problems dealing with interpretation of medical information head the list. Most family members want to know "the name of the illness," even though the name itself may have little meaning to them. Even when they are familiar with the meaning of the diagnosis, the anxiety produced by the illness frequently distorts the picture, so that family members think only of the liabilities, fear the worst, and ignore the real potentialities that the patient may have. The presence of the social worker when diagnosis is discussed accomplishes a double purpose. The social worker is able to interpret the meaning of the illness in social terms and thus to give a more accurate picture of the patient's strengths as well as his handicaps. As a result of such interpretation, the patient emerges, not as a disease entity, but as a functioning, living human being, with strengths and weaknesses, potentialities and limitations. Seen in this light, the frightening aspects of the patient's illness lose some of their terror, and the patient resembles more closely the person the family knew before the illness, who had his limitations, even when well.

At the same time, the social worker can use the very way in which family members react to a diagnosis and its implications as a tool in the better understanding of existing relationships and the treatment of the problems they create. Some families are utterly unable to accept the fact that a patient can maintain a certain level of usefulness to himself, his family, and the community even in face of a poor prognosis. Others are equally unable to accept a diagnosis of a serious disabling illness, denying the illness and continuing to expect a level of performance from the patient above what is actually possible. This inability to accept a diagnosis often indicates that the relatives react to their own fear of what the diagnosis means. They need help in arriving at a more realistic understanding of the patient and the restrictions imposed by the illness, so as to assure for the patient a milieu where he can function to his maximum ability.

Family members sometimes try to protect the relative most intimately concerned from the knowledge of a serious or fatal diagnosis. Influenced by their own fears, they try to hide the truth, not realizing that the unknown is often the greater threat and failing to appreciate the reservoir of strength with which reality, once known, can be faced. The social worker, familiar with the family relationships and able to draw upon existing strengths, can increase the relatives' capacity to meet problems and to carry the burden the illness imposes.

The question of discharge is another area where social service help is frequently needed. Admission to a hospital devoted to the care and treatment of long-term illness means that the patient, as well as the family, has gone through a period of doubt and indecision and has finally made peace with the idea of a prolonged hospital stay. However, modern methods of treatment and expansion of medical services into the home have made it increasingly possible to shorten perceptibly the period of hospital stay. This modern medical approach to the treatment of long-term illness is, as yet, not understood by the community at large. Families confronted with the fact that the anticipated prolonged stay is not necessary and that the patient can return home may react with bewilderment and anxiety.

The important factors in these situations are the nature of the patient's illness and his concern about his ability to maintain himself at home and, even more important, the family's reaction to his return. On the one hand, there are families which, having reconciled themselves to the need for prolonged hospitalization, have transferred the responsibility for the patient's care to the hospital. Faced with the necessity of assuming the burden once again, they need the help both of the medical authority, for assurance that the patient is ready for the return home, and of the social worker, in readjusting their lives to include the patient.

There are other families which, motivated by their own guilt feelings, may wish to remove the patient long before discharge is medically indicated. Because of the conflict inherent in these situations, the importance of the medical authority in determining need for hospitalization or lack of it and in setting a date for leaving the hospital cannot be overestimated. This authoritative approach, helpful and essential as it is, may leave the family with feelings of frustration and anxiety, regardless of whether or not they accept the decision. In the past, we have found that these feelings were often responsible for the family's playing the doctor against the social worker and vice versa, with resulting delayed discharges and numerous conferences to straighten out the conflicting reports. These feelings on the part of the family, unless handled, may be reflected in the type of treatment the patient receives upon his return home. He may be either neglected, made to feel his uselessness, or overprotected and shielded, with consequent exclusion from participation in family living. In either case, little can be expected in the way of continued improvement or the patient's use of himself to his maximum capacity. The social worker can anticipate some of these difficulties and help in preventing them. Fortified by the authority of the doctor's recommendations and trained to discern attitudes and understand motivations, the worker can help the family members articulate their problems, their resentment against the hospital and the doctor's decision, and, through acceptance of their questioning and offer of help, can strengthen their ability to meet the very real difficulty with which they are confronted. Once the patient returns to a family ready and willing to take him, his chances for a better adjustment and real participation in the life of the family are more adequately assured.

Many of the questions brought up for discussion during these evening sessions are concerned with the patient's hospital adjustment. The patient may be afraid of a proposed form of treatment and demand to be taken home against medical advice. He may complain about the medical or nursing care he is receiving or about his diet. When such complaints have a basis in reality, steps can be taken to remedy the situation. In a great many instances, however, they may be but an expression of the patient's reaction to his illness, his dissatisfaction with the need for hospitalization, or his attempt to control or punish his relatives. Family members, unaware of the true facts and reacting to their own feelings about the patient's illness, may identify with the patient and, by so doing, fortify his dissatisfaction.

Once again, through joint interpretation by the doctor and social worker, all aspects of the problem can be handled at the same time. The medical explanation of the need for certain medical procedures, restricted diet, and so on, is reinforced when supported by the worker's ability to understand the real meaning of the complaints and to handle the feelings involved, with the result that attitudes can frequently be changed and relatives may become active supporters in helping the patient accept the doctor's recommendations.

EVALUATION OF GAINS

In broad outline these are some of the problems handled. Whatever the nature of the problem, we have found that, with the doctor providing the medical authority and the social worker interpreting the medical information in social terms, thus releasing tensions and bringing fears, doubts, and anxieties out in the open where they can be discussed and dissolved, the difficulties they are likely to create are minimized or even completely obviated.

The program has been in operation for more than a year, and an evaluation of what it means to all those concerned with the care of the patient can be attempted. The most obvious advantage is the saving of time, a saving not lightly to be dismissed in a busy hospital schedule. Thus, during these 49 one-hour sessions, a total of 3,915 interviews were held, or an average of about 80 interviews per session.

The doctors find that the Tuesday night sessions remove the pressures of lack of time and privacy of which they were previously aware. In addition, referrals are facilitated and controversial questions settled at the time they arise, thus eliminating misinterpretation of information. Most important, these sessions serve as a living demonstration of the value of medical social work team relationship. The doctors gain a better understanding of the patient, his family, and his social situation. They are helped to see the patient not merely as a sick organ but as a functioning human being. The problems created by his illness assume significance as they are seen in relation to the complexity of family relationships and adjustments to be made in the community. The informal discussions bring out, more clearly than any formal instruction can, the interplay between the physical and emotional components of illness, between the patient and members of his family, as well as the effect that family members have upon the patient's physical condition.

These joint sessions serve as additional demonstration of the value of the teamwork approach not only to the doctors but to the patient and the family as well. Patient and family see the two professional groups working as a team and get a sense of the co-ordination of the services on the patient's behalf and are aware of the resulting higher quality of service thus secured. They respond to the individualization by the doctor, made possible by the latter's awareness of the patient as a whole and of the natural family group of which the patient is a part. The knowledge that the time with the doctor is available to them without interruption, that their questions will be answered, and that the social worker is there to help them with any difficulties which these answers may bring to the fore gives family members a feeling of security. With this joint help they are better able to handle the patient's questions, anxieties, and dissatisfactions.

The social workers see the sessions as an unusual opportunity to offer a real, meaningful service to the patient and his family, to interpret their role to another professional group, and, in so doing, to strengthen the understanding of each other's contribution, which makes working together profitable.

While it is true that in a medical situation the authority of the medical recommendation is as important to the relative as to the social worker, it tends to evoke fears, anxieties, and guilt. Perhaps one of the most important values of the joint session is the opportunity it gives the social worker to handle these feelings at the time they arise. The worker is thus able to discharge the dual responsibility most effectively. Allied with the institution and its limitations, the worker can, at the same time, identify with both patient and family members in helping them work out the problems these limitations create.

The Essential Partnership of Medicine and Social Work[1]

BY OLLIE A. RANDALL

IT SEEMS obvious that medicine and social work must establish a partnership, functioning actively for each of the disciplines party to it, if the elderly patient or individual is to have the full benefit of their common knowledge. Yet it is impossible not to be struck occasionally by the lack of recognition of the role which the social situation, if not the social worker, plays in the management of an old person's health.

Historically it has been the co-operative working relationship between members of the medical profession and members of other scientific groups, such as sanitary engineers, physicists, and chemists, which has resulted in the present controls of infectious and contagious diseases, as well as certain acute forms of illness. In these common endeavors there have been efforts to develop controls which would benefit the health of the masses, as well as improve the situation of the individual patient. It therefore seems rational to consider the effect which the tremendous change in the social environment of older persons has upon their personal health and upon the public health. Unless older people, now constituting a large proportion of almost any community, are physically, emotionally, and mentally healthy, the general level of community health suffers. That society is notably dilatory in establishing appropriate measures for coping with the results of scientific advances is axiomatic. No more dramatic examples of this can be found than those which typify almost any phase of the social provisions, or lack of them, for our older people. In considering the illness or even the health of an older person, the social factors, which often determine both *what* he can do and

1. Reprinted from *Geriatrics*, January–February, 1950, with the permission of *Geriatrics* and the American Geriatrics Society.

how he can do, must be weighed as seriously and as carefully as the physical factors.

An episode at a conference held a short time ago in New York illustrates this point. Hospital needs were discussed, and there was agreement among representatives of both the voluntary and the municipal hospitals that the groups offering the greatest problems in the way of sufficient and suitable hospital accommodations were the tuberculous and the chronically ill patients. In the interchange of comments Dr. George Baehr, former president of the Academy of Medicine of New York, said he had recently made rounds in several hospital wards and was much impressed by the fact that in one ward there was no patient under the age of forty-five; in another, no patient under sixty; and in still a third, no patient under the age of seventy. These older patients are admitted to the hospital, receive treatment, and are discharged, returning to their miserable or inadequate homes, only to come back again and again, because they cannot manage to improve or even to maintain the level of health at which they were discharged. And he added: " 'Geriatrics' is *not* a special branch of medicine—it is medicine applied to the treatment of disease as it occurs in older people. In reality it is *social medicine*." Dr. Baehr was emphasizing that in the practice of medicine with older people there can be no arbitrary separation of the person or patient from his social environment, if the maximum or optimal measure of health is to be attained or maintained. This is true to some extent for patients of all ages, but for older people, who have less opportunity and possibly less ability to control the external circumstances of their living arrangements, it is nearly always true.

Dr. E. J. Stieglitz points out that today clinical medicine must have its primary focus on "the individual rather than the diseases which beset him" and that "the person must be treated, not his illnesses," whether it is physical or mental health which is the concern. "Social medicine, on the other hand," to quote him further, "is concerned with man as a member of society."[2] This, in a broad and comprehensive sense, is the sound interpretation

2. E. J. Stieglitz, *Social Medicine: Its Derivations and Objectives* (New York: Commonwealth Fund, 1949), pp. 76–89.

of the new concept of the science of medicine. However, for the purposes of this paper a somewhat narrower interpretation may serve—one which is predicated upon the desirability of partnership *through the exchange of skills and knowledge* between the physician, who is apt to limit his work to the clinical aspects of the case, and the social worker, who must deal with the social adjustment of the patient and often that of his family.

Social workers are increasingly conscious of the need for help from the physician in understanding the implications, for the patient and for their own approach to him, of a diagnosis in terms of physical health. They are also becoming aware of the significance of disease as a determining element in the individual's personality structure and his reaction to social and economic demands—although this is less often the case in their work with older people than with younger adults and children. Members of the medical profession are responding with less reluctance than formerly to requests for medical guidance from social workers in services with children. Even here the teamwork between the two groups is, at best, very spotty and, in all probability, is usually initiated by the social worker reaching out for all the facts and assistance possible which can be useful in helping the client to help himself. It is probably treading on dangerous ground to venture the opinion that in the care of older people the amount and degree of voluntary teamwork between the two professions is negligible, for *neither* profession has as yet tilled widely or deeply enough in the field of geriatrics to have acquired substantial experience. Social workers as well as doctors function under a handicap which in many instances prevents their serving the best interests of the elderly client—the preconceived notion that all old people are sick anyway and that old age is a period of progressive ill health. The physician's usual contact with disease in the elderly, whether in medical school or with patients who are paying well for their care, has been as indifferent or casual as that of the social worker. In few cases has there been a strong desire for better understanding on the part of either the social worker or the doctor.

Today, however, there is a deepening sense of the interrelationship of the two disciplines. Current studies and programs, based on work with the patient in his own home (where the greater majority of older people will continue to be, not only because they *must* remain there, but because they wish to do so and because it is now being proved it is the *best* place for them, given certain conditions), are attracting the attention of both professions. Doctors and social workers are being challenged to re-examine their established procedures, since these must be used in the new settings and situations replacing the social institutions considered essential in the early years of the twentieth century.

The Syracuse study of follow-up care in the home after discharge from the hospital demonstrated, according to one of the physicians, that most of the social workers needed much more medical orientation and knowledge than they started out with. But, as a prominent social work leader reminded the doctor, the participating physicians also realized they needed much more social orientation than they had received in their medical training or practice. The several home medical-care programs now being conducted in New York, such as that at Montefiore Hospital and in the New York City Department of Hospitals, indicate conclusively the educational as well as the service value of such programs. As one of the medical men put it: "What I have learned about the home situations of patients, and the part the home and the family can play either favorably or unfavorably in their treatment, is extremely valuable. I have also come to realize that for some chronically ill patients and for many older people, the social worker is more essential in effecting treatment and improvement of the patient's condition than is the doctor. For practically all patients in this program she is *just* as important to the patient, and if he is a wise man, is always important to the doctor!"

This development, with the extension of medical care and auxiliary social services to the home of the patient as a substitute for the institutional or hospital care (which simply does not exist for elderly infirm persons) is further indisputable evidence that man-made institutions can be modified or adapted by man in the extremity of his need. In this search for methods of working with the difficult medical and social problems of the chronically ill and the infirm aged may come the strengthening of the

teamwork between the two professions as a new benefit to everyone concerned.

Most of us who have spent much time with older people, either
as individuals or as professional workers, are conscious of the
painful readjustment which most of this group have had to make
in a society so completely unprepared for their continued presence on earth. If their lot is to be improved—and with it the lot
of us who will take their places sooner than we would like—then
there must be immediate and intelligent planning for education in
the schools of both medicine and of social work. This planning
must inevitably map out the interdependence of the two professions. Possibly social workers could have medical men give them
their orientation courses, and medical students could have social
workers in a similar capacity. There must be clear and definite
emphasis upon the fact that a person in his old age tends to suffer
greater social and health losses than at any other time and that
those losses tend likewise to be less compensable then than at any
other period of his life. This implies that, first of all, both the doctor and the social worker must be taught to find the individual
old person—not just the disease, or the patient, or the socially dislocated person—and that, after finding him, they must be willing
to endow him in their own minds with those perquisites which
make for status and which merit the best which each profession
has to offer. This also implies that the medical man must be willing to recognize the social worker in the hierarchy of the disciplines and to accord to her or him the place which the
individual situation may call for. All of us are accustomed to the
attitude which consigns the social worker in the hospital setting
to a kind of clerical or nuisance role or to one getting less attention than either of these, in working out the total situation of
the patient. Education of the social worker as to how and when
to use her skills and how to assume the role for which she is
trained and equipped, and of the doctors as to the potentiality
of her services for the good of the patient, will ultimately produce the kind of partnership without which, in this complex
world, we cannot expect older people as patients to adjust.

If the doctor's only experience with social workers is that
acquired in the hospital setting in which the major burden of

treatment, as well as of judgment or decision, quite properly rests with him, then it is small wonder that there has been little or no progress in mutual handling of cases in the patient's own home, in which often the burden of judgment might more logically rest with the social worker. Here many of the social workers are under the spell of the superior knowledge which the doctor has of the human body and the ailments thereof, so that they have probably not felt free to question or to share with the doctor knowledge which might be of help. One classic example of this remains vividly in my memory. A physician told a little old lady of some seventy years, French by birth, that she could not expect to live more than a few days or weeks if she insisted on going daily to her work as a seamstress in a small shop. The diagnosis and prognosis were shared with us. The recommendation that work be discontinued was taken very seriously, although all of us who knew *her*, knew that giving up work, not the illness, was the real death sentence for her. However, every attempt was made to help carry out the doctor's orders, but to no avail. This little lady had set herself a goal—that of working to a certain point in order to repay some imagined debt of gratitude to the United States for what had been done for her. And in spite of illness and doctor's warnings and the social worker's unhappy failure to satisfy the doctor, that little lady lived seven years, going to work almost constantly, sewing the finest seam one could imagine, meeting her daily quota regularly, and supporting herself to within a few days of her death by the work of her hands. In the search, or research, for the controls of chronic disease we may need to pay more attention to the personal and social factors, to the psychological "will to live"—that intangible something which defies definition but which can, if detected, be used to advantage by both physician and social worker.

In another case the patient was an elderly farmer who had suffered for many years from some form of hay fever and who had spent most of his life on the particular farm on which he was still living. It was found by the clinician that the difficulty could be overcome by the "simple" device of having the old man move away from his home to another part of the county.

The statement was cavalier in its complete dismissal of the whole life-experience of the old farmer. Does it not raise questions, not as to the cure, but as to the *simplicity* of achieving it? And does it not raise the further question as to whether perhaps the cure might prove worse than the disease? Does an old man move easily from his home place of many years' standing?—or could it not be that continuing to endure the suffering might be "simpler" than making the move? Manipulation of environment often sounds practical and easy, as well as subject to more direct controls than bringing about inner or personal adjustments, until there is realization that the interdependence of the inner and outer environments makes cleavage between the two an impossibility. Perhaps the doctor was more aware of what was involved than the report indicated, but the use of the word "simple" to describe this step, which has been such a major one for the hundreds of older people whom I have known, made me suspicious that here it was the patient's disease, not the individual, that was being treated. In both these situations better understanding of both the medical and the social factors was needed by everyone, including the patients.

Today we hear of dramatic examples of return to some degree of self-service or employment by older patients, long condemned to helplessness by their own lack of motive or interest on the part of others. Not only are the new rehabilitation procedures exciting and stimulating in themselves, but they result in healthy attitudes in both patients and those working with them and create a new climate of opinion about old people and about old age. With the future locale for much of our work in the person's own home, some observations made during a medical study in England are exceedingly pertinent. The physician who visited old people in their modest homes found an amazing amount of what he called "autorehabilitation." Patients upon whom others depended or who refused to succumb to disabilities simply kept on going—a fact which demonstrated that their desire to continue living and doing was strong enough to overcome seriously crippling handicaps. The willingness of sick old people in hospitals and institutions to yield to frustrating handicaps may in some cases be attributed to the lack of a reason to get better there, may be lack of interest on the part of personnel or friends or family, lack of anything to do for themselves or for others, the lack of opportunity of going anywhere else even when able—with all the lacks adding up to a "what's the use" attitude. Both the doctor and the social worker, especially in those cases in which disease is not the dominant but rather a complicating element, need an understanding of the dislocations which have taken place in the social environment of the individual, as well as his physical, biological, or pathological dislocation, a knowledge of how these may affect the person's inner being.

Given sufficient personal motivation, the limitations imposed on the older persons by disease may often be discounted, to the end that a very satisfying social adjustment is made. Providing social activities for the older patient and the opportunity for association with persons who take the time to talk with him and who assume, without question, his ability to take part—these are undoubtedly preventive mental health measures which have not yet been successfully isolated or defined. Psychological and physical needs appear capable of satisfaction through some of the same means, although obviously in varying degrees. As personal adjustment improves, there is a new capacity for accepting and dealing with the difficulties of the social environment, to the mutual benefit of the old person and of his family.

The ultimate objective of therapy is to restore the patient to the maximum of human dignity of which he is capable; the aim of the social treatment is to assist the individual in realizing as fully as possible his capacity as a person and as a member of society. With this common goal—to be attained through different skills and methods—partnership between medicine and social work is not only essential, it is inevitable.

Group Counseling with Mothers of Children with Cerebral Palsy[1]

BY HARRY V. BICE AND MARGARET G. DAVITT HOLDEN

THROUGH co-operative planning on the part of the authors and officials of a Parents' League, counseling services were provided for mothers of children with cerebral palsy. This article presents a summary of discussion in two series of meetings, in each of which ten mothers were enrolled. A series was comprised of six sessions, each lasting an hour and a half.

These were diversified groups, with the three major religious sects and several nationalities represented. In education, the mothers ranged from eighth grade to completion of college, with an average equal to a completed high-school course. In occupation, the fathers varied from truck driver to physician. The youngest cerebral palsied child was 2 years of age, the oldest, 10. But one common denominator for the group could be found: all were mothers of children with cerebral palsy.

Some of the mothers were already acquainted with the counselors through professional contacts, a fact which helped to account for the ease with which rapport was established. How readily rapport can be destroyed by changes in the composition of the group has been indicated by Regina Elkes.[2] From the outset it was made clear that everyone was to participate. While many people seek authoritative advice from counselors, much as they would on health problems from a physician, these meetings were not to be of that nature; the counselors expected to contribute anything they could from their experience and training, but emphasis was placed on participation by the mothers.

1. Reprinted from *Journal of Social Casework*, March, 1949, with the permission of the Family Service Association of America.
2. "Group-Casework Experiment with Mothers of Children with Cerebral Palsy," *Journal of Social Casework*, March, 1947, pp. 95–101.

Since each mother present was well acquainted with only the type of cerebral palsy represented by her child, counselors opened each series with an outline of the major classifications of the condition as described by Dr. Phelps.[3] Cerebral palsy, often erroneously designated "spastic paralysis," is the name for a number of conditions that have at least two features in common: the brain has suffered damage; as a result there is some limitation of the movements or control of movements of which the child is capable. The most common types include: (1) spasticity, in which muscles are contracted, stiff, and tense; (2) athetosis, a condition characterized by involuntary motions that are variable and without definite pattern; (3) rigidity, in which muscles respond to manipulation with a "lead-pipe" resistance, quite unlike the tense condition of the spastic muscle; (4) ataxia, discoverable chiefly through the individual's lack of balance and co-ordination; (5) tremor, characterized by rhythmical involuntary motions.

THE PROBLEMS

The counselors' responses to three questions asked by parents in other connections are reported here because of their direct relation to definition and classification. These questions dealt with the characteristics of the ataxic child, the problem of mixed dominance, and the mental level of the cerebral palsied. Responses to questions that were primarily medical were brief summaries of Dr. Phelps's conclusions. The mother who asked about ataxia was chiefly interested in her child's constant dizziness and his inability to engage in such activities as bicycle riding. It was explained to her that the different types of cerebral palsy are correlated with differences in the location of the brain injury; the part of the brain involved in ataxia governs the ability to balance one's self and to make movements exactly as one needs or wishes. Whether the child is climbing stairs, trying to ride a bicycle, or learning to walk or typewrite, he cannot readily tell just where his legs, arms, or fingers are, nor how much power he needs to get them where he wants them.

To the question about mixed dominance, counselors responded

3. W. M. Phelps, "Let's Define Cerebral Palsy," *The Crippled Child*, June, 1948, pp. 4–6, 28.

that, with commission cases, several professional people pool their efforts. The physician depends largely on the psychologist, the occupational therapist, and the physiotherapist to determine which should be the leading hand. It is the responsibility of the physician to determine whether or not physiological conditions permit the use of this hand as the leading one and to prescribe the means—medical, mechanical, or educational—by which dominance may be established. There are differences of opinion on the subject of lateral dominance, and evidence from closely controlled experiments is lacking. Clinical evidence has led to certain tentative conclusions: (1) development of a dominant hand has, in the case of the cerebral palsied, a significance in some respects different from its significance in certain other children; (2) which is to be the child's leading hand depends in part on inheritance; (3) in many cases the cerebral palsied, because of structural conditions, early developmental factors, or for some other reason, want to use as a leading hand the one that cannot be used because of the physical disability; they must therefore shift to the other hand; (4) in the course of shifting dominance and before the process is complete, one or more of the following conditions may be observed: convulsions or convulsive equivalents, such as temper tantrums or periods of excitement; confusion; failure to develop speech; slow mental development; a feeling of insecurity; or fears which seem to be without adequate basis; (5) treatment not in accord with that which is recommended in these cases has been accompanied by development or aggravation of the symptoms mentioned; (6) cases in which dominance has been established through treatment have shown decrease and eventual disappearance of such symptoms.

When dealing with the mental ability of the cerebral palsied, the group discussed the changing beliefs on the subject in recent years. Formerly most people believed these children as a class to be mentally deficient. The pendulum then tended to swing to the opposite extreme; articles appeared in popular magazines, and public addresses were made stating or implying that the percentage of feeble-minded in the group was negligible. This was unfortunate, since, as a result, parents found it difficult to accept an unfavorable diagnosis. The present more realistic concept recognizes that each child represents many conditions peculiar to himself and decision on mental status can be made only after extensive study. The general picture is best represented by the conclusions of J. T. McIntire,[4] who found that in over 10 per cent of cases, physical limitations were so extreme that no diagnosis could be made; in addition, 27.6 per cent were feebleminded.

The first subject offered for discussion, one to which allusion was most frequently made later, directed attention away from the mothers and emphasized the shortcomings of others from whom they had sought advice regarding the cerebral palsied child. Reference was made specifically to bias and ignorance of the subject on the part of lay people and members of such professions as medicine, nursing, psychology, social case work, speech therapy, and occupational therapy. While mothers did not expect on the part of others the intense concern that they themselves had by virtue of being mothers, they did expect from professional people accurate and comprehensive information, objectively expressed. The physician who veiled his lack of knowledge behind critical statements directed at the mother, the home teacher who was unable to conceal facial expression of horror upon first acquaintance with her pupil, the visiting nurse who, because of her lack of knowledge, was unable to give any constructive help, were pertinent examples which justified the critical attitude of mothers.

This rationalization was accepted by the counselors as a necessary preliminary to statements of problems of more personal nature. They acknowledged the fairness of the criticisms and introduced a statement by Dr. Perlstein, explaining that, with few modifications, it would also apply to professions other than medical: "The blame for neglect, past and present, rests to a great extent on the doctor's doorstep. In general, most doctors are still abysmally ignorant concerning the nature of cerebral palsy and are unaware that most of the afflicted can be helped to a rewarding degree."[5]

4. J. T. McIntire, "The Incidence of Feeble-mindedness in the Cerebral Palsied," *American Journal of Mental Deficiency*, L, No. 4 (1946), 493–94.
5. M. A. Perlstein, *The Problem of Cerebral Palsy Today* (New York: Association for the Aid of Crippled Children, 1947).

Faced with such uncertainty concerning medical care, how do parents attempt to meet their needs? The most common practice reported was that of going from one doctor to another, hoping to find one who could help. This shopping around was motivated by the criticisms of friends and neighbors as well as the mother's inability to accept an unfavorable prognosis. In a typical case the mother assumed that her child's disability, which was unlike any condition of which she knew, would respond quickly to treatment; when it did not, she ascribed the failure to what she assumed to be the incompetence of the physician rather than the nature of the disability. Some parents in this dilemma were careful to go only to reputable physicians, but others went to charlatans. One mother was told by a person with no professional qualifications that her child could not walk because all her strength was going to her hair; the child's long braids should therefore be cut. Another was assured that her child would be healed if she were baptized. The conclusion stated by the counselors and approved by the mothers was, since the names of physicians who are doing the best work in the field of cerebral palsy are available, the wise course is to seek out such medical authorities and accept their advice.

The use of glutamic acid, which is prescribed in some cases of *petit mal* seizures, was discussed. Some mothers had tried Dr. Phelps's suggestion and found that children were more willing to take it if given in cold Jello or applesauce; one tried successfully the addition of liberal amounts of cinnamon to the fruit to disguise the taste of the glutamic acid.

Some mothers stated that when their children took this preparation, they had better color and seemed to feel better. One said her child "acted as if relieved of some annoyance." These good effects were reported lost when the use of glutamic acid was discontinued. Unfavorable results reported included sore gums, constipation, and periods of excitement. The counselors urged that such problems be referred to physicians. They also explained Dr. Phelps's conclusion that only children with seizures or epileptic equivalents improved generally when treated with glutamic acid; he had not found the widely reported gains in intelligence.

All mothers reported unfavorable attention accorded their children when taken on the street. Some curious neighbors merely stared, others made unkind remarks about the child or about the wisdom of the mother who would allow him outside the house. One mother said that, when people stared at her child, she simply stared back at them. Another remarked that, since children as well as parents offended, she arranged a meeting with a group of parents and explained the child's condition to them. When she felt they understood, she asked them to spread the information among family, friends, and neighbors.

Much more serious was the case of a child of 11 whose presence in the neighborhood was much resented; even adults prevented him from passing their houses. A half-dozen children pretended one day to accept him as a playmate. When they had taken him some distance from home, they buried him in mud and afterward held his feet in a fire, loudly asserting that he was a Jap and they were Americans at war. As a result, the afflicted child was not only afraid to leave the house, but could not listen to a radio program lest he hear something about war. The mother was told by the counselors that such a problem could not be treated in group meetings but individual psychological help was available as a commission service. This was accepted, and the mother later reported the child's almost complete return to normal social activities.

Among the problems that occur within the family circle, none appeared as urgent as that of discipline. It was introduced by a mother who had used spanking as a means of securing obedience; she did not think it effective, but was unable to devise a more satisfactory method. The consensus was that not only was whipping ineffective, but in some cases, especially with the athetoid, the punished child became more tense and nervous. One mother, while disapproving disciplinary measures that would cause pain, thought it all right to "slap him lightly, knowing that it will not really hurt." This was challenged by other mothers, who believed that a resulting feeling of humiliation and resentment on the part of the child would defeat the parents' purpose in administering discipline. More satisfactory disciplinary measures discussed included isolation, diverting attention, making a game of attaining the desired end, giving praise and rewards for good behavior, and, when possible, ignoring the bad, avoiding threats that could not be carried out, and making certain that the child did not gain his goal by unsatisfactory behavior. Consistency on the part of the entire household was considered essential if discipline were to be effective.

Extended discussion of the reasons for difficulty in applying discipline led to the following conclusions: Many parents make an ineffective start; father and mother may not agree on what to demand; either parent may be inconsistent in application of the means used, or may be swayed by too much sentiment. As one mother said, "The trouble with mothers is that they can't stand to discipline these children"; or another, "They can wind you around their finger, and you give in." The presence of grandparents in the home may further complicate the problem. At the outset, because of the palsied child's disabilities, parents have to do more for him than for the child of normal physical development. The line of demarcation between what the mother must do for the child and what she should expect him to do for himself is a difficult one to discover. Solicitude, care, service, and protection beyond what is actually needed give so much satisfaction to the child (and the mother) that he demands that they be continued. The parent knows the child must lead a circumscribed life; it is hard to take anything from him because his disability has robbed him of so much; discipline may take from him even his sense of security. The counselors admitted there was much truth in the mothers' points of view. Nevertheless, failure to do all that is possible to develop desirable personality traits only adds one more liability to the already badly handicapped child. The mother need not fear that the child will lose his sense of security. Like other children, he will learn to accept discipline from those he loves, and the spirit in which the mother does so many things for the child need leave no doubt that she loves him.

Teaching the child to care for his personal needs involved much discussion: "What about dressing and feeding?" "Can he be toilet-trained?" Consideration of toilet training elicited several suggestions: rewards for good behavior could be used; the mother should avoid attempts to train before adequate muscular control is established; she must be alert for clues from the child himself that he is ready for training. The muscular weakness of the cerebral palsied may indicate need of a specially constructed toilet seat to give the child the needed support. The manner in which conclusions were reached may be illustrated by reference to a mother's problem with her 5-year-old. When she related that she had found it impossible to train him, another mother asked, "Does he wear diapers?" When told that he did, she continued, "You are just keeping him a baby; he couldn't take care of his needs if he wanted to. Why don't you try training pants?" The suggestion was tried and found practical.

In considering the problem of a child learning to feed and clothe himself, the majority of mothers admitted that when either process takes a long time or the child is untidy about feeding, it is much easier for the mother to take care of the needs herself. Most of the group perceived that such help merely deferred the time when they must insist on training.

Mothers tended to characterize much unsatisfactory behavior as "peculiar to the cerebral palsied." One described these children as "perverse and unwilling to think as others do," a statement reminiscent of a Werner and Strauss reference to brain-injured children as "erratic, lacking control and discipline."[6] One mother's belief was illustrated by reference to her child who had been treated for Vincent's angina with gentian violet. Afterward he reacted violently to anything purple: he would not wear anything that color, nor could he tolerate it on other members of the household. In responding, a counselor stated that, although the relation of unusual physical conditions to thought-processes must always be considered, the thinking of these children, like that of others, is largely developed in many subtle ways. The dislike of purple was explained in terms of the conditioned response, a process applicable to child and adult, to the physically normal as well as to the handicapped. The constructive use

6. H. Werner and A. A. Strauss, "Impairment in Thought Processes of Brain-injured Children," *American Journal of Mental Deficiency*, XLVII, No. 3 (1943), 295.

of the method by employment of pleasant associations was described.

Several mothers verbalized their resentment against public schools for rejecting their children, even though they meet the required age, and, in some cases, intelligence level. Explanation was given by the counselors of the limitations of most public schools in terms of personnel, methods of education, and equipment, as a result of which they cannot serve the needs of the handicapped. The need for thorough individual study of the child prior to school placement was emphasized.

Late in the series, mothers found it possible to discuss their emotional conflicts about the presence of a cerebral palsied child in the home. A counselor prepared the way for this phase of the discussion by reporting a conference with a mother, not a member of the group, who answered quite fully the question, "What does the presence of this cerebral palsied child in your home do to you?" The mothers' responses included embarrassment and feelings of guilt.

Two major causes for embarrassment were reported—financial stress and criticisms by neighbors. Financial problems develop on a twofold basis: current costs of caring for these children are very high; and often parents must make complete provision for the child's future in event of their death. The counselors interpreted this by reference to the general acceptance of the fact that people who can meet all ordinary financial obligations cannot pay fully for expenses incurred during chronic illness. It has not been uncommon for neighbors to criticize parents, accusing them of being responsible for the child's condition either because the parent was assumed to have some inheritable disease or because cerebral palsy itself was thought to be inherited. Dr. Phelps was quoted as saying that he knew of only five cases that might be considered inherited, information which mothers believed should be widely disseminated.

Upon first mention of feelings of guilt, a mother exclaimed, "Oh! That! That gets to be a part of everything we think. We just take it as something we have to stand and can do nothing about." This led to a discussion of causative factors for this feeling which included parents' concern over sexual mores, specifically, contraceptive practices; religious ideology concerning the relationship between sin and suffering; and the reinforcement of already existing guilt feelings by the tendency on the part of medical authorities to impute responsibility to parents, thus exonerating themselves.

A progression could be observed in which parents moved from a negative point of view to a positive one in which their conflicts were resolved. One mother said, "You can't keep on feeling sorry for yourself; I'm not going to sit at home and cry over it." Another said, "Both my husband and I come from large families. I have thought about the different brothers and sisters and decided that it is good that I am the one with the cerebral palsied child. I am better able than any of the others to bear the burden." "We ought to look at it this way," said another, "there are other handicaps besides cerebral palsy; it must be a lot worse for the parent who has a child who has been normal for years and then suffers a crippling condition such as polio or an accident." Still another comment was, "I went in circles for a year after I found out he was a cerebral palsy; then I realized that the child is the one who has the real struggle and I should not take it as a personal hurt." Several mothers were helped by their religious beliefs. One said, "The counselor will probably think this is silly, but I can understand this experience only by relating it to religious convictions. There is a reason for everything that happens. . . . If we and our friends come to understand better and do something about the cerebral palsied, good will be accomplished that otherwise never would have been."

CONCLUSIONS AND EVALUATIONS

At the end of the series, the mothers had the opportunity to tell what values they had discovered in the meetings and how they believed the service could be made more effective. The mothers admitted their hesitancy in participating, at first, in the counseling sessions, for they felt so much apart that it was difficult for them to see beyond the needs of their own child or any relation between the solution of their problem and the problems of others. A feeling of unity developed and an unexpected recognition of interdependence and mutual support by reason of their interest in a common cause. A spontaneous expression when not in formal session emphasized how real was the feeling of identification: "We even have a language of our own that outsiders do not understand." One found the greatest value for her in "just coming here and talking about it, saying things you never before thought you could. Then when you feel free to say anything, you find that you say something that helps another parent." The practical suggestions offered were found to be of so much worth that members asked that they be published in popular form so that other parents might profit by them. They suggested that counseling sessions be held for fathers.

Since there have been numreous requests that counseling service be continued and extended, the counselors have attempted to evaluate what was done. They recognize that they could not have assumed responsibility for leadership in this project, were it not for their association and opportunity to learn about cerebral palsy from Dr. Phelps, medical director of the Cerebral Palsy Division of the New Jersey Crippled Children Commission and Dr. Sidney Keats, assistant medical director. This association enabled them to answer many questions immediately and to secure additional information when necessary.

It was the privilege of the counselors to suggest some further consideration of problems that had not been fully discussed or to emphasize some point, the importance of which had seemed to elude some member of the group. It was such unobtrusive guidance that helped mothers achieve their feeling of unity and satisfaction with the entire project. If at times the counselors could make suggestions, there were other times, they felt, when they were obliged to listen in silence, to accept what was said, and indeed to learn from those they were attempting to guide.

We have not attempted to evaluate the fact that there were two counselors, man and woman, with equal responsibility for leadership. The mothers may have identified the counselors as understanding parents who accepted without criticism any statement they made. The re-enactment of the family situation may have contributed to the freedom of discussion.

That the mothers made progress in dealing with their problems was shown in the following ways: They began their participation with statements of resentment directed at professional groups, making a point of their lack of adequate knowledge; they ended with a new appreciation of what professional people have accomplished in the field and a new feeling of individual responsibility for spreading accurate information. They emphatically rejected the counselors' first reference to the fathers' share in responsibility; later they themselves reintroduced the subject and were able to discuss their resentment against fathers. At first they could only blame the child for infractions of discipline; they attained an understanding of the relationship between the child's behavior and their own attitudes. Their inability to verbalize guilt feelings was succeeded by frank discussion of developmental factors which preceded such feelings and of individual methods of attaining some degree of objectivity.

However much may be accomplished in group counseling, some specific needs cannot be met. In such cases individualized professional guidance is indicated.

Community-wide Chest X-ray Survey

III. Social Work[1]

BY SOPHIA BLOOM

M ANY efforts have been made to meet the medical problems and some of the personal problems of sick people, but only rarely has a community had, or taken, the opportunity to consider and try to meet its social responsibility for health. The community-wide chest X-ray survey offers such an opportunity for one public health responsibility—tuberculosis control. In the survey cities the efforts to mobilize the social resources of the community help bring together the sick person in trouble and the community which wants to assist him.

In the earlier community-wide surveys, social work was represented through the selection of a social worker or representative of the council of social agencies to serve on the executive committee of the survey. Her principal responsibility was to help facilitate the referrals to community social agencies. No formal plans were worked out whereby social work was included as one of the professional services contributing to the over-all planning for the total survey, nor were social workers used in the health department and survey activities.

The first time social work as a profession was introduced into a survey organization was in 1947, when the community-wide survey of the District of Columbia was planned. In this program a committee of social workers was set up as part of the formal survey organization. This committee concentrated upon two major questions: (1) the existing and new ways in which the social agencies of the community could help meet the needs of patients and their families and (2) the contribution that social

1. Reprinted from *Public Health Reports*, LXVI (February 2, 1951), 139–56, with the permission of the Public Health Service, Department of Health, Education, and Welfare.

work could make through community planning for a major health program. In other words, just as medicine has a responsibility to the total health of the community over and above caring for patients and just as nursing has a community responsibility, what is the over-all responsibility of social work?

As a result of the efforts of the Washington group, a basic pattern of social work in community-wide surveys emerged. The pattern of social services has since been modified and expanded in each community in accordance with particular needs, but the basic structure remains the same. It is this structure, service, and philosophy which the following sections will describe.

THE PRESURVEY PERIOD

When the local official health agency considers having a survey, ways to meet the social needs of the patients who will be discovered are explored as part of the presurvey planning.[2]

In all communities there have been, to a greater or lesser extent, attempts to evaluate and deal with the social problems of people in need, and public and private social agencies have long been concerned with these problems. The services provided reflect both the community's understanding of, and its ability and willingness to meet, the health and social needs of its people.

Health departments have daily faced the problems caused by illness in the lives of individual patients, and hospitals bear a share of the social dislocations created or aggravated by tuberculosis. The health and social welfare agencies, in dealing with patients and their families, have had to do so in terms of the law, regulations, and attitudes of the community. The need to know these factors is not created by the survey; this need exists whether or not there is a survey. However, the survey, because of its scope, precipitates an immediate opportunity for pulling together the existing information, so that the survey planners may have the benefit of all available information about the social potentials of the area, its resources, its lacks, its plans and trends. Over and above facts or figures, what is of utmost im-

2. For a description of survey planning see "Community-wide Chest X-ray Survey. I. Introduction," *Public Health Reports*, LXV (October 6, 1950), 1277–91.

portance to the survey planners is the community attitude toward its responsibility for the people.

A medical social consultant from the Division of Tuberculosis visits the city to pull together the kinds of information listed below:

1. Health and medical programs—general and specific, related to tuberculosis.

2. Laws and regulations affecting the eligibility of the tuberculous for medical care and public assistance, such as means tests, residence requirements, administrative policies on hospital admissions.

3. Local social resources and present social agency structure in the community, including public assistance, public child welfare, medical and psychiatric social services, private family and children's services, and other social services. Adequacy, co-ordination, and standards of such services.

4. Special programs or provisions for the tuberculous, or others from which the tuberculous may benefit (e.g., vocational rehabilitation services, social insurance, disability insurance, special financial assistance).

5. Sociological data—culture patterns and trends, minority groups, current intergroup relationships.

6. Major medical social problems of the tuberculous (e.g., discharge against advice, bed shortages, financial assistance, etc.).

7. Number and location of medical social workers, scope of activities and quality of medical social services in medical settings where tuberculous patients are being served, including the health department.

8. Number of tuberculous patients receiving social services, sources or types of such services, and adequacy of coverage.

9. Methods of correlating medical and social planning and care.

10. Relationships between medical social work and other professional groups within and outside the health department.

11. Methods of handling social problems in the absence of social services in medical diagnostic and treatment centers and health department.

12. Research projects, completed or anticipated, relating to

the social factors in tuberculosis and potentialities for other studies.

13. Trends or definite plans for development of the community social resources.

14. Other special factors which might affect the survey.

This presurvey period, if so utilized, can offer a genuine opportunity for consideration of mutual problems and for joint planning between the health, medical, and social agencies, and the doctors, nurses, and social workers. Good co-ordination between the social agencies and health and medical-care facilities and among the social agencies themselves will mean a more effective total service to the people of the community. The community must ask itself whether it will take advantage of the opportunity offered by a community-wide program to plan for extension of needed services.

In one large community presurvey, discussions were held with more than 25 people from federal, state, and local agencies: public health officials, tuberculosis control officers, state health department social workers, medical social workers in tuberculosis agencies and in other medical settings, public assistance and child-welfare workers, social workers in the community, schools of social work, Veterans Administration, social workers from professional organizations, rehabilitation workers, administrators, welfare council representatives, and tuberculosis association representatives. It became clear that these people were keenly aware of the tuberculosis problems: many undiscovered patients, a bed shortage, a severe housing shortage, inadequate public assistance, inadequate child-care facilities, insufficient medical social case work services, differing admission policies among the tuberculosis hospitals, so that some patients were not eligible for admission anywhere.

There was great strength and forcefulness in the medical, public health, and social work leadership in that community. Determined efforts had been made for years to deal with the problems, and many people looked forward to the possibilities offered by the survey to find the unknown patients and to meet the specific medical and social needs of the tuberculosis population. In other words, the local people were prepared to use the survey not only for the immediate benefits to be gained by case finding, but to help them plan to meet the long-time health and social problems revealed in a major community health program.

THE PUBLIC HEALTH SERVICE MEDICAL SOCIAL CONSULTANT

The medical social consultant of the Public Health Service participates in the early planning of the survey and is available throughout the program. She serves in an advisory capacity to the health department and helps state and local health departments, tuberculosis associations, and community social workers work out plans to mobilize community social resources and develop any additional needed social services for the tuberculosis-control program and the survey. She brings to them the experiences gained in previous surveys.

THE STATE MEDICAL SOCIAL CONSULTANT

In most of the states there are medical social workers in one or another of the state health or medical-care programs. Their customary consultative relationships with local areas have made it possible for them to contribute greatly to the local program, and the Public Health Service consultant works closely with them. They serve on various social work committees of the survey and help particularly with over-all planning. In a number of states, they have assumed considerable responsibility for helping the social worker in the local health department in the development of the service.

SOCIAL WORK CO-ORDINATOR

Because of the many survey interests and activities of the social workers in the community, it is essential, especially in the larger communities, that some one social worker be designated to co-ordinate the social service activities involved in the case-finding program, including those in the health department, retake center, and community. This may be a social worker from an official or other agency. On one occasion a medical social worker from the Division of Tuberculosis was assigned as the co-ordinator. The full-time services of one person may be required if the community is large.

Social work functions in the survey as part of the professional services division of the survey. This division is concerned with the professional services offered to persons discovered in the survey. As the survey is of short duration but intense activity, additional services, particularly contributions of service by persons outside the official health agency, are required. The professional services division is responsible for stimulating these contributions. It helps set the professional standards of the survey and is responsible for interpreting it to the various professional groups involved. It is generally agreed that joint thinking and planning of the three professional groups involved—medical, nursing, and social work—will result in greater co-ordination of community services and in more effective services for the individual in need of help. It is in this regard that the professional services division can be very effective when joint medical, nursing, and social work considerations are brought together and merged into the over-all problem of adequate care for tuberculosis patients and their families.

Social work is represented in the professional services division by a social work committee. Since no one professional organization represents all the social workers, the health officer calls together representatives of the various social work organizations, such as the council of social agencies, schools of social work, key social agencies, and the social workers in the state and local official health agencies, explains the program, and asks them to choose the chairman and vice-chairman. This original temporary group then dissolves, and the newly appointed chairman and vice-chairman (usually one medical social worker and one social worker from another field) appoint the social work committee consisting of social workers from public and private social agencies, hospitals, and other health and medical settings, all of whom have a contribution to make to the tuberculosis-control program of the community. The committee varies in size, each community choosing the number it finds is appropriate; membership has ranged from 13 to 54. This over-all social work committee of the survey can be used in an advisory capacity by the health officer if he wishes.

The social work committee is responsible for the effective mobilization of the social workers of the community but needs the help of the health department and the rest of the survey organization. The health officer, the tuberculosis-control officer, the public health nurses, the survey program manager, the health educators, the survey publicity representatives, all contribute, together and individually, to the social workers' knowledge of the total program and to their understanding of the ways in which the health department functions. As social workers become familiar with the objectives of the tuberculosis-control program and the methods by which the tuberculosis-control officer hopes to achieve control, and as they learn how the problems are dealt with, they begin to see their own roles more clearly.

Moreover, the growth of understanding is mutual. The health workers and the lay people in the survey organization learn more of the objectives, methods, and problems of social work and utilize the social workers in other phases of the survey program, such as community organization. In the survey cities greater mutual understanding and co-ordination between the health agency and the social agencies has developed as a result of joint activities. A number of health officers have expressed gratification for the support given them by the social agencies; and, in turn, the social workers feel that they have a part in the health program. In several cities, after the survey, the health divisions of the councils of social agencies have developed permanent committees of social workers interested in the health programs of the city.

The committee as a whole considers specifically the social needs of tuberculosis patients and families, determines whether there are sufficient resources for the patients who will be discovered in the survey, points out gaps in services, and helps with recruitment of social work personnel for the health department and the retake center. The social workers in the health department and retake center can bring to the committee data on social problems of patients which, because of the number involved, will throw greater light on the total problems of the community. The committee is in a position to focus the attention of the social workers in the community and other professional and lay groups on the specific medical social problems which the survey emphasizes.

SOCIAL WORK SUBCOMMITTEES

There are usually a number of subcommittees of the social work committee. These vary with situations in the survey cities and with the specific needs that arise as the survey progresses. The chairman of the social work committee appoints the chairmen of the subcommittees, and their membership may be drawn from the full committee or include other social workers from the community. Sometimes the chairmen of the subcommittees serve with the chairmen of the social work committee as a steering group, so that it is not necessary to have frequent meetings of the full membership. Long-range planning to meet community needs revealed by the survey is, of course, a function of the full committee, but preliminary work on it can be handled by the steering group. In every city, however, there has been a subcommittee on interpretation, which has had responsibility for bringing to the social workers of the community facts about the survey, facts about the control of tuberculosis, and suggestions as to the role that social agencies can play. This committee informs social agencies about the program, provides social workers for neighborhood committees and for the speakers' bureau, and helps develop some of the publicity materials—press, radio, television —on social needs, so that the community will learn more about them. One of its important responsibilities is to sponsor an institute in which the social workers in the community can learn more of the medical and social factors in tuberculosis. An example of this kind of institute is the program sponsored by the Greater Cleveland Chest X-ray Survey Foundation. Many of the agencies in the city operated with skeleton staffs for the day, so that all the social workers could attend and there would have to be only one meeting instead of many small ones. In most of the communities the institute follows this general pattern.

Subcommittees to consider problems requiring further study

have been established in every survey. Consideration is given to the effect on tuberculosis patients and tuberculosis control of such matters as the following:

1. Adequacy of local public assistance allowances
2. Adequacy of provision for child-care and housekeeping services
3. The residence laws
4. The means test
5. The effects on patients of long waiting periods for beds
6. Problems of the single, homeless person
7. Emotional factors contributing to acceptance or rejection of the diagnosis
8. Financial factors contributing to refusal to enter the hospital
9. Effects of disciplinary discharges from tuberculosis hospitals
10. Vocational needs of patients
11. Income of patients

There have also been subcommittees appointed to carry out certain other responsibilities, like the compilation of a list of social agencies available for tuberculosis patients, indicating the specific kinds of services offered, recruitment of social work personnel, pointing out gaps in services.

As in all the survey committees, activity among the social workers is great during the planning of the survey and during its operation. Considerable enthusiasm and excitement are engendered. Committees, large and small, meet frequently and spend hours working out problems and outlining procedures. That the range of interests is broad is indicated by the subjects and reports described in the minutes of one meeting of a social work committee.

1. A statement of social needs of patients with a list of social resources—to be included as part of a larger statement of medical, nursing, and social information to be printed in the local medical journal.

2. A letter containing current reports on the survey, such as the number of persons X-rayed, and current social work activities to be sent to all social agency executives in the area.

3. A presentation by the health department social workers of some of the social needs as revealed in the health department activities.

4. Report of social work activities in the retake center.

5. Publicity to be released to the newspapers, radio, and television on social aspects of tuberculosis.

6. Discussion of a proposed study project on unattached men and women.

SOCIAL SERVICES IN THE HEALTH DEPARTMENT

An increasing number of local health departments are employing social workers to serve patients. This number, however, is still limited, and in most of the communities in which chest X-ray programs take place social service has not yet been established in the health departments. Our discussion here is concerned with those health departments which have not had social services before.

During the planning period for the survey the social problems of tuberculosis are discussed with the health department officials, the experiences of other survey cities are examined, and the health officers have time and opportunity to decide how they wish to initiate social services for tuberculosis patients and plan for service through the follow-up period. Recruitment begins early, so that the service may be started as far ahead of the survey as possible. This enables the health department to set up an administrative structure and enables the social worker and others in the health department to clarify functions and work out procedures and methods. Because the survey is tuberculosis case finding, social service is usually started in the tuberculosis division of the local health department. Care is always taken to so organize that later extension of service for other diagnostic groups is possible and expansion into a social service department is feasible.

Social workers for health departments have been secured by various means. Some are employed by local health departments, some with survey funds, others have been loaned by state health departments, and, in two cities, the local tuberculosis association has provided funds. Medical social consultants from the Public Health Service are loaned upon request, and on one occasion the National Tuberculosis Association made one of its social workers available. In some of the surveys only one social worker has been available at a time; in others there have been as many as six on the staff.

The problems confronting the social workers who are starting service in the local health department in preparation for the tuberculosis surveys are essentially no different from the problems involved in initiating social service in a local health department at any time, except for the necessity of preparing for the immediate survey case load. After the social worker comes, there are additional conferences within the health department, again with the health officer, the tuberculosis-control officer, and the director of nursing. During these discussions there is clarification of the needs of the patients served by the health department, and a beginning is made toward the determination of the ways in which the social worker will function. Because the service is new, flexibility in development is essential. Basic principles of social work are discussed and an administrative structure is established. One of the purposes of these conferences is to try to determine the kinds of social problems with which various people in the health department have already been dealing and the ways in which the social workers can help. The health department physicians, social workers, and nurses together arrive at a mutual understanding of how social service can add to the services already given by the health department and try to delineate the specific functions and various activities of the social workers. It is usually determined that the social worker will offer social case work services to patients and families and consultation services to other health department personnel and to the community social agencies.

Administratively, the social workers are always responsible to the physician in charge of the division of tuberculosis for the work in the tuberculosis program. In most of the survey cities, the health officers have taken considerable responsibility in the development of over-all policies which will influence further social service developments in the health department.

Usually, a statement of the functions of the clinic social worker is worked out. There is no set pattern and the functions are adapted to each clinic. The following kinds of services are usually included:

1. SOCIAL CASE WORK

The social workers give direct case work services to patients who need help with those social, emotional, and financial factors which affect their ability to accept the diagnosis and to follow recommendations for medical care. The following are thumb-nail examples of the kinds of problems requiring social case work service:

Acceptance of the diagnosis.—The social workers have found that, along with the doctors and nurses, they must devote much of the first interview or interviews to consideration of the patient's fears about himself—fear of death, of physical deformity and crippling, of permanent incapacity. After patients are given ample opportunity to release their emotions and to gain reassurance, the related social problems, such as the need for financial assistance or planning for the care of children, are more easily faced and solved.

Hospitalization.—They have also found it necessary to deal with the factors creating resistance to entering the hospital. A certain amount of resistance is, of course, normal, but some patients require help in working their way through the mixture of reactions of fear, resistance, and acquiescence so that they can come to the decision to enter the hospital and can find the way, with help from the clinic social worker or community agencies when necessary, to care for their children, make financial arrangements, etc.

Financial problems.—The social workers in the clinics often devote much time to helping patients and their families plan to meet the severe financial strains caused by tuberculosis. Some need immediate referrals to public assistance agencies; a large number of tuberculosis patients, it has been found, do not apply for such aid, and, indeed, many are not eligible. Because of the disaster created in the majority of families, patients need a great deal of help to face the necessary readjustments, such as reduced living standards, curtailment of education, employment of wives and children, and the necessity to seek relief. Much time may be required before patients can make the practical and emotional adjustments necessary to enable them to enter hospitals or follow other medical recommendations.

Along with the actual cost of maintaining their families, many patients must meet some of the costs of hospital care. Although there may be efforts to rate patients according to ability to pay, the sum charged may be more than the patient can handle, especially over a sustained period of time. Some people, when frightened and unaware of the length of time required by treatment, will agree to almost any charge. To be certain that the illness is understood and that plans are not made on the basis of 6 months when it is more likely that 2 years will be required, social workers help patients with the necessary planning. Much bitterness among patients and much leaving hospitals against advice can be prevented when patients have an opportunity to absorb the impact of the diagnosis at the beginning and to plan in terms of reality.

Residence laws.—In all but a very few of the states these laws are a genuine source of difficulty to the patient, to the health department, to the hospital, to community social agencies, and to the control of tuberculosis. If the nonresident patient has legal residence in his former home, the social worker can help him accept the necessity of returning there for treatment. Sometimes the social considerations, along with the patient's medical needs and the community's public health responsibility, make it possible for the responsible authorities to waive the residence requirements. On occasion, nonofficial hospitals will admit the patients. Sometimes, especially when the patient has no place of residence, he can receive no medical care until a year or more has passed. During this period, he often needs considerable help from community social agencies.

2. COOPERATION WITH COMMUNITY SOCIAL AGENCIES

Although all the patients referred to the social workers have social difficulties which are intertwined with the illness and therefore need some help in the medical setting as part of the medical treatment, others need additional social services from other agencies. Bed shortages can create the need for additional social resources. For example, when sick people must remain at home, it is often necessary to remove the children, sometimes to foster-homes and institutions.

In the survey cities, up to one-third of the patients have been referred to other agencies for services. In one city the range of services required by patients necessitated the use of the following agencies:

Vocational Rehabilitation
County Tuberculosis Hospital—Social Service
County Welfare Department
Family Society
Juvenile Court
Guidance Council
Mental Hospital
Three other county health departments
Marine Hospital
Social Security—Old Age
Four local health departments in other states
Social Service Exchange
Urban League
Veterans Administration
Tumor Institute
Visiting Nurse Society
County Veterans Aid Bureau
American Red Cross
Disabled American Veterans
Convent of Good Shepherd
County Hospital
County Health Department
Public Welfare Department
Children's Home
St. Vincent de Paul Clinic—Social Service
Catholic Church
Catholic Children's Bureau
Municipal Court
Memorial Hospital
Medina Children's Service
Traveler's Aid

The social worker in the health department develops a close working relationship with other social agencies in the community. At times she functions by bringing to them an interpretation of the medical conditions and the social factors involved. By dealing with the patients from the point of diagnosis, referrals to community agencies are made earlier, and some further social strain is prevented. The social agencies in turn learn through these experiences to use the health department more effectively for all the people under their care.

3. CONSULTATION SERVICES

In addition to giving direct services to some patients, the social worker also functions as a consultant to other health department personnel. As pointed out earlier, she deals directly with a limited number of patients, those who by the nature of their medical problems and the related social situation particularly require a specialized social case work service. Very often, the social worker is used by other staff members in a consultative capacity. At times this is in relation to over-all administrative policy; at other times, it is in relation to specific patients.

In some clinics the tuberculosis-control officer calls case conferences at intervals to discuss individual patients. Doctors, nurses, and social workers have an opportunity to think and plan together for the patient's benefit. These are the more formal conferences. In every clinic there is, every day, a constant informal exchange of information and thinking. This is essential, so that the patients can receive the most effective help.

4. COLLECTION OF SOCIAL DATA

In addition to dealing with the individual patient, the social worker in the clinic has the means of collecting the social data which the community can use to develop additional resources. Community needs may be highlighted. The health department is in a particularly strategic position to acquire the data as many patients pass through its doors, either for some kind of medical service or on the way to the hospital.

The problem of single people, particularly men, is an example of this kind of activity. Community attitudes toward the single, unattached people, particularly the men, vary and are frequently hostile. It seems to be generally assumed that the single person can draw upon unknown intangible resources and should be able to get along somehow. In public assistance programs, for example, there are often provisions which set up different standards for the single person as opposed to the rest of the population. It is frequently harder for him to prove his need, and he often receives less than other people. In the tuberculosis field, single men are often assumed to be, and said to be, the most irresponsible and socially undesirable segment of the total population—the wanderers, the alcoholics, the feeble-minded; and they are often believed to refuse hospitalization. Reports from social workers in various surveys show that, in fact, the single men are often eager, because of their homelessness and need of care, to enter the hospital. In one survey city nearly 60 single men, most of them from the skid-row area, were interviewed. Almost all entered the hospital. Reports from doctors and social workers in many tuberculosis hospitals show that the single homeless people are among those who find it hardest to leave the security and protection of the hospital. Data such as these can enable a community to approach the problems of sick, homeless people more realistically.

Even before the arrival of the social worker certain essentials in the physical setting are considered. Privacy for interviewing is very necessary. A private telephone is also an essential. Adequate secretarial assistance is essential, because much of the value of social case work is lost unless it can be transmitted quickly in usable form to others: the doctors, the nurses, the hospital or clinic caring for the patient, and the other social agencies. Face sheets are developed so that social data may be systematically gathered and kept. Records are usually written in descriptive form. The records need not necessarily be long, but they must be adequate to meet the needs of the patient and the medical and social personnel caring for him. Conversations between the social worker and the doctor or nurse will not meet this need, as the risk of losing the continuing value of the material is great.

Patients are usually referred to social service by the clinic physicians, clinic nurses, public health nurses in the field, private doctors, the community agencies, and others. Some come on their own initiative. In most surveys, the doctors are the principal source of referrals, with the nurses the second largest source. The use of the social workers by other personnel in the clinic increases steadily as experience begins to show the kinds of services that are given and as others begin to see how this service fits into the total tuberculosis-control program.

Priorities for services must be established because of the size of the survey load and because there are usually not enough social workers in the clinic. For example, it may be agreed within the clinic that social workers will see all the newly diagnosed patients and all of those for whom hospitalization is recommended. These two groups are usually given priority because it is obvious that among the newly diagnosed and among those who are to go to the hospital there are many personal problems. Adequate attention paid to these problems at the start will cut down resistance to entering hospitals or refusal to follow medical recommendations. Social service, however, is not restricted to these two groups and is available for other patients referred by doctors, clinic nurses, field nurses, other clinic personnel, and outside agencies. Often patients who know of the service will come themselves to ask for help.

In many clinics, after the doctor sees the patient he sends him to the nurse and then to the social worker. This is not necessarily a set pattern, and at the discretion of the doctor or nurse or the wish of the patient, the social worker may be called in at any time. The doctor explains the reason for referral to the patient and makes the referral to the social worker in person, so that the social worker has the opportunity of learning what social problems he believes require attention. The start of joint medical social thinking about the patient takes place at this time.

The length of time necessary for interviews and the number of interviews required per patient cannot be standardized. Many social workers estimate that approximately an hour should be set aside for the first interview with the patient. Sometimes less time is actually used; on other occasions more may be necessary. With some patients one interview is enough in which to gain an understanding of the patient's problem, his attitudes toward his problem, and the effect of this on his social situation and to help him begin to make his plans. In other instances more than one interview is necessary. There are some patients whose understanding and acceptance of the diagnosis and the demands it makes upon them in terms of hospitalization, jobs, and families is such that they can begin to chart their courses relatively quickly. Others, whose fear and uncertainty is greater, need help for a longer period. Sometimes it is necessary to see these patients more than once, and it may be necessary to speak with relatives.

On occasion, home visits are needed. This is comparatively infrequent, but again circumstances indicate the need. In a health department which serves primarily an urban community where transportation is good and where people have easy access to the clinic, most of the interviews can be conducted in the office. If the health department located in a city also serves a rural area, it may be necessary for the social worker to make home visits to people in outlying districts—to housewives, for instance, who would have difficulty in arranging care for their children while they made long daytime trips. On other occasions, too, the social worker may feel that an interview with the patient and his family in his own home may be more productive and may give her a better understanding of the whole situation than she can get in clinic interviews. This is particularly true where there have been indications that the interpersonal relationships between the family members are disturbed. Because the sick person is so dependent upon those who are closest to him and because his sense of security or insecurity will affect his attitudes toward the diagnosis and toward the recommendations for medical care, it is often important that the social worker secure sufficient firsthand understanding of the family relationships to enable her to help most effectively.

RETAKE CENTER

The social worker in tuberculosis has worked in a variety of medical settings, as it has been recognized that patients have problems in different phases of treatment. The needs of the patient who was preparing to return to work were first recognized. Experience with patients at this time pointed out the need for help earlier, at the time the patient was in the hospital. Then, because of the problems which arose in the hospital, it was apparent that there was a place for the social worker earlier, in the clinic, where the patient was undergoing diagnosis. Now we are exploring the needs of persons who are suspected of having tuberculosis, in order to determine how much social breakdown can be prevented from the very beginning of the long course of treatment.

In the retake center there is medical consideration of the problems of the suspected cancer and cardiac patients as well as the suspected tuberculosis patients. The principal focus of the social workers in the center is in the interest of furthering medical care for those suspected patients who are referred to the social workers by retake center personnel because of specific social and emotional problems.

The problems presented by persons suspected of having tuberculosis are, of course, similar to those already described in the preceding section, with emphasis on anxiety and occasional need for the services of other social agencies. The experiences with those suspected of cancer or cardiac disease are the same.

This is an example of the way social service functioned for the suspected cardiac patients in one retake center. The state health department provided two social workers for the retake center, primarily for the suspected heart patients, although they also gave service to others. The following outline shows the basis of selection of patients and the kinds of services rendered:

PERSONS TO BE REFERRED TO THE SOCIAL WORKER

1. Persons who, following the small film, return for confirmatory films or consultation related to suspected cardiovascular disease and who express marked concern or fear.

2. Persons who need help in finding and using appropriate medical facilities.

3. Specific referrals from private physicians for plans for social care or with the request that a different medical plan be worked out.

SERVICES PROVIDED BY THE SOCIAL WORKER

1. Effecting a referral to appropriate medical resources in the community.

2. Helping the patient overcome obstacles affecting the medical plan.

   a) Discussing with the patient his attitudes, problems within his home, work, or school situation, and other factors which affect adversely his ability or readiness to follow recommendations for diagnostic procedures and treatment.

   b) Determining with the patient what help he may require through family and community facilities and helping him to make the best possible use of all resources.

   c) Sharing social information with other professional staff.

CONCLUSION

The social needs of the tuberculous cannot be considered as an entity. They stem from and are created by the over-all problem of the necessary adjustments of man to his physical, social, and economic environment. Because there has been more and more emphasis in recent years upon the individual needs of people, we have learned more about helping them to make satisfying adjustments.

We have learned not to do things "for" and "to" people, and we know that we are of genuine assistance only if we help them to help themselves. Although the helping process takes place between individuals, the person who is helping reflects the desire of society to provide for the person in need. However, society must provide not only the person who helps—the doctor or the social worker—but must also provide the hospital, the foster-home, the social agency. Progress is being made in many directions, but there are still wide gaps in our social provisions. This has been repeatedly demonstrated by the community-wide surveys.

The continuing economic and social changes of our industrial economy inevitably produce inequity and imbalance; and in our complex modern society, our social customs and laws are not always at the level of our modern scientific knowledge or even with modern social knowledge. We may know, for example, that prompt hospitalization is the best way to care for a person with positive sputum and the best way to prevent further spread of the disease, but our residence laws may prevent us from providing such hospitalization for the sick person who needs it, even when we have empty beds in our hospitals. We may know that a man cannot easily rest in bed if he is worried about the deprivations his children suffer because of his illness, but we do not always provide adequate support for them. Medically, a particular program of treatment may be clearly indicated and outlined, but cultural and psychological attitudes about tuberculosis in particular, and dependency in general, may operate against the acceptance of scientific knowledge on the part of both the patient and society.

Our society has conflicts about dependency and people in need. Although we retain some archaic laws and customs, we want to meet the needs of people, to provide for the individual and the group, medically and socially. Our laws governing health and social welfare, our institutions, our development of public education, our social historical precedents are all evidences of this desire to meet the universal needs of people. But as individual persons and as a group, we are all subject to many contradictory impulses. We may recognize that a given person needs help; we may provide the means for such help; and we may then think the less of the man who takes it. In a culture which places such a high value on independence, most people, the well and the sick, are not able to set this aside easily and accept dependence themselves, or see others do so. This is one of the reasons why it is difficult to accept full community responsibility, even though we may acknowledge the needs of individuals and even though we know that in our complicated social order no man can be entirely self-sufficient.

In tuberculosis, our responsibility lies in two areas: first, to provide public health services and, second, to meet the social needs of patients. The first is accepted far more than the second. As a result, a very large portion of the social burden has fallen upon the shoulders of the sick and their families, and many tuberculosis-control efforts are thereby substantially weakened. We must ease the load if our efforts to control tuberculosis are to be fully successful.

The Participation of Medical Social Workers in Professional Education

1. Of Social Workers

Content of Field Teaching in Medical Social Work[1]

BY MURIEL GAYFORD

FIELD work is a part of the total educational process for the profession of social work. It cannot be thought of as a separate entity in itself, as it is inevitably related to classroom study from which it is, at the same time, clearly distinguished. In any discussion of the subject it seems important to repeat and stress the fact that field work is concerned with the student's doing something, as contrasted with his knowing something. In field work the student must translate into activity, which he initiates and directs, the knowledge, the thinking, and the emotional responses he has acquired in the classroom. This fact of doing, as distinguished from knowing, is the basic reason for field work's having developed a content and a method of its own. In the field the student has his opportunity to learn facts of a kind and range different from those that can be taught in class, to co-ordinate all his information into a usable whole, and to put the total sum of this information into service. If the maximum value is to be had from the time allotted to field work, there should be as little duplication of classroom activity as possible and a conscious effort not to cover areas which could as well or better be included in classroom study.

Field teaching is focused upon the application of generic case work concepts to a specific situation. A complete description of the content of field teaching would attempt to cover all aspects of the student's learning situation, the growing under-

1. Reprinted from *The Family*, April, 1942, with the permission of the Family Service Association of America.

173

standing of an ability to use basic concepts, as well as proficiency in meeting the specialized problems that are inherent only in the specific field placement. Content might thus be thought of as being composed of two general areas, that which is basic to all field-work experience and that which is peculiar to the specialized field. Valuable as it may be to see the student's experience as a whole, rather than to break it into parts, space in this article does not permit such a complete approach to the subject. Only the specialized content of field work in medical social work will be discussed. The large and basically important area of the concepts and skill common to all case work must be taken for granted. An article published in *The Compass*[2] is a helpful reference in considering what the range of such knowledge might be.[3]

Discussion of the methods of teaching in field work will be held to a minimum in this presentation. Consideration of the advisable content of a field-work experience will inevitably raise questions as to the processes of teaching in such a situation. It can only be stated that the methods of teaching which have developed for field work are those of supervision and that, as such, they are basically the same in all social case work. Generic principles of supervision apply in medical social work as in any other field. If soundly used, they can give guidance with difficulties met in any specialized field placement if the supervisor has the ability to analyze the problem and to highlight its essential meaning for the student.

SPECIAL CONTENT IN MEDICAL SOCIAL WORK

There are probably few field-work placements as complex and difficult for a student as one in a large hospital with its variety of professional and technical personnel, its numerous lines of authority and relationships, and its many rules and regula-

2. Committee on the Study of Field Work, Boston Chapter, American Association of Social Workers, "Supervised Field Work in Education for Social Case Work," *The Compass*, November, 1940, pp. 7–9.
3. An article by Florence Hollis in *The Skills of the Beginning Case Worker* (New York: Family Welfare Association of America, 1941), pp. 1–12, presents extremely helpful material regarding the total knowledge and skill which a group of young workers in a family agency had acquired or should have acquired in their previous training.

tions. As one sees a succession of students passing through periods of field work in a medical social service department, one can pick out recurring situations inherent in the setting or in the special areas of maladjustment with which medical social workers deal. Time and again these situations give the student particular difficulty, and for this reason they show the need for her to learn special adaptations of her developing case work skill. They vary considerably in number and intensity with individual students, but occur with sufficient frequency to be considered, in their broader aspects, as typical. There are many of them, too many to present in detail here; but brief discussion of the more important ones should point out for us the specialized content of medical social field work.

There is, first, the difficulty of understanding the large, highly technical, medical institution. There are, second, the problems related to the student's use of the specialized medical knowledge she is being taught and that both patients and doctors expect her to know. Third, there are the uncomfortable struggles during which she learns the application of case work concepts in an illness situation, relating herself professionally to a sick person, finding a new meaning in the technique of giving reassurance and of helping a person to gain insight, and achieving a balance between self-determination for the patient-client and the authoritative aspects of medical practice. Later comes the impact of the need to understand clearly her function as a part of the total hospital setup, so that her decisions about what is and what is not appropriate can be made with assurance. Finally, there is the matter of learning to take full responsibility for her own case load, particularly as regards intake and the relative emphases to be given various activities.

The supervisor may be much more consciously aware than is the student of the existence of these difficulties in the form described above. This, however, is to be expected in the teaching-learning relationship and is the reason the supervisor can give the guidance, support, and stimulation necessary. The problems are so interrelated that progress, when it takes place, is likely to occur in all areas simultaneously, and increasing understanding in one direction should result in improvement in the others.

THE HOSPITAL SETTING

Some students will have had previous working experience in hospitals or clinics or brief periods of field work in a medical social agency before they begin their second year of study during which they specialize in medical social work. A large majority will have had personal experience with hospitals as patients or, at least, as members of patients' families. All of them, whether they are aware of it or not, will have deeply intrenched attitudes toward the sick and toward forms of medical treatment, which attitudes are part of their cultural heritage. Coming into a hospital for field work, the medical social work student finds herself faced with having to achieve an orientation to the background against which her activity will be carried out, a process which may mean unexpected changes in her beliefs.

The first difficulty for the student will be that of becoming comfortable among myriads of people none of whom she knows, many of whom she never meets, and all of whom seem very busy and purposeful. Her own role may not be clearly understood by these others. She may, as a result, become too aggressive or too retiring. Until she can gain some security as a social worker and also as a student, she cannot overcome her self-consciousness and begin to function adequately. This is true even for the student who has had some years of experience in a medical social agency; she also will, as a rule, with the impact of new ideas regarding psychoanalytic concepts and psychosomatic medicine which she is learning in the classroom, find conflicts arising in the very areas where she felt most secure.

The student's understanding of the organization necessarily develops slowly. It must go further than an awareness of the locations and functions of the various departments. It must be consciously expanding toward a knowledge of some breadth of the mores and ethics of medical practice. New concepts must be integrated with the changes in personal attitudes which the student finds taking place. She must understand the purpose of the administrative regulations of the hospital before she can help the patient to use them constructively. She will otherwise see them as something to be bowed to or to be circumvented, rules against which she is the patient's advocate and intercessor. The value in which human life is held, even for the poorest, weakest, and least important, can be quickly respected by the average social work student. The strength of the medical profession's belief that "while there is life there is hope" and the lengths to which this belief will carry them is understood more slowly. Awareness of the meaning of the traditional doctor-patient relationship and the reasons for its development become more real as there is opportunity for firsthand observation. Psychiatric information regarding social attitudes can later be applied to the concept of the doctor as the father-person, so that the depth of feeling on the patient's part can be seen more clearly. The customary practice of protection of the sick from responsibility, worry, and strain takes on new meaning as the student's knowledge of the emotional factors in illness develops. The many people who are responsible for the ill person may seem at first to be too loosely bound together, but later perspective can be gained, so that their larger co-operative aims can be glimpsed.

The activity of the field-work supervisor in this situation will be to individualize the student's experience to the extent of giving her an opportunity which she can use. This will probably be done by a judicious selection of cases, a controlled introduction to the institution, an understanding and supportive attitude during difficult periods, and stimulation and encouragement in thinking through the implications of what she is seeing. Many of the student's experiences will arouse conflicts for her in connection with her own highly personalized attitudes toward sickness in general, toward certain diseases, and toward certain forms of medical treatment.

It cannot be expected that the inexperienced student will have complete understanding of these problems by the time she finishes her field work. Two years' working experience in a hospital is usually considered the minimum in which complete orientation to the setting of medical practice can be achieved. The supervisor of field work can, however, give the student a beginning awareness of her needs and a method of approach in learning to relate her job to the whole.

USE OF MEDICAL INFORMATION

The second specialized area in medical social field work mentioned above is in regard to the technical medical information needed by the medical social worker. This problem has two aspects: first, learning how much and what kind of knowledge a social worker should have and, second, acquiring professional ways of using it.

It might be expected that sufficient information regarding medical conditions and their treatment would be learned in the classroom. The fact is, however, that each medical social case is likely to demand some special knowledge that cannot be secured from textbooks or lectures. No matter how comprehensive the courses, they cannot give the student all the information she may need at any time. They can give the necessary factual background and can teach methods used in studying certain diseases in greater detail. Field work, on the other hand, provides the student with the opportunity of seeing what kinds of medical knowledge she needs under different circumstances in order to achieve a more sensitive understanding of the patient's situation. She can then extend her fund of knowledge by selective reading. The whole setup of the field-work placement also allows the student to find ways of supplementing her information by consultations with doctors, nurses, and others, by discriminating observation of what is going on about her, and by participating in case discussions with groups of medical personnel.

The matter of learning how to use this medical information in case work with patients is the more difficult area, perhaps because even now this aspect of medical social work is not well understood by the field as a whole. The student in her insecurity and self-consciousness is likely to feel under pressure to use what medical knowledge she has prematurely and superficially. She explains (she may say she "interprets") the condition or its treatment to the patient, primarily because she has such a desire to do something concrete, to "give," and, it must be admitted, to show what she knows. Continuing experience in seeing patients going through the ordeal of an illness and growing understanding of and proficiency with other case work techniques will help the student to be more restrained in waiting to learn what the patient's deeper needs are and to be more observant as regards the meaning of the illness in the patient's terms, not in those of the medical textbooks. Here skilful supervision is important for the student. Although it is not the purpose of this article to discuss methods of supervision, it seems permissible to point out that the average supervisor may be faced with two temptations when dealing with these problems. One is to give the student, directly and in some detail, more factual information about a medical condition than the student can absorb or is ready to use. The other is to stop there, without giving continuing help in using such facts skilfully and in integrating them with developing concepts of human behavior and case work treatment. The student may fail to relate what medical information is available on a case to the "social" problem as she sees it, and the "medical social" focus is lost. On the other hand, she may take flight from the conflicts aroused for her by the patient's situation and lose herself in a useless accumulation of details regarding the medical condition. The phenomenon of undue energy being put into finding out all that the medical specialists can tell is frequent enough with students in field work and with workers on the job. It is not always recognized, however, that such preoccupations have meaning, either in terms of the difficulties the worker is having with other aspects of the case or in terms of the personal and emotional responses which the patient's condition is stirring up in her.

WORKING WITH AN ILL PERSON

The third area of difficult adjustment for the student in medical social work lies in the fact that it is in an illness situation that she must make practical application of case work concepts. Such use of these concepts in this field requires special adaptations that are sometimes difficult to understand and to achieve. The student in medical social work has presumably been motivated in her choice of this special field by a desire to help the sick or by some other identification with the medical profession. She learns, gradually perhaps but no less surely, that her ideas of both "help" and "the sick" must change, together with her other ideas about the way people behave. Even when she has mastered these new concepts intellectually, a great deal of reorientation of her emotional responses must take place before she can put her classroom theories into practice. An awareness on the part of her supervisor as to what these difficulties will mean and a willingness to give direct help in meeting them may make it possible for the student to begin to overcome them. The supervisor and the student should strive toward such control of the student's urge to help that the power behind it is not lost, as it is being refined and redirected.

As regards the case work relationship, the student must gain, or begin to gain, two attributes before she can achieve such professional control. These are (1) awareness of her own anxieties regarding illness and (2) ability to understand the real meaning of an illness to a patient, that is, the meaning of the symptoms and the treatment, and the meaning of his having sought medical care, all in terms of the purposiveness of human behavior. Medical social work deals with conditions that are among the most elementally disturbing to mankind—dependency, pain, mutilation, and death. They are bound to frighten the student in some degree and may arouse deep conflicts for her. She cannot, however, be given complete protection from them or from finding her own way of dealing with them, if the development of superficial attitudes is to be prevented. This experience of illness is something we have all had personally, and we have our firsthand ideas of what it has meant. We all, therefore, even during student days, have great potential ability for identification with the patient. The danger is that there may be overidentification. There may also be insufficient individualization. The patient may be endowed with feelings which are entirely the student's or which are generalizations.

The facts of emotional regression occurring in illness and of physical dependency arousing conflicts for the patient may be learned in the classroom and accepted theoretically. In field work the student is faced with the need to develop and use a case work relationship which must be based upon her own judgment as to the degree of the patient's regression with the varying stages of his illness and as to the patient's ability to mobilize physical and emotional energy to cope with the dependency situation. Acquiring skill in estimating the extent of control, authority, or responsibility which the social worker should take at any given time for the sick person, who will inevitably have his own way of meeting his problems and whose illness itself may be an attempt at a way out, is the continuing aim of even the most experienced worker. The student will have an exceedingly difficult time acting in these areas, but she should exhibit a beginning development which will eventually lead to a firmly woven pattern of professional performance.

The processes of interviewing, which the student may feel she has mastered to a certain extent, may be difficult of application in the medical setting. There are several factors that enter into this situation. In the first place, many of the interviews, first ones especially, are not private. They may be held in an open ward or in a busy clinic, even in the presence of the doctor or nurse. In addition to having a disturbing effect on the patient, this lack of privacy tends to confuse the student, increasing her self-consciousness and fastening her attention on her own situation rather than on the patient's. Until she has acquired some poise and self-control, she is likely to rush ahead too fast, instead of making what attempt she can to arrange a contact under more favorable circumstances. Second, because the patient's exact purpose in having related himself to the medical institution is sometimes difficult to define, it may take the student a little time to learn to "meet the patient on his own ground." The social worker's role does not stand out as clearly as it does in the family agency, for instance, and there may be necessary a period of orientation on the part of the worker to the problem that brought the patient to the institution, before she can begin to find out what brought the patient to her. The student, in her eagerness to be of service and to have her service wanted, may begin her interviews at a point the patient has not yet reached. A third factor that may make interviewing difficult is related to the problem of learning how to use medical information. The student in her conversation with the patient may be fearful of encouraging talk about the patient's symptoms. Even though they constitute the condition that brought the patient to the agency, the student may feel she has no right to question regarding pain, cough, bleeding, and so forth, because she is not to treat them directly. She may even be as afraid of them as is the patient. Conversely, the student may lay too much stress on the purely medical aspects of the symptoms, whereas she should think of the interview as an opportunity to find out the use the patient is making of them.

Throughout the period of medical social field work the supervisor can help the student to learn to use more varied and skilful methods of interviewing, both for study and for treatment purposes, if there is progression in the student's comprehension of the total meaning of the patient's situation and the social worker's relationship to it.

Some of the special techniques of social case work treatment may give the student trouble, notably reassurance and helping the client to gain insight. These are, of course, problems of all fields of social work and are not peculiar to the medical setting. The point to be made, however, is that there are special temptations to cheer and support the patient because he is ill and to think that insight has been given when the disease and its treatment have been "interpreted."

The sick person is usually seen as someone who needs to be protected and to be comforted. The custom is to say, "I hope you feel better," "I'm sure you'll feel better soon," and so forth. Such remarks may be quite appropriate in a particular case work situation, but we cannot call them "reassurance" unless the full facts tell us that the term is warranted. The student, again because she wants to be liked and wants to help, tends to use such phrases without discrimination and because at first she thinks they are really effective. She will undoubtedly need assistance in seeing that they usually do not take into account the meaning of the illness to the patient. The most reassuring kind of situation for a sick person may lie in being allowed to talk about the negative aspects of his illness, even to the point of getting excited, with someone who will not tend to shut off the flow of feeling and who will not herself become disturbed. The patient may want his symptoms to continue. He may want to criticize the doctor and revile the hospital. It may be most comforting for him when the social worker lets him do so. Or it may be that simple interest and acceptance, expressed in action rather than in words, will be more reassuring than any carefully verbalized phrase could be.

In helping a patient gain insight, the student must use all the understanding of personality development and of the meaning of illness which she has. She cannot interpret a situation to another unless she has some awareness of it herself. The patient's overt symptoms and his ideas about them, whether they have any basis in scientific fact or not, should be resources to which the student learns to turn for her knowledge of the kind of person the patient is and the kind of problem he has. Here again the student may find it difficult not to take an authoritative attitude, correct the patient on misinformation, and give out instructions prematurely. Her attitudes as she grows more mature in her role as a social worker, and the security and control she should be achieving, will help her gradually to identify with what is reality for the patient and eventually to use case work techniques to more purpose.

As the student's understanding of the medical organization in which she is working broadens and as her knowledge of case work theory develops, she may become aware of another conflict with which she will need guidance. Reference here is to the difficulty she may have in harmonizing the case work concept of self-determination for the client-patient with the semi-authoritative attitudes of the medical institution. This problem of a conflict of ideologies is one that is not characteristic of the medical social work field alone, but it is more sharply defined and more frequent in the medical setting.

Identification, on the student's part, with the patient as against the institution may occur if the student has not had opportunity to understand the historic purpose and traditional methods of the hospital. On the other hand, her problem may be one of not yet having had a sufficient background of experience to be able to judge the patient's ability to make his own decisions. The student must be able to see the effect on the patient, if she should become disturbed and antagonistic toward the organization because it does not fall in with her plan to be of service. The student or social worker can do nothing apart from the institution, and it is, after all, the institution as a whole to which the patient has appealed. The student must also be acquiring some ability to estimate the long-time effects on the patient and his family, as well as on the community, if he does not follow a prescribed course of treatment, and to use her conclusions in these areas constructively in planning with the doctor. A sense of balance, understanding, and persistence needs to be developed in this setting, as in no other.

RELATIONSHIP WITH THE DOCTOR

Learning to work in a co-operative relationship with the doctor and at times with other institutional personnel will undoubtedly have been part of the experience of the medical social work student from the first. Some of this experience will have been helpful and inspiring, and some of it may have been frustrating. The student should learn to make what she can of each such relationship with a doctor, in terms of a real sharing of understanding and plans, and of a separate professional function for each. Obstacles to the student's learning may be either her resistance to the doctor's prior "claim" on the patient and a sense of competition with him, or a too full submission on her part to his orders and a limitation of her activity to the finding of answers to his direct questions. Many students vary between these two reactions before they find assurance in their own ideas of their roles. Eventually, it will not matter much to a student if the doctor does not accept completely her professional status and ability, as long as she feels some security in them herself. The supervisor may be able to stimulate the student to use initiative in demonstrating her service to the physician and in actively going after his co-operation.

As has been mentioned so many times before, the student's personal feelings in this situation must be taken into account. Her prior conception, perhaps unconscious, of the doctor as the father-person and her early experiences within her own family will directly affect her ability to work pleasantly and effectively with the physicians of her patients. In many instances a student has found it disconcerting to be associated with a young doctor who is as insecure and self-conscious as she is herself. Perhaps it might be suggested that the social work student has, in this situation, a special responsibility to show herself able to understand and to adapt to another person. She will, however, probably need the support of her supervisor if she is not to feel presumptuous.

The student's previous relationships to a doctor with herself as the patient may reflect constructively or destructively here. Unless, however, she has an overwhelming need to continue to be possessive, retiring, or resistant to authority, she should show progress in her ability to share her patients professionally. This triangular relationship between the doctor, the social worker, and the patient may develop very significantly for the patient into a reliving of the father-mother-child relationship. The student, with the supervisor's help, can gain some awareness of the meaning of this situation in terms of its assets and liabilities for social case work and some capacity for assuming the responsibilities involved.

Acceptance of the function and adjustment to the policies of the agency in which field work is taking place is part of the learning situation for any social work student. In medical social field work these matters become particular problems and need to be stressed separately because of the fact that in this special form of social work practice the worker's area of performance is only one of many within the same institution. Questioning of the role the worker selects may come from within the organization and from those with whom she is closely associated. The complexities in the setting of the field-work placement will contribute to the student's confusion. In small matters, as well as in the broader aspects of her work, she needs experiences which will give her a basis for sound judgment as to what her procedure in any given situation should be. There is, for instance, no universally accepted practice as to when a medical social worker stays in the examining room with a patient or when she accompanies a patient to the operating room and remains until the anesthesia is administered. Her understanding of the traditional policies of the institution and of the attitudes of the doctor, together with her estimate of the patient's need and what she has to give, will make it possible for her to plan action which uses to a maximum extent opportunities for being helpful without embarrassing or making uncomfortable either the patient or the other institutional personnel.

The fact that the possible types of activity for the medical social worker are varied and the fact that the need for her service is sometimes indefinite may add to her difficulties. There are many pressures, which the student will feel, to divert the medical social worker from her theoretical intentions and to dissipate her energies in inappropriate and even purposeless activities. It is, therefore, essential that the medical social work student be gaining, as early as possible, integration of her knowledge of the medical setting with her understanding of case work theory, sufficient for her to be able to make a conscious choice as to her role in any given situation and to defend her choice soundly.

If the student's manner of working with the medical personnel and with the administrative officers of the hospital is showing an increasing proficiency and flexibility, she will automatically be achieving some basis for her decisions. A further measure of her grasp of the problems in this area might be called, briefly, her diagnostic ability. She should realize the value of cultivating a form of diagnostic approach which takes into account the patient's total problem—the social and emotional factors, the medical factors, the plan of treatment, and the meaning for the patient. The understanding thus gained should be considered in relation to the part to be played by the social worker, by the doctor, and by the other institutional personnel.

PROBLEMS OF INTAKE

There is one final area of the specialized content of medical social field work which will be mentioned briefly and that is the matter of the student's learning to manage a varied case load, planning, herself, for intake and for the types of service to be given. It seems advisable for the student of medical social work to have some experience with these problems when it can be arranged. She cannot otherwise be ready for her first position, which is likely to be so set up that she will be responsible for giving all types of service required in certain clinics and wards. Definition of a problem, determination of the focus of social treatment needed, and decision as to intake will be areas in which even a young worker may have to perform immediately. The situation will often be complicated for her by the fact that she will be exploring a problem with a patient who has been sent to her when he has no request for a service in mind. Ability must be acquired to carry on sympathetically and with understanding in minor services on the rather uninteresting cases, in the face of the demands of a fascinating and intensive problem. Supportive treatment for the chronically or incurably ill may seem to involve a comparative waste of effort unless the student can see it as part of the total plan of the hospital's operation to meet the community's needs. The student whose field-work experience can give her some knowledge of these problems will be fortunate.

As can be seen, there is a large area of specialized content in medical social field work. Any one student cannot always be given sufficient contact with these various problems and with all the future phases of her work to become fully aware of them. The supervisor's perspective can, however, make it possible to guide the student toward some conception of their existence and to broaden the range of her thinking. The temptation to give the student too much is real and should be guarded against. Even in two years of professional training she can absorb only so much knowledge. The changes necessary in her outlook, in her habits, and in her behavior inevitably require time. There are so many situations in which a total reorganization of the student's ideas and of her emotional responses is necessary that she may achieve only a beginning toward the point of being fully equipped.

The final conclusion must be that adequate supervision of the worker on her first job is as important in the process of her development as are the guidance and assistance she receives during field work. If the worker is to continue the growth that the period in school began and if the employing agency is to have the service of an adequate, well-balanced worker, she must have help, not only with the management of her day-by-day job, but also with understanding the broader implications of the way her work relates to the institution of which she is a part; with grasping the meaning and the importance of her activities; with deepening her understanding; and with the continuing incorporation within herself of the attitudes and knowledge which a social worker must have when she is prepared to function competently in the medical setting.

The Relationship between Field and Schools of Social Work in Training for the New Function of the Hospital[1]

BY BESSIE G. SCHLESS

MEDICAL social work for many years was the stepchild of social case work practice. Its rise in status, in recent years, can be attributed directly to the growing importance that the medical profession itself attaches to social and emotional factors in the study and treatment of disease. It is no longer enough for the medical social worker to know about the patient and his environment. She is now expected to use her knowledge of the patient dynamically toward helping him effect a recovery commensurate with his functional capacities. A goal so allied with treatment calls for a thorough understanding of disease processes and the meaning of illness to the individual patient, an appreciation of the environmental situation which the patient faces, and a comprehensive knowledge of the resources available to him. Medical social work training must thus, of necessity, be generic in terms of developing understanding of human behavior and social forces and specific in terms of offering the student special knowledge of sickness and sick people and familiarity with hospital procedures.

To decide who has the greater responsibility in training of this nature—field or school—is as equivocal as the old chicken-egg controversy. The fact is that the two areas share a mutual interdependency and together make of the whole of student training a configuration more meaningful than its component parts. Like

1. Presented at the National Conference of Jewish Social Welfare, Atlantic City, May, 1948. Reprinted from the *Jewish Social Service Quarterly*, 1948, with the permission of the *Quarterly* and the National Conference of Jewish Communal Service.

all reciprocal relationships, that between school and field proves most effective when it is most clearly defined.

Student training, as it has been established in the schools of social work, combines two major areas—theory and practice. The field-work placement is the alleged proving ground for the theoretical knowledge supplied by the classroom. In medical social work it offers, in addition, actual exposure to the setting in which the medical social worker operates, a setting which the classroom cannot be expected to reproduce. A co-ordinated approach to student training thus imposes the necessity for practice to keep up with theory and vice versa. Where a dichotomy exists between the two areas, the student can only be caught up in a whirlpool of confusion and tossed about without ever reaching the shore of professionalism.

In these days of changing concepts of hospital function, it is not enough for school and field to rely on established medical practices for the knowledge they impart to students. Intramural social work is now only a part of medical social work practice. The medical social worker of a nearing tomorrow will be involved in group medical practice, home-care programs, public health measures, and medical social research. The goal of training must be to equip the student with enough fundamental understanding to enable her to relate to practice not only as it exists at present but to a future as yet more envisioned than real.

Basic to the ability to offer case work service effectively in any setting is the understanding of human behavior. Good student training encompasses not only an understanding of the client-patient's behavior but thorough self-knowledge as well. Schools of social work through their "personality development," psychiatry, and case work courses broaden the student's vision by enabling her to see the relationship between overt behavior and inner feelings. As her knowledge of others deepens, the student begins to view her own development in a new way, so that theoretical material becomes personalized to her. It is important for the field supervisor to know at what pace the school is moving, so that she does not expect more from the student than the student is being prepared to give. Criteria for the student in each quarter of training, as have recently been developed by the schools of social work, serve as a helpful guide to the student supervisor. I cannot emphasize too much the importance of the student supervisor's identification with school as well as agency in successful student training. Knowing what the school expects from the student is another means of clarifying for the student supervisor what the school expects from her and gives focus and purpose to her job. There is perhaps no more reassuring moment in the professional life of the student supervisor than that in which the student volunteers that what is being said in supervisory conferences coincides with what is being taught in the classroom, for it assures her of the accuracy with which she times her contributions to the student's learning. To the student the visible evidence of correlation between field and school serves to strengthen her concept of professionalism and gives her confidence in the goal to which she aspires.

The student in a medical setting is expected to achieve understanding of ill people as well as generalized understanding of human behavior. The specifics, however, grow out of the general. Unless, for example, the student understands the dependency-independency drive in all personality development, she cannot evaluate the way in which hospitalization may serve to enhance this conflict, nor know how she herself relates to the dependency inherent in illness and supervision. The school can only point up the forces that serve to make and keep people ill. The student supervisor, through the cases assigned to the student, can make the concepts described in the classroom live as they are demonstrated by Mrs. L. or Mr. Z. Even the medical content of the school courses in disease and public health takes on, for the student, real meaning only as she identifies symptomatology with a particular patient whom she knows.

We are all geared to the term "psychosomatic medicine" these days and would certainly see the acceptance of its principles as vital to medical social work practice. Sometimes, because the student is so intellectually oriented to the validity of such medical thinking, she is disillusioned when she finds that doctors are less ready than she is to accept the relationship between emotional factors and illness. While certainly the school has a responsibility to share with the student the psychogenic origin of illness, that responsibility extends to pointing up the controversial aspects of this philosophy as well. Medical social work is still in the formative stage of working out its own part in the practice of psychosomatic medicine and, in the application of it to individual cases, can move only as fast as the physician is ready to go. The student needs to know this and to learn to accept the sometimes grim reality of the doctor who cannot see beyond what the fluoroscope and X-ray reveal or hear more than what his stethoscope tells him.

School and field must both recognize the meaning that medical authority can hold for the student and help the student see how she is using it. I have found in my experience as student supervisor that learning to be comfortable with doctors is, oftentimes, the most threatening aspect of placement to the medical social student. While the school can discuss intellectually the differences in doctors as human beings, only through working with a variety of doctors can the student appreciate just how human and different doctors can be. As the student gains security in her own place in the hospital, she grows able to articulate her job to the doctor. She begins to develop a respect for her own professional convictions, even when the doctor, because of the difference in his orientation, questions them.

Often the medical social student tends to minimize the so-called "little things" in medical social work, such as the braces and dentures, and yearns for the more exotic as represented in the patient who refuses surgery or cannot accept psychiatric help. I think that all of us, in our zeal to jump on the psychosomatic band wagon, have erred in the emphasis we have put on medical social work function as being related primarily to emotional factors in illness. That goes for field and school alike. In the selection of case material for classroom use, I would make a plea for more frequent discussion of the dynamics of helping the patient secure an appliance or arrange convalescent care as a way of preparing the student for what the field of practice will offer her. If we are agreed that the giving of medical relief calls for the same critical evaluation of individual need as any other case work service, such classroom discussion is vital to sound preparation for medical social practice. This does not remove the student supervisor from responsibility. In selecting cases for the student, she must be aware that good learning can spring from any source germane to the medical social work job. I am sure that any one of us who has supervised students must know the temptation to select for the student the case that exemplifies the most esoteric aspects of case work practice. Only as we ourselves come to accept the fact that the ability to deal with environmental factors effectively requires skill and understanding, can we impart to students similar satisfaction in a simple job, well done. The reality is that not only do teeth and braces and eyeglasses make up a large part of the patient's living with his illness, but actually I know of no better approach to the psyche than through the soma. Often the patient cannot be comfortable in discussing his deeper problems until he is offered alleviation of some of his environmental difficulties. The student can best acquire sensitive hearing through being helped to see that the patient's attitudes toward any aspect of his medical care reflect his general attitude toward himself and his illness.

The emphasis I have thus far put on the importance of school and field's being attuned to the reality of practice may seem to negate the earlier definition of the goal of student training as developing vision broad enough to encompass a widening medical social future. It is my feeling, however, that no program of the future is unrelated to the past and present, but represents instead an evolutionary process. Group medical practice has come into being out of a growing awareness of the inequalities in the distribution of medical care; hospital home-care programs were inspired by the realization that the building of more hospital beds was not the total answer to the problem of increasing demand for hospital care; the use of medical social work in the treatment of private patients has developed out of the cognizance that money alone cannot alleviate the anxiety which illness creates. Unless the student shares in the conceptual thinking on which these developments are based, unless she is made aware of the negatives as well as the positives in present-day medical social practice, she is in the doubtful position of the child who begins to walk without having learned to crawl. It is, to my mind, a serious error to fail to give the student stimulus for developing her own ideas about what is good and what is bad in our present social scheme of things. The school can stimulate the student to think in terms of social programs by introducing such controversial subjects as socialized medicine, private social case work practice and group insurance plans into the curriculum. Similarly, the student supervisor can help the student in her understanding of the inner workings of hospital and community by exposing her to the realities of practice as influenced by present social conditions.

It is no small charge to ask that the schools incorporate into their programs the developments in practice, particularly these days when the tempo of change is such a rapid one. There are, however, several ways in which the field itself can contribute to curriculum-making. We are all oriented to working with the schools on an individual student basis. We are accustomed to share with the field consultant the problems we are encountering in working with a particular student and in seeking from her help and reassurance for going on with the student's training. We talk more frequently of case than program. Yet we expect the schools to be aware of the problems in practice itself and often accuse the schools of dwelling in a never-never land. If we feel a responsibility for medical social education, do we not have a like responsibility to contribute to its content? I recall the satisfaction expressed recently by a student at Montefiore Hospital when her classroom instructor asked her to report on the Montefiore Home Care Program. Not only did she gain status from her close identification with a new program, but the program itself gained status from the school's interest in it. Because we at Montefiore felt that we were embarking on a new course in our home-care program, we discussed its step-by-step development with the faculty of the New York School, inviting the field consultant to attend a regular departmental meeting, sending the school the literature we were developing on the subject of "home care," and making material available to students who expressed interest in writing their school projects on some aspect of home care.

The whole area of the relationship between field and school in the student project is one that might well be explored further. The research project is too often both a headache and a bore. It is not unusual to see a student who has blossomed steadily during her training period begin to wilt as the last quarter approaches and the unfinished project looms ahead. The student supervisor may question what more she can do, in this trying time, than to tolerate and reassure. If so much trauma has set in, it may indeed be too late for anything more than a supportive role. If, however, the agency is program-minded, it can play a preventive role in warding off project-panic by helping the student to choose a project related to the student's interests, the agency's practices, and of sufficient value to the agency to make the work involved seem worth while. What better way of bridging the gap between agency and school than through the student herself?

From the school's point of view, the project can serve as an excellent means of preparing the student for participation in medical research. While psychiatric social workers have for some time played an important role in psychiatric research, medical social workers have more recently begun to function in this area. Since there is much in medical social thinking that can add greatly to present-day investigation of social factors in illness, the school and field should encourage interest in research and give students sound preparation for investigatory activity.

The correlation of agency and school program this paper suggests is dependent on the development of a sound working relationship between school and field. The school, in such a working relationship, would view its student supervisors as part of its faculty, drawing them into curriculum planning, encouraging them to contribute their thinking to the school program, sponsoring meetings of the student supervisory staff where ideas are freely shared. If the student supervisor w re to derive from the school a sense of the significance of her contribution to student training, she would be readier to assume a dynamic part in the educational process and to think beyond the individual student to the whole of student training. The student supervisor is, after all, a practitioner. Her daily work experience serves as a continual testing of the theory the school propounds. Because she herself is a part of the changing function of the hospital, she is in an excellent position to help the school keep up with change, for she has firsthand awareness of change as it is needed and takes place.

Problems Faced by Beginning Medical
Social Workers[1]

BY ADDIE THOMAS

BEGINNING medical social workers face not only the adjustments inherent in any first social work placement but also those peculiar to the medical setting and the functional relationships within which the medical social worker practices. We are interested in the total adjustment of the worker, but we shall be concerned here with the development, in the latter aspects, of three workers in their first medical social placement.

In accordance with the standards of our department, established three years ago in a teaching hospital, all three workers had already completed at least the two-year graduate social work curriculum, specializing in medical social work. The requirement of a Master's degree was waived for two workers because of the wartime shortage of fully qualified personnel. The case work unit of the department included, besides these workers, an experienced worker, a part-time student supervisor, a case supervisor (both supervisors carry some intensive cases), and medical social field-work students from the school of social work in the university of which the medical school and hospital are a part.

The three beginning workers brought to this department similar backgrounds of professional training but their range of previous work experience varied. One worker had public welfare experience as an untrained worker, one had a longer business experience, and the third had only part-time work while attending school. Because she had less previous experience, the third worker's induction period has been more extensive. It was more difficult for her to make the transition from "feeling like a glorified student" to feeling herself a responsible and in-

1. Reprinted from *The Family*, January, 1946, with the permission of the Family Service Association of America.

dependent member of the staff who uses the supervisor as supervisor-consultant rather than supervisor-teacher. The experienced workers were a threat to her, and she required much reassurance and demonstration in her own cases to gain the realization that her accomplishments were as appropriate to her stage of development as were those of the more experienced workers for theirs.

INITIAL PROBLEMS

The medical social workers, like recent graduates in any field, brought to their first jobs intellectual understanding, obtained in the classroom and in field work, which they were impatient to apply. Immediately they met frustration in being able to do so only partially, not realizing that their knowledge was not yet so integrated a part of themselves that they could use it securely and effectively. They were impatient with many of the mechanics and relationships of practice because of their retarding effect. There were the clinic and hospital admitting workers, for example, whose function they must not assume and to whom they must demonstrate their own function so that proper referrals of social problems would be made. They had given practical assent to the value of supervision by wishing to be in a department where it was available, but it also seemed a hampering procedure.

Recording was laborious and frustrating because they were confused about its purpose. They tended to see it primarily as a tool for supervision and an end in itself rather than as a means of writing down their activity to clarify their own thinking as a part of their case work practice. For instance, two of the workers at first showed resistance to recording the medical social impression (or problem) and plan because it required extra time, but later they found that it improved their diagnostic thinking and treatment and saved time in the long run. It was more difficult than they expected to get acquainted with the hospital—the wards and clinics, their personnel and procedures. Many of the doctors, nurses, and others did not understand the social worker's function and were not easily available. Conferences with them were not always satisfactory. It was as though the new workers felt a great rush against time to use their knowledge while it was still fresh in their minds; yet circumstances conspired to deter them. Being unaware of the fact that the principal cause of their difficulty was lack of integration of intellectual knowledge into practice, or being unwilling to give full significance to it, they were prone to project the reasons for their frustration.

There was, too, the pressure of their desire to make good, not only to demonstrate their right to be in the profession but also to win the confidence of the director by showing that they could perform in this high-standard program. On the worker rested the responsibility for gaining acceptance of herself and her function, as well as of her specialty in the profession—or perhaps of the entire profession—by doctors and hospital personnel whose knowledge of, or experience with, social work had not enabled them to understand its contribution to good medical care. Confusion resulted, and the workers wondered whether they really had any status in this program.

All three workers had some security in case work, so that the supervisor had a base from which to begin to help them gain status that would not be threatened by the numerous pressures. This was fairly easy when the patient was well referred and the case worker's role was clear to the doctor and patient; for instance, in effecting discharge arrangements, helping to pay for an appliance, securing financial assistance, planning for children during hospitalization of a mother. In such cases, the worker needed only to be encouraged to voice her own findings and opinions rather than to proceed merely on the doctor's recommendations. Her security was established or increased when she was able to plan co-operatively with the doctor, especially when he adjusted his recommendations to the social situation she interpreted. Our least experienced worker found her first real security when she was helped to uncover the feelings that were keeping an adolescent boy from wearing the appliance for which she had authorized payment and so to interpret them to the surgeon that a compromise, but successful, plan was worked out.

The beginning worker's insecurity was most obvious in her

functional relationship with other hospital personnel. She was especially threatened by referrals from nonmedical staff when her role was not clear to the doctor (whose concurrence is required by department policy before a case may be accepted) or by those in which the referring doctor had not properly prepared the patient. It was comparatively easy to help the worker to learn to explain the basis of referral to the patient, but much more assistance was needed before she gained facility in interpreting her function in such a way that the doctor would release part of the responsibility for the patient's treatment to her and discuss the medical findings in relation to her activity rather than give directions or "orders" in his customary manner.

It was helpful to learn from one pediatrician that he had refrained from referring patients with emotional problems because he felt incompetent to give direction to treatment in this area and had thought that the workers would expect guidance from him. When the case work supervisor's responsibility for giving such guidance and the use of psychiatric consultation were explained, he began to make referrals and to encourage his staff to do so. The two workers on adult services profited from being encouraged to ask the doctor to tell the patient that he was ready for discharge in order to prepare him for the social worker's discussion of postdischarge plans with him. Increased security in her status and successful conferences usually resulted when the worker was helped to clarify her own thinking, to bring her focus back to the patient, to appreciate the doctor's lack of knowledge of how she practices, to understand how the insecurity of the young practitioner sometimes made him reluctant to give the patient disturbing information, and to demonstrate to the doctor that she had no desire to "take over" his prerogatives. It was sometimes necessary to help the worker resolve her conflict between guilt over her failure to contribute to the doctor's understanding of the patient or to his understanding of her function and her annoyance that her service was rejected or that she was given "orders." Occasionally, so simple a thing as suggesting that the worker time her contact with the doctor at an hour when he was less rushed or was not concentrating on something else insured a satisfactory conference with him.

Another supervisory device, used infrequently, was to join the worker in a conference. She was left free to reject the offer to do this, and it was withdrawn if it seemed she would be threatened by self-consciousness in the presence of the supervisor or thought this might give the impression that she was inadequate to carry on alone. Each of the workers has been able to use this type of assistance to gain security with doctors with whom she felt ill at ease, or when she was not sure of the content of the conference. (This was most likely to be felt when interpretation of the worker's treatment was involved.) The supervisor referred to the worker matters that she knew the worker could discuss and handled the others herself. Security with workers of other agencies has often been gained by this device, the supervisor speaking for agency policy but leaving the worker free to discuss the case work factors.

It is normal for any beginning worker to tend to let the pendulum swing between identification with the client and identification with the agency. The medical social worker, like the social worker in any setting where case work is not the primary function of the organization, can never work alone in relation to her patient and thus faces many more possible identifications. Unless she can bring all these into proper perspective with her own function and status, she runs the risk of conflict, of losing her objectivity and, consequently, her ability to be of maximum help to the patient directly or through those to whom she interprets the effect of, or his feelings about, his environment and social relationships.

DIFFICULT SERVICES

Many threats to the beginning worker are inherent in any case load; so the supervisor must be constantly alert for indications of blocking or undue emphasis. The pressure of a full case load and the impossibility of giving much protection in a department where demands for service are heavy are so real that as complete service as desirable cannot be given in each case. Medical social review of all patients with cancer and all children with diabetes has been requested by the respective medical staffs. With the pressure of referred cases, it has been impossible to make the 100 per cent review, creating a sense of guilt and partial failure on the part of the two workers covering these services, particularly for the one whose salary is paid by the cancer committee. They have been helped by reviewing the relative importance of their cases, in service to the patient, in demonstration of their function, and in their own development. Reassurance that they were properly selective and were carrying larger case loads than desirable and that the supervisor and director shared the responsibility for the selection has not been so effective.

In addition to the lack of sufficient time for complete review, the workers have shown reluctance to initiate this, because there was no specific reason to be given the patient for the interview. This has been particularly difficult for the worker on cancer service, because many patients do not know their diagnoses and she has been fearful of their questions, especially, "Do I have cancer?" She was able to proceed upon being reminded of the technique of turning the question back to the patient or inquiring what the doctor said and basing her interpretation on that. Discouragement has also come from a feeling that she is not helping the patient specifically and because so few medical social problems have been revealed in the review. However, she has been able to accept its value as contributing (1) to the establishment of a relationship that will encourage the patient to return when he desires help and (2) to information leading toward improvement in methods of early diagnosis and treatment.

This worker and the one on surgical service have been threatened by the pressure of discharge situations and were inclined to neglect everything else for them. They were helped to learn how to be selective, and pressure was lessened following conferences with the residents in surgery, in which the supervisor and director participated, to explain necessary delays and request more time between referral and probable date of discharge. All the workers have used supervisory help in becoming more objective about criticism directed toward them for delays due to lack of resources or slowness of community agencies, in learning to interpret the reasons for this to hospital personnel, and to obtain co-operation of other agency workers through allowing them to participate in planning as well as in service. When pressure on other agencies was necessary or matters of policy were involved, the workers all readily accepted the principle that further clarification or pressure was the responsibility of the supervisor or director.

The two most difficult types of medical social cases for the beginning workers have been those involving serious or terminal illness and those where direct treatment of children was needed. In these situations they sometimes blocked to the extent of failing to see the patient. The pediatric worker found it frustrating that parents of seriously ill children were not being referred to her. When cases have eventually come to her, she has seen the often serious implications of delay in case work treatment and has felt pressure that would not have been present, had they come to her attention earlier. On the other hand, when cases with serious emotional components were referred, the workers have not always been able to follow through constructively. This particular worker, who has good insight, usually remarks that she has no right to feel resentful because a case was not referred early when she has not always followed through on similar ones that were.

One worker was less threatened by serious illness but resisted pediatric cases as such. She has been willing to carry a sufficient number to gain experience in this area and sufficient other cases to indicate that her aptitudes lie elsewhere. She has been able to use supervisory assistance to clarify her own interests and skills and gain security to accept them as different from, rather than inferior to, those of other workers, and to know that her greatest contribution will come from functioning within her skills and limitations. The worker on pediatrics has developed from having to be pushed into interviews with children to being able to enter direct treatment comfortably and carry it successfully. The third worker has little opportunity to work with children but has shown this same resistance. There has been difficulty, also, in getting into cases where a crisis could be anticipated (such as

surgery, death, or a disturbing diagnosis) if the crisis was not
so imminent that it must be faced immediately.

Reluctance to undertake and continue treatment stemmed
from the worker's fears that she would not know how to relate
to the patient without some tangible entrée, that she would not
be able to obtain significant material or know what to do about
it if it was produced. It has been obvious that all three workers
were in the stage of learning described by Miss Reynolds as "understanding the situation without power to control one's own
activity in it."[2] These same factors contributed to the workers'
discouragement after treatment had begun. Additional factors
were their feeling that movement was not obvious, seemed slow,
or that their part in effecting improvement was obscure. Workers sometimes remarked that the current improvement would
probably have been attained without case work help.

In attempting to alleviate the worker's discouragement, the
supervisor often began by granting this possibility and then went
on with some or all of the following: citing examples of similar
cases lacking case work in which there were negative results;
reminding the worker of the values of just listening even if she
could do nothing more—a concept the worker usually accepted
at least intellectually; if the worker's fear was that the patient
would not talk at all, helping her to feel secure enough to handle
that directly, even to the point of terminating the interview until
the patient was ready to discuss his problem; helping her to think
through what she already knew in the situation and how, indirectly, to secure further information, suggesting that she write
out the interview in process immediately afterward, together
with any impressions which she had about it for supervisory
conference in preparation for the next interview; helping her
review and evaluate her activity in relation to any movement
that had occurred and the possible part she might play in
furthering movement; guiding her to see, or actually pointing
out to her, the relationship of specific activity or content to
concepts, procedures, and techniques she had mastered in theory;
giving her reassurance that what she was doing was right, or, if

2. Bertha Capen Reynolds, *Learning and Teaching in the Practice of Social Work* (New York: Farrar & Rinehart, Inc., 1942), p. 79.

an impasse or plateau in treatment had been reached, suggesting techniques for standing by or cutting through it; suggesting consultation with the psychiatrist; having the case presented in staff case conference.

When it appeared that the worker was over her depth, she was permitted, if she wished, to transfer the case to one of the supervisors and encouraged to follow the handling of it. When indicated, referral to a psychiatrist was discussed, preparatory to consultation with the doctor on the case.

RELATIONSHIPS WITH PHYSICIANS

Two of the workers were disturbed by the content of records involving emotional and behavior problems because of the meaning they might have to the doctors. (The medical social history is filed in the unit medical chart.) The use of psychiatric and technical case work terminology, except that in common usage in the hospital, is discouraged because it is not easily understood and is sometimes threatening. Other threats were evident in the recording of case work judgment that differed from medical judgment (such as the case work knowledge that placement is not always the only or best solution to convalescent or behavior problems or to poor family situations), and in handling hostility toward the doctor or hospital.

However, one of the functions of the medical social worker is to participate, through case work demonstrations and consultation, in helping the medical students become aware of social and environmental factors and their importance in diagnosis and treatment. For this reason and also in order to demonstrate the function of the medical social worker in dealing with emotional and behavior problems related to illness, as well as because detailed material is needed for constant re-evaluation of the case work itself, the worker is encouraged to record completely as well as concisely.

The workers have been and should be concerned when nonprofessional personnel have had access to the medical chart and about inclinations to gossip about patients' personal affairs. On the other hand, they have been encouraged to see that the manner in which they record the material has resulted in intelligent

referrals and the calling of pertinent information to their attention. The workers have been helped to obviate their fears of the
doctors' rejection of the handling of emotions, as well as to develop clear diagnostic thinking, by taking care that all impressions, plans, and recommendations were founded on sufficient,
obvious, and reasonable evidence. They were permitted to
speculate in the supervisory conference but not allowed to forget
that they were speculating. Interestingly, the worker who most
resisted incorporation in the record of material regarding her
handling of emotional problems and expressed the strongest
opinion against use of technical terminology as irritating to
the doctor omitted the material and terms except in her less well-
founded impressions, being quite unaware of doing so until it
was called to her attention.

A TERMINAL ILLNESS

The records of two cases, carried by workers with one and
six months' experience, respectively, when case work was
undertaken, incorporate and illustrate many of the points discussed above.

Mrs. N, 29-year-old mother of four children, was referred for plans
for her children during her hospitalization for treatment of terminal
cancer. The husband had not availed himself of service offered by a former
worker, and Mrs. N had left the hospital, against advice, to be with her
children. Our worker, Miss E, entered the case when the visiting nurse
reported home conditions poor and the husband unable, even with the
help of a neighbor, to keep up his full-time job, the housekeeping, and
the care of the children. Miss E obtained the promise of a community
agency to furnish a practical nurse if a housekeeper were provided. The
family agency accepted responsibility for supplying a housekeeper. The
family worker, distressed by the serious illness of the mother and the behavior problems of the children, began immediately to bring pressure for
hospitalization of the mother, although this was not yet considered medically necessary. When the visiting nurse's concern over the delay in
furnishing housekeeping service was discussed, it was discovered that, although Miss E had made the referrals for service and participated in
numerous conferences, she had had no contact with the patient or family.
She saw no service for which she personally was needed because the patient
knew of her impending death, and the worker considered that reminding
her of it would be an unnecessary cruelty. Miss E accepted the suggestion
that, on the contrary, a relationship established now would enable the
family to turn to her readily when a crisis arose.
When an impasse resulted from pressure from the family worker for

hospitalization of the patient and the decision of the doctor from the county hospital (where patients are hospitalized if beds are not available in the University Hospital) that admission was not necessary, Miss E felt helpless. The problems in the situation were reviewed with her. She admitted that they were principally medical social but that she felt inadequate to handle them or to clarify her function with the experienced family worker. She agreed to assume her proper responsibility; and the supervisor clarified it with the family worker. They concurred in the opinion that it would be advisable to learn to what extent the older children had been affected by their mother's illness. Assistance was given in working out the mechanics of seeing the oldest child while the nurse was occupied with the mother. Miss E found the boy upset by his fear that his mother would die in her sleep and was able to establish a relationship with him which made his feel appreciated and feel that he could call on the worker when he needed her. When hospitalization was indicated, Miss E was helped to see her supportive and steering role, which she handled well.

It was unfortunate that a case with so many threatening aspects came so early in the worker's experience, but, because of her personal maturity, her real desire to be of help, and her ability to use supervision constructively, this case proved a positive experience in overcoming her fear of situations in which the illness was cancer.

TREATMENT OF AN ARTHRITIC CHILD

Mrs. D was first referred in the fall of 1944 during one of her periodic episodes of dissatisfaction over the care of Dolores, aged 12, who had been under treatment for a number of years for rheumatoid arthritis. Miss M was helped to accept the mother's right to reject medical care, even though her action would be detrimental to the child. However, it was decided that if Mrs. D brought her back, an effort would be made to help her accept Dolores' illness and, possibly, care outside the home, since she was never skilful with her and in many ways openly showed rejection. In January, 1945, the case was referred by the orthopedist for placement of Dolores away from her mother, where she could receive physiotherapy, and for arranging transportation for physiotherapy pending placement. At that time the arthritis was active, limiting motion in practically all joints, and she "walked like a crippled old lady." Her expression was dour and her responses, if any, were curt and negative. The father had recently died but left a small income for Mrs. D and the three children.

The mother accepted the recommendation for placement. The Crippled Children's Guild paid for taxi transportation, saving time and energy for both Dolores and Mrs. D. Miss M made application to the convalescent home on the basis of the recommendation for physical care, but she did not accept it as the solution for the poor family relationships. She and the supervisor hoped (off the record) that there would be delay in placement because need for case work treatment was indicated to help both Mrs. D and Dolores accept and adjust to the illness and to develop a positive relationship between them.

When insufficient physiotherapy staff, however, precluded Dolores' acceptance by the convalescent home, Miss M was hesitant about undertaking treatment, especially of Dolores, feeling inadequate to handle it. Her interest in the social and medical problems as ones in which case work therapy should be effective and her desire to develop her treatment skills were stronger than her doubts, and, having fortified herself with the promise of close supervision, she was able to offer the kind of treatment needed. She consistently recorded each interview immediately in order to have help in understanding the meaning of the material produced, the trends, and the possible nature of the next interview. Her first concern was how to relate to this negative child, and she was reassured that it was valid to take several interviews to get acquainted.

Mrs. D's hospitalization for a diabetic reaction resulted in her beginning to accept not only her own condition and need for medical care but Dolores' also. Consequently, need for regular interviews with Mrs. D was not indicated. There were weekly interviews with Dolores during her subsequent physiotherapy. The personality of the physiotherapist was ideally suited to this arrangement and was part of the dynamics of case work therapy, which was carried on sometimes in her presence and sometimes alone with Dolores. In March, Dolores first expressed her feelings of hostility toward her brothers when Miss M told her she could swear (as her brothers did) or say anything she liked in her presence without being thought "unladylike." In succeeding interviews, modified play therapy, which had been suggested to Miss M, brought expression of resentment at the "unfairness" of her illness, the cruelty of children who teased her, and her inability to participate in active play. Hostility toward her brothers continued paramount. Such things as evasion of the word "leg" and her guessing games related to fast-moving objects of drab or dark colors were interpreted for Miss M to indicate conflict about walking and running and suggestions were made for gearing treatment to the feelings indicated.

In May the orthopedist "noticed a definite improvement in Dolores' attitude, a relaxation of tension which she feels is very important to the physical improvement which has been shown." Mrs. D was happy when the pediatrician also noted improvement. Miss M had conferred frequently with the orthopedist but had almost no contact with the pediatrician. When questioned about this, she said she had had no specific reason for the latter and hesitated just to report her activity as she was doubtful of her ability to interpret her case work treatment understandably and acceptably. She readily accepted the supervisor's offer to join her in the conference but needed little participation by her to carry on the discussion, which included helpful information from the doctor.

Interviews continued with greater freedom of expression on Dolores' part. Clinic personnel began to notice her increasing friendliness, and she was participating in more normal activities. When Miss M went on vacation in July, she asked the supervisor to assume responsibility for continuing treatment in order especially that she might be able to see the relationships firsthand and interpret them. Dolores accepted the substitution well and there was no break in treatment. The more rapid movement evident in that month (Dolores even talked about her legs) was later evaluated with Miss M in relation to her months of treatment. The dynamics of the three-way relationship were interpreted to consist of: the patient, accessible to therapy; the physiotherapist, as the mother-person receiving the overt demonstrations of affection and hostility; and the medical social worker, as the accepting, understanding, and steering person. By the time Dolores could be accepted by the convalescent home in September, Miss M and the supervisor considered she was ready for the experience of group living.

This case had satisfactions for the worker not only in its benefit to the patient and in her development but also in its use as interpretation to the pediatrics department as the first medical social case to be presented in its medical seminar. It was gratifying to have the orthopedist acknowledge the contribution of the case work treatment to Dolores' improvement and cite instances of the correlation between favorable social and emotional factors and the rapid or complete recovery from rheumatoid arthritis. Another doctor advocated early medical social treatment of social and emotional problems.

We have been reviewing fifteen months of the development of beginning medical social workers—their problems, their satisfactions, and their supervision. Their problems were created primarily by their lack of facility in putting theoretical concepts and techniques into practice. Their insecurity in function, in turn, brought insecurity in the functional relationships peculiar to their specialty. It also made them fearful of undertaking treatment of difficult situations, particularly those in which relationships were hard to establish or in which there were serious physical or emotional problems. Having entered treatment, it was difficult for them to make conscious use of their techniques, to see the effect of case work methods even when they were used intuitively, and not to be threatened by the record of their own activity and judgment. Their satisfactions came from anything in the case situations or relationships which increased their security, facility, and independence. The purpose of supervision was to assist them to make conscious integration of theory and practice so that they could function securely and effectively, to minimize their problems and increase their satisfactions. It was necessary for the supervisor to help the workers achieve this through a variety of techniques—reassurance, encouragement, support, explanation, interpretation, suggestion, illustration, demonstration, and evaluation.

2. Of Other Professional Workers

The Preparation of the Medical Student in the
Recognition of the Social Component
of Disease[1]

BY ELEANOR COCKERILL

THIS is the commencement season, when universities and
colleges are holding exercises which celebrate the end of
a period of academic training and mark the beginning of new
and broader experiences for the graduate. Recently, I attended
the exercises of a college of medicine and saw a class of young
men and women solemnly take the Hippocratic Oath, thereby
pledging themselves to a life of service and devotion to the
practice of medicine. I was deeply stirred as I listened to this
dedicatory service and thought of the broad responsibility to
be assumed in the future by this class, individually and collec-
tively. As one who had participated in their training, I wondered how much real understanding of human nature, of the
sources of human ills, of the complexities of modern civiliza-
tion and human relationships these students had acquired during their long years of study in the laboratory and classroom.
The fact that they were being awarded the degree of Doctor of
Medicine was evidence that their knowledge of anatomy, physi-
ology, pathology, bacteriology, biological chemistry, and clinical medicine was sufficient to allow them to move ahead into
their period of internship. I was cognizant, also, of their familiarity with the phenomena of disease and death as they had

1. Reprinted from *Hospital Progress*, November, 1941, with the permission
of the Catholic Hospital Association.

discovered it at the bedside of patients and at the autopsy table. I could only speculate, however, about their knowledge of the phenomena of life as it is manifested and expressed through the living human personality. This capacity for perception and understanding of man is part of what we refer to as the "art of medicine."

Eighty years ago, James Jackson in his *Letters to a Young Physician*[2] said:

> From this day you must realize more and more the difference between the study of the sciences and the application of them to the business of life—to the practice of your art. . . . First, because many principles on which we act are not established on certain ground; and therefore they must be followed with great caution and constant watchfulness. Second, because there are few principles which are universal in their application.

Later, in the same letter he compares the art of medicine to that of navigation:

> In the practice of each of these arts we avail ourselves of the laws of nature to produce certain results. The seaman places his ship upon the waters, and avails himself of the winds to propel it. These winds are uncertain; they are not, in any way, subject to control, so that he cannot be sure as to the duration, the comfort, or even the safety of the voyage; he cannot furnish a pupil with positive rules by which to conduct his bark across the Atlantic. The captain must have regard to the qualities of his ship, the strength of his crew, and to the constantly varying circumstances of the weather. The complexity here is much less than attending the treatment of a disease; for in this we have to do with a living being.

Dr. George Reynolds, of the Harvard Medical School, has said:

> Medicine is not, and never will be, an exact science which can be practiced by the precise methods of reasoning and deduction of the mathematician, the chemist, or the physicist. The reaction, both mental and physical, of the human being to any external or internal factor is an ever present variable which prevents the accurate and unfailing relation between cause and effect that characterizes the work of the scientist. The engineer who wishes to construct a bridge that is to support a given weight can, through his knowledge of the strength of its component parts, prophesy with considerable accuracy the strength of the whole structure. The chemist can foretell the reaction that must result when two compounds are brought together under given conditions. But where living organisms are involved, individual variation precludes any such exactitude, and in medicine the innumerable social, economic, psychiatric, and phys-

2. Boston: Phillips, Sampson & Co., 1855.

ical elements of each situation make this variation an ever-changing factor in the reaction of the human being at various times in his life and even during the course of a brief illness.[3]

THE PREPARATION OF THE STUDENT

We are perhaps overwhelmed as we consider the task of medical education. How may the student be given this broad base of understanding during his relatively brief course in medical school? My own observation has led me to believe that when this kind of understanding is not developed during the formative years spent in medical school, it cannot readily be "grafted on" at a later point in the training process. It is important, of course, to stimulate and encourage the development of keener perception and greater understanding during the internship, but it is more fundamental that the habit of thinking of patients as social beings become established before internship is begun. This attitude or philosophy can be most effectively integrated with the student's whole concept of the practice of medicine if it has thoroughly permeated the entire curriculum of the medical school. When this permeation is lacking, the usual result is that the emerging young doctor regards the consideration of social factors as belonging to an allied field of social endeavor. He tolerates social service departments in hospitals as channels for the expression of a charitable interest in the poor and unfortunate. He defines social problems in terms of financial need and is oblivious to their presence in patients of sound economic status.

For the past two years, I have been associated with the dean of the Long Island College of Medicine and the professor of preventive medicine in an effort to develop a program whereby third-year students would have an opportunity to discover for themselves the value of knowing patients as persons and of understanding their environment in its fullest sense. A very important part of the plan which has been developed is that the major responsibility for its formal teaching aspects is invested in the professor of preventive medicine. As an instructor in his department and as director of the Department of Social Service

3. "The Teaching of the Medicosocial Aspects of Cases," *New England Journal of Medicine*, CCXX, No. 1 (January 5, 1939), 1–7.

in the hospital, I am available for consultation and guidance as the students carry on their case studies. Patients are selected during the third year, when these students are assigned to the clinics of the outpatient department. It is their first direct contact with patients and provides a real opportunity for the stimulation of a broad interest in patients as human beings. I shall not elaborate upon the details of this specific plan because it will be modified from time to time as we become more aware of the needs of our students. In passing, I would like to add by way of explanation that during some of the lecture hours which are assigned to the third-year course in preventive medicine selected case studies are presented by the students before the entire group and are discussed by the group. The professor of preventive medicine is in charge of the discussion period, and I am invited to participate at points when my help seems to be indicated. I am stressing this point because I think that it is fundamental that discussion of case material should always be clearly focused upon the medical problems presented and that leadership should be assumed by the medical profession itself.

I am going to devote the remainder of my paper to a consideration of the contribution which the medical social worker may make to such a program of teaching and to a brief enumeration of some of the results which have emerged from the case studies of these students.

THE FORMATION OF ATTITUDES

In the first place, it should be emphasized that good medical social casework practice should prevail in the clinic or hospital where this kind of teaching is being done. Otherwise the validity and therapeutic effectiveness of a sound plan of medical social treatment cannot be demonstrated, and theory becomes as "sounding brass and a tinkling cymbal." It is during these student days that later attitudes toward medical social service are in the process of formation, and it is important that the students have an opportunity to observe the finest quality of professional practice.

The most direct contribution of the medical social worker in this kind of program, however, is made through her consultative relationship with the students throughout the process of case study. Soon after the plan was initiated, I found the students eager and interested but also fearful and questioning. The process of selecting a particular patient for study was provocative of considerable anxiety for many students. I was frequently asked: "What will happen if I choose a patient and make a study and then find there are no social problems?" This type of question seemed to reflect the insecurity which all medical students feel as they approach the problem of diagnosis. They feel safe only when it is possible for them to demonstrate a direct correlation of the patient's symptoms, clinical findings, and laboratory reports. As they approach this new task of exploring the life-situation of their patient, there is something of the same fear—a fear that unless very obvious social pathology is revealed they will find themselves stranded in the midst of a fruitless search. Reassurance may be given by suggesting that they approach this study with an attitude of inquiry and that evaluation will come as a later step in the process. It is essential, I feel, that this anxiety of the student be recognized and relieved as much as possible, in order to enable him to establish a relationship with his patient and the family group which will be productive of real understanding. If he is driven by his own need to establish certain correlations, he may succeed in accumulating an impressive array of information and descriptive material without arriving at any real understanding of the patient or any real appreciation of how it all fits together in terms of the patient and his illness.

Another source of anxiety for the student is the whole problem of how an outsider may relate himself in a helpful and effective way to patients and their families in order that the process of social study may be carried on. It is not uncommon at all to find a student seriously questioning his right to inquire into the more intimate aspects of his patient's life. Many students wonder how they will be received at the time of a home visit and whether they may not be regarded as an intruder. At this point, emphasis is focused on the fact that the patient has expressed a desire for help by coming to the clinic to obtain relief from a distressing symptom. If he is assured of the doctor's real desire to be helpful, he will welcome this extension of the doctor's interest. My own experience as a case worker was frequently cited as evidence of how readily people respond to an attitude of interest and helpfulness. Many students subsequently express warm appreciation of the truth of this statement as they discover it for themselves. Later, they arrive at an appreciation of the fact that the physician has a real responsibility for knowing the problems of his patient and a realization that this responsibility has been overlooked in recent years because of the way in which medical care is now administered.

THE STUDENT'S REACTION

The selection of a patient for study and the initiation of the process of study are not the only points, however, when my help is needed. It is important to remember that each student brings to this experience his own personal equation which has evolved throughout his life. And so we find students reacting in varying ways and with varying degrees of feeling to the social situations which their studies reveal. It is not surprising that the student identifies rather quickly and intensely with some member of the social group he endeavors to study. It is this ability to identify which will help him to become the sensitive, intuitive, understanding type of physician later. It is only through identification of this sort that he is able to sense the feelings of others. Edna St. Vincent Millay has described this beautifully in her poem "Renascence" in the lines:

> A man was starving in Capri
> He moved his eyes and looked at me.
> I felt his gaze: I heard his moan
> And knew his hunger as my own.[4]

The student whose early life was disrupted by the separation and ultimate divorce of his parents may react rather violently to the discovery that his patient, a mother of six young children, is contemplating separation from her husband as a means of escape from an intolerable marital situation. Or the student whose early security was constantly threatened by the drinking escapades of

4. In *Renascence and Other Poems* (New York: Harper & Bros., 1917).

his father may assume a very critical and punishing attitude toward his patient if chronic alcoholism is discovered.

The following excerpt from one case study is illustrative of this type of reaction:

> In conclusion, we feel that Mr. A's condition as well as the plight of his family are due to his own stubbornness, stupidity, and evil habits. We don't feel that he can be helped by Social Service or by medical care, since he refuses to help himself or give up the habits that are slowly undermining his constitution. We do suggest, however, that an attempt should be made to assist Mrs. A and her daughter in ridding themselves of him.

Another problem concerning which great feeling is frequently expressed is that of financial dependency and the whole subject of public and private relief. Many students find dependency in patients very difficult to accept and are inclined to attribute this situation wholly to personal inadequacy and failure on the part of the patient. Others deplore the inadequacy of relief programs and identify strongly with the patient who they feel has not received just consideration from those upon whom he is dependent. In these varying attitudes, we find reflected each student's own cultural pattern and basic concept of what constitutes adequacy, as well as his own fears about financial security and the forces which threaten it. Another area which is very provocative of conflict in the student is found in the problems of patients which have to do with the relationship between parents and children. In one instance the possibility of foster-home placement of a greatly deprived child was under consideration. With great feeling the student commented that if he had discovered at the age of 21 that his own mother had allowed him to be placed in a foster-home, he would have killed her. At the same time, he expressed great hostility toward social workers who would permit such a thing to happen.

Another student became interested in an adolescent boy with diabetes, who refused to co-operate in the details of his care. Before becoming acquainted with the boy and his family group, the student expressed the feeling that this would be a simple problem to handle because all that the boy needed was to receive a good beating at the hands of his parents. He explained that that was the way such matters were handled in his own home. It was interesting to note that this student's final conclusions made no reference to physical punishment as a solution of the problem and placed special emphasis upon this boy's need of a big brother who would provide a more wholesome relationship than he could have with his aged and erratic parents.

THE SOCIAL WORKER'S OPPORTUNITY

As a consultant, the medical social worker has a real opportunity to help these students gradually arrive at a more mature, objective point of view. By the use of carefully selected questions, she is able to help them discover the reality factors in the patient's situation and sift out their own subjective interpretation of it. It is essential that students become aware of the external as well as internal factors which contribute to social distress and that they develop some understanding of our present social order, as well as an appreciation of the dynamics of human behavior. As physicians, they will need to have an understanding, tolerant attitude if they are to help individuals extricate themselves from life-situations which have made them ill and unhappy. This attitude is developed as a part of a growth experience and leads eventually to the kind of philosophy so admirably demonstrated by Will Rogers, who was often heard to say: "I never knew a man I couldn't like."

SOCIAL FACTORS IN THE PATIENT'S ILLNESS

In conclusion, I shall summarize briefly some of the evidence reflected in these case studies of a broadened understanding on the part of the student of the following:

1. The importance of the social aspects of medicine to the practice of their art
2. Their responsibility as physicians not only to the patient but to his family, the community, and humanity
3. How the social factors in an individual case may be elicited and evaluated in a scientific fashion
4. How a plan of treatment that is socially as well as medically adequate and applicable to the peculiar circumstances of the individual patient is evolved.

The diagnostic groups studied included those with tuberculosis, rheumatic heart disease, syphilis, diabetes, and nephritis, as well as a number of patients with no demonstrable evidence of physical pathology. One conclusion which appeared repeatedly in these studies had to do with the discovery of other health problems in the families of patients and indicated a realization that the physician must consider the total health problems of a family group. The observation frequently made was that many health problems had been neglected because of the financial inability of families to procure adequate care, and several students commented that even when the family income seemed sufficient to provide for maintenance needs, there was not enough surplus to pay for medical care. There was frequent reference to the influence of poor housing upon the development of rheumatic fever and of the role played by an inadequate diet. When the medical problem was that of tuberculosis, the students showed an active interest not only in arranging adequate care for the tuberculous patient but also in searching for the sources of infection in order that others might not be exposed. There was increased understanding of the so-called "unco-operative patient." One student discovered that a tuberculous patient signed herself out of a hospital ward because of her reaction to isolation technique and its implication that she was "unfit" to associate with others. Another student found that a mother, who had a healed tuberculous lesion, was emotionally unable to complete an examination of her daughter because of her feeling that if she was found to be tuberculous, the mother would be considered responsible and subject to blame from everyone.

There was increased understanding, also, of some of the reasons why certain patients attend clinic so frequently, even in the absence of demonstrable pathology. In the beginning, one student was quite intolerant of a young woman who had attended practically every clinic in the outpatient department for relief from fatigue and general weakness, which could not be accounted for by the usual studies. In conversation with a nurse, he learned that the patient seemed to be seeking companionship, attention, and sympathy. Greater familiarity with the details of this patient's life-story led this student to the following conclusions: "She has had a very unfortunate and depressing environmental background. She lacked love, guidance, and security.

Although the various charitable organizations tried their utmost to help her, we wonder if the help was more detrimental than beneficial, since in every case the home or institution in which she was placed never seemed to advance the sought-for love or affection."

Practically all of these studies included a medical social plan of treatment and reflected a real awareness of the need for constructing a plan which would insure adequate physical care and happiness for the patient. In the group of patients suffering from rheumatic heart disease, many students discovered factors at home which made adequate care impossible, and they evolved a plan for care away from home. Other students recognized the need for occupational or school adjustments and were quite resourceful in their attempts to bring this about. Some of them were quite startled by the degree of social adjustment which seemed indicated, and one student commented: "The solution of the problems of the S family will be very difficult, since successful management of the case would necessitate complete rearrangement of their family life."

THE PHYSICIAN'S UNDERSTANDING OF SOCIAL PROBLEMS

Dr. George R. Minot, professor of medicine of Harvard University, has so aptly described the combination of characteristics needed by the successful practitioner of medicine that I am going to close with a quotation from an article he has written:

It would seem as if individuals dealing with medical social problems needed a greater breadth of knowledge than workers in almost any other field. Besides the specialized knowledge of medical sociology and medicine, they must become students of men and recognize the uniqueness of each human being and his possibilities for growth. They must be fully alert to the stream of the world's thoughts as influenced by different cultures. An intimate knowledge of life's problems with ability to interpret another's life without prejudice is essential and this demands infinite tact and experience. Empirical and intuitive skill in managing one's relations with others is of great value. Those persons with a favored personality, whose perceptions, appreciations, and sensibilities are well suited to the task, have the character to make particularly successful practitioners or investigators of social problems.[5]

5. "Investigation and Teaching in the Field of the Social Component of Medicine," *Bulletin of the American Association of Medical Social Workers,* X, No. 2 (April, 1937), 9–18.

Training of Interns in the Social Aspects of Illness[1]

BY ETHEL COHEN AND HARRY A. DEROW

SINCE 1929 a plan for the training of interns[2] in the social aspects of medicine has been carried on at the Beth Israel Hospital, Boston.[3] The purpose of this paper is to present an evaluation of this plan following ten years' experience.

The plan has aimed to develop an appreciation that (1) the practice of medicine is not merely the treatment of sickness but the care of sick persons, (2) the everyday circumstances of life play an important role in creating illness, (3) illness with its accompanying problems often disrupts normal existence, and (4) consideration of social factors is consequently an inseparable part of the process of diagnosis and treatment. The objectives of the plan have been met by requiring the senior intern to (*a*) acquire comprehensive social knowledge himself about each patient in his ward; (*b*) discuss these data at regular weekly medical social ward rounds with the resident and the medical social worker assigned to the particular service; and (*c*) share the responsibility for plans for therapy or aftercare based on the realities of each patient's social as well as medical needs.

During his six-month period as senior at this hospital, the intern studies and treats approximately 300 patients. By the systematic consideration of every patient in the ward in the manner described, he realizes, through the many vicissitudes in the treatment of patients, that there are interrelationships between the

1. Reprinted from the *Journal of the American Medical Association*, November 22, 1941, with the permission of the American Medical Association.
2. H. A. Derow and Ethel Cohen, "The Training of Interns in the Social Aspects of Medicine," *New England Journal of Medicine*, CCIX (October 26, 1933), 827–31.
3. A two hundred and twenty-five bed voluntary, nonsectarian, general hospital and outpatient department, with teaching affiliations with Harvard Medical School, Tufts College Medical School, and the Simmons College School of Social Work.

patient's personality, his social environment, his illness, and his response to medical therapy. The practice of considering each patient individually in his social as well as his physical aspects becomes an established habit of thinking, persisting in private practice or medical teaching.

A procedure of this sort places on the intern additional responsibility beyond the technical medical study and treatment of patients. It is time-consuming. It involves for most interns a new orientation in thought concerning patients and illness, for during most of four undergraduate medical years the student has, with some exceptions, concentrated largely on the physical and scientific aspects of disease.

During undergraduate study, treatment has been viewed usually from the standpoint of drugs, surgery, roentgen ray and other technical procedures. The great amount of technical medical knowledge which must be crowded into the short time available to the students during the latter part of their undergraduate study makes it increasingly difficult for them to see each patient in all his dimensions and with perspective. Instead of the hospitalization period being an episode in the patient's life, it frequently occupies the full range of the student's view. Though patients have been seen by some students with their individual physical and even psychic differentiation, not enough emphasis has been placed during undergraduate study on (*a*) the patient in his social setting, (*b*) the interaction of the patient's social situation and his illness or disability, (*c*) the patient's attitude toward the situation created by his illness, (*d*) the difficulties involved for the particular patient in a proposed plan of care, and (*e*) the possibilities of the recommended plan being carried out.

In certain teaching hospitals, conferences on the medical and social interrelationships of illness in the case of a few patients have been carried out.[4] These discussions have been of value in demonstrating to the medical student the existence of another important phase of medicine. This experience, though valuable,

4. Ethel Cohen and H. A. Derow, "Teaching Medical Students Objectives for Care of Patients and Social Aspects of Illness," *Archives of Internal Medicine*, LVI (August, 1935), 351–59.

is brief and usually not comprehensive enough to help him with the individual problems he meets later during his internship and in his private practice.

During the internship period the young physician becomes responsible for the care of patients; then the need for understanding sick people and helping them with their problems becomes vivid.

MEDICAL SOCIAL WARD ROUNDS

The procedure that serves at the Beth Israel Hospital is known as "medical social ward rounds'" and is conducted at a specified time each week. The resident physician, the senior intern, and the medical social worker assigned to the service meet and discuss each patient. The senior intern presents a statement of the social data which he has secured himself in interviews with each patient, including facts relative to home conditions, economic stability, and factors for consideration of aftercare. The intern is expected to know the type of home and neighborhood from which the patient comes and the suitability of this environment for convalescence. He must know whether the patient has a dependent family or whether there are children at home without care, about whom the patient may be worried. The possible existence of emotional factors or conflicts within the home must also be appreciated. In regard to economic stability, he should learn whether or not the patient has financial worries, is unemployed, or is in fear of losing his job while ill. From the beginning the intern should realize that he will be asked for advice as to the patient's aftercare, and he must therefore consider whether the patient can understand and will follow instructions and whether he will be able to carry heavy housekeeping duties or be able to provide for a special diet or appliance, if necessary. Also he should study the possibilities of the need for adjustment of occupation or of school work. In addition to these social data, the intern describes the medical aspects of the patient's illness during medical social ward rounds. This includes a statement of the patient's physical and mental condition, the probable duration of hospitalization, the outlook for the immediate present and for the long-range view, a statement relative to ability to resume activity or need for its limitation at home, at work, or at school, and recommendations as to the type of care that the patient will require following discharge from the hospital.

This material is discussed by the three participants in this procedure, and a decision is made as to which of these patients present problems which the medical social worker should take up for further social study and case work service. During these rounds the medical social worker also reports on the developments in the patients still in the wards whose problems had been taken up on previous rounds. After all the cases have been presented, they are reviewed briefly to determine which seem to call for immediate attention and which may be deferred. This joint evaluation and discussion, valuable for its own sake in promoting further thought on these problems, is necessary also because of the social service department's policy of limitation of intake and selection of problems accepted for service.

In the intervals between these weekly rounds, the intern, and frequently the resident and the medical social worker, have numerous informal discussions concerning progress in the patients under their care. In addition, the interns often request the medical social worker to join a discussion of the patient's condition and future care with the relatives after the regular ward visiting hours.

The medical diagnoses, prognoses, and general questions of aftercare are, of course, taken up by the visiting staff on the regular daily morning ward rounds with the interns in attendance. The data secured during these daily visits with the staff physicians form the basis for the material which the senior intern presents at the medical social ward rounds. The visiting physicians are occasionally consulted by the senior intern and the social worker in special types of cases. These include the following situations:

a) When the recommendation is made for a radical change in the patient's work or general way of life.

b) When the medical social plan is not accepted by a patient seriously ill and a safe compromise is needed.

c) When social plans involve large expenditures of money, either by the patient or by the community, for chronic or convalescent care.

d) When the diagnosis is still in doubt, and the patient does not require further hospital care for an acute condition but home facilities seem inadequate.

e) In a small miscellaneous group of complex and delicate problems which require more mature judgment.

It is to be noted that this procedure has been carried on in both the surgical and the medical ward service. Initially, we accepted the common opinion that the surgeon's preoccupation with the technique of operative and postoperative care precludes interest in the social and emotional aspects of his patients' illnesses. We no longer hold this view. Some of the most thoughtful, imaginative, and responsive men have been interns in surgery. Despite the exigencies of urgent operations and the unexpected postoperative emergencies, surgical interns have served as well in this procedure as the medical interns.

THE LEARNING PROCESS THROUGH JOINT THINKING AND DISCUSSION
BETWEEN INTERN, RESIDENT, AND SOCIAL WORKER

When the intern begins his experience with medical social ward rounds he is apt to disregard social data as unimportant and to dismiss certain patients with the remark "there is no social problem here." He may believe this because of his inability to evaluate the social history he has secured. The social worker, however, appreciating that the intern has not yet had the experience to justify this statement, asks him what he found the situation to be. Sometimes the intern has adequate information and believes that he is able to make a judgment as valid as the social worker's. However, because of the difference in training and professional orientation, the same facts often have different significance for the intern and the medical social worker. Two brief examples are presented here for illustration:

Case 1.—A man aged 42, a moving picture operator, was unable to resume work because of severe malignant hypertension. He earned, when employed, $90 a week. He owned the home in which his wife and four young children lived. The intern believed that an intelligent patient of this economic level required only medical care from the physician with no further concern by the physician or anyone else. The serious nature of the illness, the patient's feelings about his situation, the need for the patient's adequate care following hospitalization, and the question as to the potential dependence of his wife and young children during the terminal phase of the illness and afterward were the implications which impressed the medical social worker from the facts as finally related by the intern, rather than the income and homeownership. A subsequent interview with the patient and family revealed the patient greatly worried because of heavy debts, no savings, threat of losing his heavily mortgaged home, dependence on friends and relatives, and serious family friction and distrust.

Case 2.—The intern learned from a ward patient that she was a dietitian, that her son was in a private school, and that she had earned $135 a month, but had not worked for five months because of illness and was living at a private club. The medical diagnosis was not clear, and, since exploratory operation was being considered, a period of convalescence would be needed before she could return to work. The intern thought it unnecessary to spend any time beyond the strictly medical care of this patient because "she presents no social problem." He considered $135 a month a large income and assumed the existence of other income or savings for the maintenance of a son at a private school. More significant to the social worker even than the patient's wages was the five-month period of unemployment because of illness. Also, she wondered what kind of "private school" would take a boy whose mother had not earned even her usual $30 a week for five months. Additional study revealed the facts that the "dietitian" was a domestic employed at $10 a week and that her illegitimate son was in an institution under the care of a social agency. The club which the intern named as the patient's home was known to the social worker as a place where unemployed working women could procure food and lodging for a temporary period. There was no possibility of convalescent care there.

It is clear that the intern had not been aware that the "facts" lacked inner consistency, nor had he been concerned with the possible reason why the patient felt it necessary to present herself in this light.

At times the intern may present social data without understanding the sginificance of the data for the particular patient discussed. The social worker asks for more information which would apply particularly to the age, marital status, occupation, responsibilities, and attitudes of the individual patient. She may raise questions about the medical data, such as: What is the significance of this illness? Is it progressive, self-limited or will it be quiescent for a period and become reactivated later? How does the type and extent of the illness affect a particular patient? The self-limited illness in a given patient may present no special problems which the patient or his family cannot manage themselves, but a chronic progressive illness of the same patient and with the same social situation may change the pattern of life of the patient and his entire family.

Through such continuous questioning the intern becomes increasingly aware of the need for relating the patient's social situation to the particular medical problem. The social worker shares with the intern the knowledge that she has gained in her social study of a particular patient through interviews with family, social agencies, school, or other relevant sources. Her data may either confirm his social history, elaborate on it, or correct it. Her contribution will be the result of her skill derived from training and experience in her own specialized field of social work. In time, the intern gains appreciation of the meaning and interrelationship of the various social and medical data. Just as the trained medical social worker through experience gains an appreciation of the prognosis and possible plan of treatment in certain illnesses, so does the intern in the course of time develop skill in gathering and evaluating social data and an awareness of the inherent relationship of potential social factors with certain medical diagnoses. This process, which was at first conscious and deliberate with practice, becomes less conscious and more habitual.

Usually one of the foremost objectives of the intern is disposition of the patient, making possible new admissions and new medical experiences. While this primary objective of the house officer is being furthered by the social worker indirectly, the intern is becoming habituated to the consideration of the social factors of each patient.

The resident contributes to both intern and social worker from his longer experience and greater knowledge. The intern and social worker each has his own particular function and professional skill, but neither can carry out his function in the care of the patient completely by himself. At certain points and many times their functions are interrelated and merge. They must think and practice in co-ordination and harmony.

The development of understanding, insight, and skill is a gradual process. The rate of progress depends on many factors within the intern and within the medical social worker: their ability to "give and take," to interpret to each other the special knowledge each has and to accept each other as professional workers sharing in the study and care of the sick.

SUBJECTS DISCUSSED DURING MEDICAL SOCIAL WARD ROUNDS

A wide range of subjects is covered in the course of the discussions during rounds. These relate to the particular problems encountered or the obstacles to the carrying out of the plans agreed on. Some of these subjects are:

1. The description of the elements of a home maintained on a marginal or substandard income.

2. The effects on the patient's immediate health and on family life of overcrowding, inadequate equipment, insufficient heat, light, and air.

3. Description of various community resources, their policies, and the conditions of acceptance for service or care.

4. The absence of necessary resources, the consequent need to devise substitutes and to consider relative advantages or disadvantages of several possible alternatives for the case in question.

5. The influence of the various racial and cultural traditions and customs on the patient's and family's relationships to each other, to certain kinds of illness, to hospitalization, to home care, to diet, and to dependence.

6. The influence of emotional strain, economic inadequacy, and other unfavorable social conditions on the illness.

7. Analysis of factors for consideration in securing "complete rest" or "modified activity" for a mother with small children; for young or old persons living alone in a rooming house or hotel; and like situations.

8. The unfavorable effect on the sick person of demands that unwilling relatives provide care, as contrasted with the more favorable opportunity for the patient's improvement when the responsibility for care is assumed in adequate community resources.

9. The need to understand the forces operating in the so-called uncooperative patient who demands discharge against advice; the hospital's responsibility to see that the patient may know how to secure sound medical care elsewhere or to allow the patient to return to the hospital again if he wishes.

10. The importance of ascertaining the physical and emotional health of relatives who will bear the burden of care for seriously handicapped or chronically ill patients.

11. The importance of weighing both the probable psychologic and the economic effects on the individual patient of recommendation to give up work entirely or to change radically his occupation even in the presence of a chronic progressive illness.

12. Appreciation of the length of time needed by the medical social worker, community social worker, or family to mobilize resources, even when all are working at maximum speed, and the variation in amount of time needed because of varying intelligence, emotional maturity of patient or relatives, and financial resources.

13. The hospital's responsibility for care of the patient as its major responsibility, as well as the advancement of the intern's opportunity for handling a maximum number and variety of patients.

These by no means constitute all the subjects discussed during rounds or in the intervals between rounds. All these concepts and undoubtedly many more are the subjects of discussion in all hospitals where trained medical social workers and interns work together. The significant difference in the plan here described is that these discussions are habitual, regular, and frequent and include a large number of patients. The cumulative knowledge and the increase in understanding derived from experience with a large number of cases tend to develop in the intern the habit of considering all his patients in terms of the nonmedical aspects.

PARTICIPANTS IN THE PLAN

THE INTERN

Interns vary considerably in the rapidity and manner in which they learn to appreciate the importance of social factors in disease. This is because of differences in personality, interest in people, administrative ability as senior wardsman, degree of confidence relative to medical knowledge, ability to accept questions from the social worker which the intern may not be able to answer and to acknowledge the need to consult the visiting physician. Interns with whom representatives of other departments have difficulty will usually present difficulties in relations with the social worker.

The integration of previously acquired scientific knowledge with newly acquired social concepts may at first be difficult. It is definitely influenced by the intern's previous social experience and in turn often involves change in his social outlook. Problems of patients often stir up problems in the intern's own life, producing subjective reactions that influence his thought and activities concerning the patient. For example, some men who have earned their way through school, college, and medical school, carrying family burdens as well, at first believe that everyone else could help himself if he "willed" to do so. Not "willing" to do so, the patient is therefore unworthy of help from society. Other men, coming from an economically well-favored environment initially, may have no appreciation of pain, want, loneliness, strife, or of the dread of dependence, while others from similarly well-favored backgrounds may be overprotective and urge assistance even when none is desired by the patient. For many patients independence and self-maintenance, even on a meager scale, are their most treasured possessions.

THE RESIDENT

Brief reference has already been made to the role of the resident. In the organization of the Beth Israel Hospital, the intern is responsible to the resident. The resident's presence during medical social ward rounds provides the medical social worker with support and authority, which are especially necessary in the early period of each senior intern's experience. The resident can often influence the intern's evaluation of the patient's condition, prognosis, and needs following discharge from the hospital. From the resident's comments the social worker likewise gains considerable medical knowledge and understanding.

A resident indifferent to this aspect of medical care may be a real handicap to both intern and social worker, while an interested resident can greatly further its development.

THE MEDICAL SOCIAL WORKER

The high degree of co-operation involved in this kind of teamwork requires tact, stability, and resourcefulness on the part of the social worker. Her contribution will be more effective as she learns how to share her specialized knowledge with the intern. She must be mature enough emotionally to accept some interns' reluctance at times to share medical data sufficient for her comprehensive understanding of the total medical situation and their unwillingness at times to accept her interpretation of emotional and social factors and their relationship to the particular patient's medical problem.

Our experience has demonstrated that the medical social worker participating in this procedure should be a well-prepared, professionally experienced, and mature person. She must be secure in the knowledge of her own function and of the philosophy and concepts of present-day social work. Unless she is able to express her ideas clearly and to demonstrate them convincingly through her practice, she will have little success in influencing the young physician's point of view or in stimulating his interest in a broad concept of medical care. She must know how to work understandingly with the intern, whose authority as senior wardsman is important to him but whose theoretical knowledge has not yet been tempered by professional experience. The knowledge acquired over a period of years by medical social workers from close working association with physicians in a procedure of this kind increases their usefulness to the patient, to the hospital, and to other community agencies.

The advantage of having the same medical social worker assigned to these ward rounds for a long period of time is considerable. Opportunity for cumulative learning and understanding of the intern's problems and psychology can be attained only by continuous experience with many different interns. Because of the periodic changes of interns, the possibilities of the maintenance of this system of rounds are greatly enhanced by continuity in service of the same medical social worker. As each man completes his training period, he is succeeded by another intern. The resident may serve for one year only. Thus the entire process is re-created anew every few months. The medical social worker is the one practitioner in this team who, because she is a permanent staff worker, can promote the purposes of an integrated service to the patient.

EVALUATION BY THE GRADUATES OF MEDICAL
SOCIAL WARD ROUNDS

Throughout these years we have been formulating our own conclusions as to the values of the plan from our observations and indirect participation, but we desired, in addition, the testimony of men who had actually had the experience and had reacted to it in various ways. A conference was held with twelve graduates. Their comments were of such interest as to stimulate us to elicit the reactions of the entire number of interns and residents, fifty-three in all, who had participated during the ten years that the plan has been in use. The questionnaire method was decided on as the most practicable because many of the graduates were practicing in various parts of the country.

As interns, these fifty-three men were graduates of a number of different medical schools. They represented a variety of professional interests, skill, and ability.

It was expected that some of the graduates would respond negatively to the rounds because of the amount of time and thought required in the whole process and because of certain psychologic reactions or social points of view. In order to secure full and free expression of opinion and comment, the questionnaire, worded so as to encourage negative replies, was sent out over the signature of the medical author only.

SUBJECTS INCLUDED IN THE QUESTIONNAIRE SENT TO GRADUATES

The graduates were requested to discuss the parts of the procedure to which they objected and to state whether they found it difficult to secure social information from the patient. They

TABLE 1

FIELD OF PRACTICE OF FIFTY-THREE GRADUATES
OF BETH ISRAEL HOSPITAL

Field of Practice	No.	Total
Medicine.............................	.....	34
Private practice:		
Internal medicine...................	20	......
Gastroenterology...................	2	......
Allergy...........................	1	......
General practice......:	2	25
Internships.......................	2	2
Residencies.......................	5	5
Full-time medical research...........	1	1
Full-time psychiatrist in mental hospital.	1	1
Surgery................................	.....	19
Private practice:		
Surgery...........................	8	......
Surgery, gynecology, and obstetrics...	2	......
General practice, emphasis on surgery..	4	14
Veterans Administration..............	1	1
Residencies.......................	4	4

were asked to evaluate which aspect of the plan they considered of value to the patient, to the hospital, and to themselves during their period of training and whether the experience had been of value to them in their private practice. The graduates who are now teaching medical students were asked to describe the method by which they bring into their teaching their consideration of the patient as a whole. They were also asked to suggest changes for improvement of the plan and to comment on any point not covered by the questionnaire.

ANALYSIS OF THE REPLIES TO THE QUESTIONNAIRE

Replies were received from every graduate, in most instances within a week. An analysis was made of the distribution of graduates as to present geographic location, field of practice and medical school teaching affiliations and is recorded in Tables 1–3.

There was considerable agreement on many points by both the medical and the surgical graduates. A selection of their com-

TABLE 2

PRESENT MEDICAL SCHOOL
TEACHING AFFILIATIONS

Medical School	Medical Graduates	Surgical Graduates
Harvard	12	4
Tufts	1	3
Western Reserve	1	....
Albany	1	....
Yale	1	....
Harvard and Tufts	2	....
Cornell	1	....
Emory	....	1
Total	19	8

TABLE 3

PRESENT GEOGRAPHIC LOCATION
OF GRADUATES

State	Medical Graduates	Surgical Graduates
Massachusetts	23	12
New York	3	1
Ohio	2	....
Illinois	1	....
California	1	....
Connecticut	2	....
Missouri	1	1
Rhode Island	1	1
Florida	....	1
Washington, D.C.	....	1
Georgia	....	1
Pennsylvania	....	1
Total	34	19

ments for this paper was made on the basis of characteristic replies or of evidence of unusual understanding of the aims of the plan.

1. *Parts of the procedure to which objections were raised.*— Seven medical graduates objected to the time taken up by the rounds from their other responsibilities. Two of these men believed that there was no advantage to be gained from rounds which could not be as well accomplished by some other technique. One of the men who had objected in the beginning that it was time-consuming with experience changed his point of view, as it then "seemed a worth-while expenditure of time."

Four surgical graduates, though they did not object to any part of the procedure, wished that they could have had more time to give to it.

2. *Difficulties in securing social information from patients.*— Six medical and four surgical graduates found it difficult to secure financial data from the patients. This was the only point about which they thought that they had had difficulty in the early part of their experience. This, they believed, without substantiating evidence, to be due to the patients' fear that the physician's knowledge of their financial circumstances might in some way adversely affect their care in the wards. A few graduates thought that the difficulty in securing accurate information was due to the patient's pride or his desire to conceal his economic state. Undoubtedly, practice in interviewing increased their skill, since the graduates who found this a problem at first stated that it became less difficult with experience.

3. *Values to the patient.*—All the medical and surgical graduates felt that the plan was of value to the patients. They mentioned the importance of appreciation of the social and economic background of the patient so that their therapeutic procedures and recommendations would be feasible. The patient was considered in terms of his total disability rather than in terms of pathologic lesions. Often asking the patient for social information opened up a general discussion in which the patient revealed emotional conflicts and their causes. It made possible a better handling of convalescence and the care of chronic disease while

at home. Adequate aftercare was secured for a great many patients who otherwise would have returned to the hospital in similar sick conditions.

Patients benefited by the interns' increased realization of the social implications. This was particularly true of those interns who had not been exposed either by their own personal experiences or by observation to the effect of low economic status, environment, and adverse relationships on people. The patients appreciated the hospital's interest, which extended beyond the period of hospitalization.

4. *Values to the hospital.*—All the medical and surgical graduates felt that the plan was of distinct value to the hospital. An adequate plan for aftercare frequently reduced the period of hospitalization and eliminated unnecessary readmissions, thus assisting the hospital in maintaining its status as an institution for the care of acute illness and in rendering maximum service to the community.

5. *Values to graduates during their period of training.*—All the medical men believed that it had value for them during the period of their training in the wards. All the surgical graduates felt that it had value to them excepting one, and he wasn't sure. The typical replies from all the graduates indicated that this experience increased their understanding of the patient; that it removed the "case" attitude; that it was a valuable adjunct in the handling of patients not obtainable from textbooks or lectures. It taught them how to plan the care of patients following hospitalization, which had not been included in their training up to that time, and gave them a long-term view of every patient's illness. It gave an excellent background for evaluating the factor of the human and environmental equation in the causation, aggravation, and recrudescence of functional and organic symptoms. It tended to establish a closer interest in the patient as an individual, enabling the intern to learn more from each problem, and at times gave the clue to the diagnosis in psychoneurosis and in other personality problems. Also, recommendations which were impossible for the patients to carry out were eliminated. Various types of aftercare were learned and the difficulties encountered in arranging for them.

6. *Values of the experience to graduates in their private practice.*—All the graduates expressed the view that a greater understanding of the patients resulted from the experience. Also, it "developed the human touch appreciated by patients" and emphasized the great part that economic factors may play in illness and in the recovery from illness. By acquiring a greater understanding of the patient, some of the graduates believed that they had been rewarded both by a broadened experience and by a greater financial return.

7. *Method by which graduates bring into their teaching their consideration of the patient.*—Among the replies from medical graduates now engaged in teaching medical students were included the following methods: Insistence on complete social data for better understanding of the presenting symptoms and intelligent treatment; consideration of disposition of the patient as active therapy, not as a finale to a temporary episode; the need for knowledge of the patient and his environment so that plans for disposition will be "feasible, adaptable, and profitable."

One of the graduates wrote:

In my third year teaching on the medical wards in the afternoon, several patients with the same diagnosis are discussed. The social aspects are considered, not as a separate entity but as part of the patient's history. When a patient's history is taken, he is not first asked about his pain, but what he does and how he lives. As the patient's history reveals economic insufficiency or unemployment or strain, then the students are told about the failure of medical therapy alone in given cases where these social elements are an important factor. For example, in a patient with a gastric ulcer, the unmet need for special diet or family troubles may prevent the medical treatment from becoming effective. As some of the patients are taken up several times, the students then see that their fancy therapy doesn't work.

8. *Changes recommended and comments.*—Practically no suggestions for change were made, excepting that one or two graduates suggested the expansion of the rounds to include the visiting physicians. Several of the graduates associated with other hospitals commented on the greater possibilities for service to patients by the procedure of medical social ward rounds in which they had previously participated and the lack of which they now regretted.

CONTRIBUTION OF THIS PLAN TO PREPARATION OF
MEDICAL TEACHERS FOR TEACHING STUDENTS
THE SOCIAL ASPECTS OF ILLNESS

During the early years of the use of this plan of training interns, both of us were responsible for teaching fourth-year medical students the social aspects of illness. However, as the interns and residents graduated and received medical school teaching appointments, a number of them became teachers in the seminars on the social aspects of illness to fourth-year students of Harvard and Tufts medical schools assigned to Beth Israel Hospital. The schedule for this teaching is so arranged that the graduates responsible for the regular medical teaching in the wards also conduct the conferences for the teaching of the social aspects of illness later the same morning. In both aspects of this teaching, as a result of their earlier training, the graduates quite naturally and without conscious effort discuss the patient's illness in terms of the particular patient's individuality. The medical social author of this paper has participated in all special conferences on the social aspects and has been greatly impressed by the understanding and enthusiasm which these physicians have brought to this teaching.

In addition to the number who have taught fourth-year students, there are other graduates who are assigned to medical teaching for second- and third-year students. The third-year students at the Beth Israel Hospital work in the medical clinic of the outpatient department, where for the first time they take histories, examine patients, make diagnoses, and suggest treatment. The Beth Israel graduates who serve as instructors put considerable emphasis on a comprehensive history, stressing the relationship of the social and personal items in the history to the past and present illness and physical examination. As the instructor senses a social component which has bearing on the health situation, he discusses this with the students himself. When the patients present complex social problems or situations which require social assistance, the instructor suggests that the student take the problem up directly with the medical social worker. She may elaborate on the less obvious social implications of the problem at the time the patient is referred to her. Later, after she has studied the situation and given some case work service, she will report her observations to the student and the instructor. At times this presents an occasion for discussion of broad questions of social import in relation to illness. All of this is carried on informally and as naturally as the student is taught the use of laboratory aids to diagnosis.

It is believed that the training which the intern receives in medical social ward rounds offers a logical opportunity for preparing potential medical instructors for their future responsibilities.

SUMMARY

Medical social ward rounds, as carried on at the Beth Israel Hospital, constitute a regular part of the official duties of the senior intern, resident, and medical social ward worker.

As a tested practice over a period of ten years, the plan has been evaluated by the authors and all fifty-three graduates who have participated in the procedure during this time. Of the fifty-three graduates from "straight" internships or residencies, thirty-four were medical and nineteen were surgical. They are located in twelve states. Twenty-seven graduates are teaching in seven medical schools, nineteen medical graduates in five schools, and eight surgical graduates in three schools.

Principal among the special features of the plan are:

a) The responsibility placed on the intern himself to secure a comprehensive knowledge of the patient's social as well as his physical history, so that he may be able to think of the patient in terms of his totality. This replaces the more usual hospital practice in which the social worker takes the responsibility for securing social data.

b) A review by the intern with the resident and medical social ward worker of the data he has learned, considering each sick person in terms of his own personality and environment.

c) Discussion by the medical social worker with intern and resident concerning significant social implications unrecognized or unappreciated by the intern to which the trained experienced medical social worker contributes insight and understanding. This aims to broaden his view to consideration of illness and disability beyond the more limited concept of diagnosis and disease.

d) Sharing by the intern with the medical social worker in the selection of patients with complex social or emotional problems requiring further social study and treatment by medical social workers or community workers equipped to provide other specialized services.

e) Sharing with the medical social worker in planning for care of the patient following hospitalization. This furthers his understanding of obstacles within the patient or his surroundings which may arise to prevent or delay execution of both simple and complex recommendations for treatment. From this cumulative experience with a large number of patients, he derives a broad knowledge of community life and its resources or lack of resources for health and social welfare.

The experience derived from medical social ward rounds has been of great value to most of the graduates as a preparation for the realities of private practice.

It has provided an unusual opportunity for the preparation of physicians for teaching medical students.

Recognition is given to the periodic change of service of interns and residents in a teaching hospital. The emphasis must be kept on the training or educational aspects of this procedure. Once initiated and developed, this plan cannot be left to progress by itself as a tradition. It must be re-created anew with each new resident, intern, and medical social worker. Therefore, the maintenance of medical social ward rounds as a service and as a training opportunity requires the enthusiasm and sustaining interest of physicians and surgeons of senior rank and of the director of the social service department.

In the ten years of the development and maintenance of this procedure, difficulties were encountered. Most of these were overcome through increased experience and professional maturity on the part of the participants. Therefore, it is believed that teaching interns the social aspects of illness by medical social ward rounds has proved to be a valid method. Further use of the method will develop deeper understanding of the problems involved and may indicate adaptations which will enhance its value.

Teaching of Social and Environmental Factors in Medicine: Some Unsolved Problems[1]

BY HARRIETT M. BARTLETT AND WILLIAM W. BECKMAN

THE challenge of the unsolved problems of medical education must reach persons who will do something about them," says Dr. Raymond B. Allen in his book on *Medical Education and the Changing Order*. The recent study of the teaching of social and environmental factors in medicine raised some difficult problems, which were not presented in the published report,[2] lest the reader be confused. We feel, however, that everyone closely concerned with the teaching of medical students must face them, since without such recognition the whole picture appears greatly oversimplified. Further progress seems to depend upon clear definition of the major issues.

This whole phase of medical teaching relating to the patient and his social environment is a live subject today. Deans and medical faculty are eager to do something about it. Early efforts took the form of separate projects initiated by individual teachers, but interest is rapidly extending to every section of the medical curriculum. In a previous paper[3] one of us discussed the teaching of the individual student—in application of knowl-

1. Presented at a meeting of the American Association of Medical Social Workers in Atlantic City on April 21, 1948. Reprinted from the *Bulletin of the American Association of Medical Social Workers*, September, 1949, with the permission of the association. The material in this paper is largely a rearrangement of material originally prepared for the Joint Committee on the Teaching of the Social and Environmental Factors in Medicine but not published in its final report.

2. *Widening Horizons in Medical Education: A Study of the Teaching of Social and Environmental Factors in Medicine: A Report of the Joint Committee of the Association of American Medical Colleges and the American Association of Medical Social Workers* (New York: Commonwealth Fund, 1948).

3. W. W. Beckman, "Some Aspects of the Clinical Teaching of the Social and Environmental Factors in Medicine," *Journal of the Association of American Medical Colleges*, XXII (May, 1947), 149.

edge in specific cases, in acquisition of skills, in relating himself to his teacher and his patient, in developing as a professional person. Now we are ready to widen our focus to consider
some of the problems involved in organizing this instruction in
the medical curriculum as a whole.

RELATION BETWEEN SOCIAL AND EMOTIONAL FACTORS

At once we face the difficulty that we are not dealing with
clear-cut subject matter, as in most other branches of medicine.

1. The social sciences are relatively undeveloped, and much of the
present understanding of human behavior is based on a limited number of
scientific concepts combined with many practical observations.
2. The knowledge with which we are concerned spreads across several
disciplines, including sociology, anthropology, psychology, and others.
3. Ideas cannot be dealt with independently but only in terms of rather
complex interrelationships.

Being conditioned to another type of subject matter, the
medical mind does not yet feel at home with this sort of material. To us it seems, however, that some of the most crucial
problems of medicine today lie in this very area of elusive concepts and complex interrelationship of ideas and that medical
educators must grapple with these unsolved difficulties.

We have observed that many medical teachers proceed on the
assumption that knowledge of the objective social and environmental factors is sufficient for the understanding of a case. But,
as the psychiatric members of our joint committee repeatedly
emphasized, social and environmental factors impinge upon the
individual's health largely through the feelings and reactions of
the patient and his personal associates; it is these mediating personality factors which give the clue to understanding. Thus it
is not what happens, by and large, that makes a particular event
important or unimportant in a case. It is *how the patient feels
about what happens* that is important.[4]

This means that every medical student must learn to understand the common range of patients' emotional responses to social and environmental problems and to evaluate the specific

4. Personal communications from Dr. Howard W. Potter and Dr. John C.
Whitehorn.

reaction of the individual patient against this range.[5] He must have in mind that people are not just physical organisms, or rational beings, but also respond emotionally in ways that often appear quite irrational to the observer and may be wholly unconscious to the individual himself. The student who has such a background will find that he is much more successful in discriminating as to the nature and causes of his patients' reactions. He is now in a position to relate social and emotional factors more pertinently to his thinking about the etiology of the illness, the present diagnosis, and the measures for treatment.[6]

The problem is, how to teach this unfamiliar type of material—how to break it down so that teachers can handle it and students can grasp it. From the experience of our recent study it is evident that there is some confusion regarding the relation between social and emotional factors. We have discussed the means for dealing with this subject matter with many medical teachers from various clinical fields (including psychiatry). Most of them believe that the subject is important, but one gets no real sense of agreement among them. A discussion which starts impersonally may run into departmental lines and break down through the feeling thus engendered. An honest effort to consider how teaching about emotional factors could spread more widely through the curriculum may be misunderstood as an attempt to devaluate the psychiatrist's role or to force a psychiatric consultant upon a general medical teacher.

One illustration may show the difficulties involved. Several psychiatrists pointed out to us that social factors affect patients mainly through emotionally charged attitudes. Therefore, they went on to say, in their opinion this makes it essentially a psychiatric problem. A conclusion to this statement, sometimes verbalized and sometimes implicit, is that psychiatrists are the only persons who can really deal with this whole area. We found some medical teachers who wanted to delegate all such teaching to psychiatrists for this very reason. It has seemed to us that such categorical thinking may block all forward movement. It

5. "Conclusions concerning Psychiatric Training and Clinics," *Public Health Reports*, LXI (June 28, 1946), 943.

6. John Romano, "Psychiatry in Undergraduate Medical Education," *Bulletin of the Menninger Clinic*, IX (March, 1945), 34.

is an oversimplification which does not evaluate adequately either the interrelationship of concepts or the relative responsibilities of the various teachers.

In the effort to clarify the picture in our own minds we have arrived at several distinctions which seem particularly important to prevent misunderstanding:

1. Psychiatry as a discipline now customarily covers not only psychopathology but also the growth of normal personality, and sometimes all emotional reactions.
2. The use of psychiatric knowledge in medical teaching by any qualified teacher should be distinguished from the specific teaching which only the psychiatrist is qualified to undertake.
3. What is necessary practice now, because of limited spread of psychiatric knowledge, should not be regarded as a pattern for all future practice.

If we examine the manner in which social and emotional problems are handled in actual care of the patient, we obtain some helpful clues as to how the subject might be handled in the curriculum. When an emotional problem is relatively simple, any one of the professional persons working with the patient—such as doctor, nurse, or social worker—is likely to deal with it directly. When an emotional difficulty seems to be tied up with social maladjustments in such a manner that change in the social environment will probably ease the pressures and modify the attitudes, the social worker is usually the one to assume responsibility. When, however, an emotional problem is too deep-seated to respond to such approaches, the psychiatrist will be expected to assume treatment.

To deal effectively with the simpler emotional problems prevalent in medical practice, the individual practitioner (from whatever profession) must acquire from psychiatric and other teachers adequate psychiatric knowledge and techniques for applying it. This is true of medical and psychiatric social workers today and is increasingly true of medical students. Once the practitioner has integrated in his own practice this psychiatric knowledge and these skills—including insight into his own personality as a professional person—he is prepared to share it with his students, recognizing always the limits of his competence and the need to turn to the psychiatrist in relation to more complex problems.

Thus it would seem that several groups of teachers—including psychiatrists and other medical teachers and social workers— are concerned with the teaching of social and emotional problems in illness. They share responsibility for a central area, representing the most common social and emotional problems, while each has his own subject matter which he alone teaches.

There is great need for the various teachers to get together in order to clarify their concepts and integrate their methods; otherwise students may be confused, rather than helped, by their uncorrelated efforts. It would seem that teachers of general medicine are in the best position to act as co-ordinators. Until the time arrives that they take active leadership, might it be that the social worker could be a liaison agent in this situation, just as she has so often in the past been the person to bring the psychiatrist and other clinicians together around the problems of an individual patient? However and wherever the joint thinking is initiated, it is hoped that it can start with a fresh unbiased attack upon these important issues.[7]

PROBLEMS OF CURRICULUM PLANNING

Another important unsolved problem is how to get this teaching started and properly organized in the curriculum. Since this phase of instruction has not yet spread through any medical school in clear enough form to be identified and analyzed, our recent study attempted only to explore those smaller units where it could be readily recognized and evaluated. These were found to be either single departments in a school or the program of an individual teaching hospital.

The first point that struck us was that continuity of leadership is essential. The phase of instruction we are discussing comes and goes without any permanence when it is dependent upon the interest of individual teachers. According to the present organization of medical education, each medical school

7. See also the concept of "comprehensive medicine" in *Medicine and the Neuroses* (New York: National Committee on Mental Hygiene, 1945), pp. 27 and 36. This combines the viewpoints of internal medicine and psychiatry but does not emphasize the social factors as much as we do.

department must see that its teachers are adequate. This becomes the responsibility of the chief. Where this teaching is really present throughout a department, it will be found that it is under a chief who is consistently taking measures to bring it about. He is usually personally interested in this type of instruction, but not necessarily so, since he may act simply because he recognizes it as a part of his administrative responsibility. The essential viewpoint is well expressed in the statement by Dr. Harry Linenthal, former physician-in-chief at the Beth Israel Hospital, Boston:

> The teaching of all the social implications in illness should begin when students first come in contact with patients. It should be an integral part of the taking of the history. . . . The approach to the patient by the staff members who do the teaching in the Out-Patient Department and later on the wards, should always include the social aspects and should be discussed in a natural way, just as the physiological disturbances caused by his disease. With this fundamental concept of what the training of medical students should be, and what should be later a part of their regular work in the practice of medicine, the specific social problems that each patient presents can be taken up in greater detail and elaborated upon at ward rounds, by the social-service worker, with the interns, staff and students, as well as in special conference of the students with the social workers. The extramural factors of the patient's life can then be discussed in great detail and the available communal agencies that might be called upon to assist in the solution of some of these problems be made familiar to the student. . . . The integration of the social problems with the patient's illness has been carried on in a perfectly matter-of-fact manner from the day the Beth Israel Hospital was opened.[8]

The development of this type of teaching requires continuous experimentation with teaching methods until something resembling a consistent program, involving a number of teachers and with several interrelated parts, is built up. The major elements of such a program as we have observed them seem to be:

1. Inclusion of social and emotional factors in the daily instruction.
2. Additional methods and projects to extend and emphasize teaching in these areas from time to time, such as case studies and group discussions.
3. Planned use of psychiatric and social service participation throughout.
4. Inclusion in the teaching of all essential phases of the subject: fundamental knowledge, attitudes and skills.
5. A co-ordinated plan combining all the above elements throughout the period of clinical instruction and carrying on into the internship.

8. Personal communication from Dr. Harry Linenthal.

The teaching at the Beth Israel Hospital is an excellent example of such a program.[9] We have observed the same development taking place in other teaching hospitals and in many medical school departments, where the chief has been interested and individual teachers responsive. While such teaching was at varying stages and employed differing methods, in every instance there was a strong trend toward permeation of the department's instruction with a social viewpoint, reinforced by specific teaching at appropriate points. The means to this achievement have been fundamentally the same. They have rested upon the assumption that basic responsibility for teaching of social and environmental aspects lies with the general medical staff. The active process has started and developed through the interest and leadership of the chief, supported by a few medical teachers and a social service department equipped to give the necessary collaboration. Growth has come through the steady building-up of a teaching staff ready and able to include this material and viewpoint in the regular instruction. To those who know the situation at first hand, these demonstrations are convincing. They show that this teaching is practical and effective; and—a particularly encouraging point—that, once started, it grows steadily like a snowball.

THE PROBLEM OF A "PERMEATING" SUBJECT

Another problem in organizing this instruction grows out of the peculiar nature of the subject matter. How is a *permeating* subject of this type best included in the curriculum? By *permeating* we mean subjects like psychiatry and preventive medicine, offering both a general viewpoint and specific technical skills which should pervade medical practice and all branches of medical teaching. Psychiatry and preventive medicine have been set up as special departments in medical schools and are reaching out into the rest of the curriculum from their respective bases. They have been confronted with many difficulties.

9. Ethel Cohen and H. A. Derow, "Teaching Medical Students Objectives for Care of Patients and Social Aspects of Illness," *Archives of Internal Medicine*, LVI (August, 1935), 351; and "The Training of Interns in the Social Aspects of Illness," *Journal of the American Medical Association*, CXVII (November 22, 1941), 1817.

While in British and Canadian medical schools separate departments of "social and preventive medicine" are increasingly being established, in this country the teaching of social and environmental factors (and related skills) has not generally been regarded as a subject to be organized in the form of a new department, but rather as something to be included within the present framework. Thus there will be interesting possibilities for new methods and experimentation along lines not tried in the past.

Meanwhile, we need to analyze much more carefully the pros and cons of assignment of specific responsibility for teaching of the social aspects of medicine, whether to a newly formed department, to already existing departments, or to individual teachers. First, the positive values of such assignment should be recognized. Every scientific subject must have some formal organization in the medical curriculum for teaching and research, if it is to advance. Such responsibilities cannot be left vaguely to all departments; they must be specifically allocated for assurance of progress.

On the other hand, the dangers of specific assignment should also be recognized. As a new subject finds its way into a curriculum, it is to be expected that it will first be handled by a relatively small number of teachers, who are personally convinced of its importance and equipped to deal with its technical aspects. By implicit but unformulated agreement, other teachers may allow the responsibility to rest there, without attempting to take it up in their own departments. In our visits to medical schools we were sometimes told, as soon as we mentioned the subject of our study, "We depend upon our department of preventive medicine (or psychiatry, or medical social service) for that. We leave it to them." The communications from the medical schools as a whole showed that much of the teaching of social and environmental factors now centers in these "special" departments, or teachers. While such a situation is understandable at this early period, it would be unfortunate if the pattern of medical teaching crystallized along these lines. Such a result could block the sound development to be ultimately desired, by which each department will participate actively in this teaching.

If the special department acts as a stimulus to the others, so that the teaching gradually spreads through the school—as can be seen in many schools today—then its contribution will be sound. It must function as catalyst rather than monopolist.

BALANCE BETWEEN TEACHING METHODS

One of the principles which has emerged most clearly from our observation and analysis of present methods of teaching social and environmental factors concerns the interdependence of the two characteristic systems for handling this instruction: (1) through inclusion in the general teaching, without any particular emphasis, and (2) through development of special exercises and projects to emphasize social aspects. The first approach is illustrated by the consistent discussion of social aspects of patients' problems by the clinical teacher on ward rounds; the second by case study projects focusing upon social and environmental problems.

At this stage in the development of the teaching, the manner of its growth creates both a problem and an opportunity. Because this teaching has in some schools grown very strongly in rather isolated sections of the curriculum, without being reflected in the basic instruction, students have been unable to benefit from it as fully as was hoped. The weakness of the special project or exercise is its isolation from the rest of the teaching. When we discussed with students the value of case studies in social and environmental problems combined with seminar discussion, some of them would always take the attitude that it was all very interesting but did not have enough relation to the rest of their work. "We don't see that this is practical for us," they would say. "We spend many hours on the study of a single case and we couldn't possibly work up all our cases this way, now in school or later when we are practicing." Because they were not seeing this method applied in abbreviated form as a part of the daily ward and clinic teaching, they could not grasp its application. The special case study inevitably seems artificial to the student unless he recognizes it as an extension, for learning purposes, of the method used in routine management of patients. Furthermore, it will continue to be either meaningless or actually confusing to many students unless they are given individual help in going through the necessary steps from one stage to the other.

The best solution for the handling of a *permeating* subject seems to be through bringing about its inclusion in the daily experience of students, particularly during their clinical clerkships. In the teaching of the social aspects of medicine our study showed that more effort has gone into developing new teaching projects than in attempting to enrich the traditional clinical instruction. It is most important that concentrated effort in the next few years should be directed toward exploration of opportunities for using the student's daily contact with his patients as a base for the desired instruction. This point is of significance not only for medical teachers but also for social workers who are participating in the teaching of social and environmental factors. The two-person informal conference initiated at the student's request in relation to some problem on one of his cases has endless possibilities for teaching, as Eleanor Cockerill suggested in a paper addressed to a social work conference.[10] Social workers need to study these opportunities for effective teaching, which have been too neglected in the past. It was the opinion of our study committee that here lay the most important channel for future exploration, by both medical and social instructors.

Thus it seems clear that the general instruction and various methods of emphasis through special projects are interdependent, each necessarily looking to the other for support and supplementation in the things which it cannot do itself. At the present stage we find that individual schools tend to be stronger in one or another method. The possibilities and limitations of each approach and the manner of their interrelationship need more demonstration and evaluation.

The perspective should be broadened so as to cover the student's total experience. The subject is too important to be left to grow through the efforts of individual teachers or departments. It requires the conscious, controlled collaboration of all departments in the medical school.

10. "Widening Horizons in Medical Education: A Challenge to Medical Social Work," *Journal of Social Casework*, XXIX (January, 1948), 3.

PLANNING CONTINUITY OF STUDENT EXPERIENCE

If the instruction is to be organized so as to give the greatest benefit to the student, serious consideration must be given to the continuity of student experience. The principle of continuity is fundamental for this teaching for a number of reasons. The stream of social and psychological events often moves much less rapidly than that of medical events. Patients and their families frequently do not know how they feel about one problem or another and what action they wish to take regarding it until considerable time has elapsed. The process by which the medical student builds rapport to the point where the patient feels free to share his difficulties may be inevitably slow in certain cases, which not infrequently offer the best teaching experience. Thus it is impossible to judge the accuracy of a medical social diagnosis and treatment plan on the basis of a few contacts within a limited number of weeks. These fundamental facts regarding the nature of social problems and the physician-patient relationship must be reckoned with more directly in planning an educational experience which has to do with the interaction of social and emotional factors in medical care.

No matter how seriously clinical teachers urge students to follow their patients, the question must be raised whether this will eventuate until two minimal conditions are fulfilled. First, the student needs to feel that he has some genuine continuing responsibility for the patient's welfare, as a basis for an extended relationship. Otherwise he becomes just an observer, in which role he cannot learn the same things that he can as a participant in the active, ongoing situation. Second, teaching methods should be so organized as to enable the student really to keep in touch with his own patients and by this very step to convince him that this is not a secondary but a primary phase of medical instruction. So far as we have been able to observe, the most persistent efforts in both these directions have been taken in connection with certain case study projects, where the importance of continued contact has been recognized. The whole question needs to be examined in relation to clinical teaching, where the student's contact with his patients on one service or another usually does not last more than a few weeks, or several months at the most. We would like to stress again that since the student learns best through his own supervised experience, it is essential that this experience should be of sufficient duration and significance that the fundamentals in knowledge, skill, and attitudes may be encompassed.

STUDENT ATTITUDES AND INTERESTS

Students are key persons in this picture. In organizing teaching for the future, more should be understood about the attitudes and interests of students as they move through the four-year course. Even a preliminary examination suggests many strategic points which are now not given full recognition.

It is evident that the method by which the student is oriented in the first few days and weeks will affect his later attitudes in significant ways. At this impressionable period in learning there is an excellent opportunity to help the student to relate himself to the profession of medicine, before he becomes submerged in intensive study of specific subjects.

The long span of time in the first two years before the student customarily begins to see and work with patients as living human beings is also a matter of concern to many teachers. During this period his basic concepts about medicine are being crystallized. How can he be expected to appreciate later the significance of the personal and social aspects of illness, if he is for so extended a period in his early studies kept isolated from them?

Toward the middle or latter part of the second year comes a particularly strategic moment for the emphasis on social and environmental factors, when the student is brought into the contact with actual patients himself instead of watching his teachers do the examination from an amphitheater seat. The manner in which he is introduced to the fundamental concepts and techniques of clinical medicine through this initial clinical course is again crucial for his later attitudes. While the importance of social factors may receive mention in connection with the teaching of history taking, such teaching is still relatively unorganized and dependent upon the interest of individual teachers. Some instructors believe that at this time the student should be consistently introduced to the full scope of concepts and skills involved in medical diagnosis and treatment, not only those relating to physical diagnosis, as is now customary, but to complete diagnosis of the problem, including the social and emotional components.

The third-year instruction brings the student to a point where he is charged with a portion of actual responsibility for the patient's care, an assignment which grows steadily through the last two years with his deepening knowledge and skill. The customary emphasis on diagnostic processes in the third year offers an opportunity for teaching the role of social and emotional problems in the etiology of disease. The student's increased responsibility for planning and participating in the treatment of patients in the fourth year, on the other hand, points to the teaching of skill in dealing with the social aspects of treatment. The interest of most medical students is usually stimulated to a high level during the period of the clinical clerkships and provides a favorable psychological base for this type of instruction, where receptivity is extremely important.

The reaction of most of the students interviewed during the course of our study confirms the preceding analysis. Many students felt that they wanted more help of this sort earlier in their course, that the case study projects usually came too late and were too brief to give the type of educational experience needed. One student commented on the unfortunate change in attitude that tends to take place in the class as the medical course goes on. He said that he would never forget his spontaneous feeling of sympathy for the first patient he saw brought into a demonstration clinic and how he found that he was more and more coming to regard patients as "cases" as he continued in his work.

A bird's-eye view of the medical course thus shows certain places all the way through where the student is likely to find the teaching of social aspects interesting and valuable in connection with his other work—indeed, to have real need of it for rounding out his experience. Objectives will naturally shift as the student progresses. Successive emphases in this teaching would seem to be: first, development of basic attitudes, awareness, and receptivity; then intellectual grasp of concepts, followed by attainment of special skills; and, finally, ability to integrate this knowledge, these attitudes, and these skills in the effective handling of individual cases of illness and of other professional responsibilities.

TEACHING OF TEACHERS

The medical teacher aims to equip his students with the knowledge and skill necessary for the best practice of medicine. Like any other teacher, he must know his subject matter and the appropriate related educational techniques. How can this be accomplished in relation to such a new and relatively undefined area? This is one of the most important unsolved problems. Everyone interested in these questions agrees that some beginning must be made through the teaching of the teachers themselves, but no one knows the answer.

It would seem that the definition of the area and the teaching of teachers must move along together. One of the most significant experiments was the institute at the University of Minnesota in 1946,[11] when medical and psychiatric teachers (with some collaboration from social workers) joined in giving instruction to experienced medical practitioners. This offers a promising pattern adaptable to the needs in medical education today. Experimental institutes and similar devices are greatly needed, as the times are moving rapidly and social change waits for no man. In the hands of the teachers lies the future of medicine.

CONCLUSION

This paper has attempted to discuss some of the unsolved problems in teaching of social and environmental factors in medicine, as revealed in a recent study. When the time arrives that the general teaching in the medical school assumes responsibility for giving the foundation and integration, while the spe-

11. Helen Leland Witmer (ed.), *Teaching Psychotherapeutic Medicine: An Experimental Course for General Physicians* (New York: Commonwealth Fund, 1947).

cial projects assume responsibility for deepening and emphasizing, then the situation will be much clearer for both teachers and students. Recognition of social aspects will appear at different levels all through the school. It may be revealed in the attitudes of the dean and administration, and through the planning of department heads. It will have its most effective realization through the active teaching of individual professors and younger members of the faculty. The more informal teaching activities of residents and others, such as social workers, will be still another channel. Whether formal or informal, explicit or implicit, it will be an ever-recurring and essential element throughout the four years. The student will recognize the logic of the whole orderly plan and move from one step to another with conviction and security. The various teachers will know what the others are doing and be able to integrate their efforts toward a shared objective. When that happens, the teaching of social and environmental factors will truly be a part of the medical curriculum—and thus of the educational preparation of the physician as a professional person.

APPENDIX

Appendix

Excerpts from "Hospital and Dispensary Social Work"[1]

BY RICHARD C. CABOT, M.D.

. . . .

III. NAME AND DEFINITION

The purpose of social work in hospitals is to obtain such understanding of the patient and of his concerns as will enable us to supplement the efforts of the physicians and nurses, both in the comprehension and in the treatment of his illness.

From this definition it follows that the chief work of the social worker is to understand the patient and to make him understand what he especially needs to know in order that he may be properly cared for and, if possible, recover his health. Ideas, then, are the material in which the social worker chiefly deals. She is to gather ideas about the patient and to convey ideas to him. Her business is to understand him and to make him understand, so far as this is necessary to fulfil the hopes and desires with which he sought the hospital. What she aims to understand is especially (*a*) the patient's state of mind, (*b*) his economic, domestic, and industrial situation, and (*c*) these same facts as regards his family and those most closely connected with him in his school, his work, his recreations, and his religious life. When she aims to enlighten and assist the patient it is chiefly (*a*) by explaining to him the nature and the future of his own disease, (*b*) by explaining what is to be done for its palliation or its cure, and (*c*) as to what individuals or agencies outside the hospital can help him either by care or by cure.

It is much easier to state these purposes than to give them a fit name. All names hitherto proposed seem to me unsatisfactory. The word *social*, which I have perhaps done as much as anyone to connect with this work, seems to me in several respects misleading; for in the first place the work is concerned primarily with individuals and *social* is a term often contrasted with *individual*. Moreover, the ideas called up by the word *social* are often entirely misleading when one is thinking of the work which

1. Read before the International Conference of Social Work, Paris, France, July, 1928. Reprinted from *Hospital Social Service*, Vol. XVIII (1928).

we are now discussing. If we think of "social hygiene," the problems of venereal disease are suggested. "Social democracy" calls up political theories with which we have here no concern. Finally, in English the word *social* is often, perhaps chiefly, connected with afternoon tea and similar functions. For all these reasons I object to the term. Yet when I consider the alternatives proposed for it I am no better satisfied. For instance, in Germany, Dr. Alter of Dusseldorf, in his most valuable and interesting writings in the *Zeitschrift für das gesamte Krankenhauswesen*, January 3, 1927, and elsewhere, has proposed the term *"Fürsorgedienst im Krankenhaus."* We all agree that this work should be connected with the hospital and that it is a *service*, but when we come to define this service by the word *"Fürsorge"* or *"Fürsorgelich"* we have a term that is as much too wide as the word *social* is too narrow. For the doctor and the nurse also give *sorge* or "care," and it is one of our chief objects to distinguish the *particular* hospital service which I am now describing from other services given in hospitals.

The English word *almoner* naturally connects itself with the giving of *alms*, which we are all agreed has little or no part in this work. The English themselves have had to supplement this word by phrases like *social service, social work,* and *the social service department,* all of which now appear in their reports.

One of the ideas which we most want to convey in the name which we give to this work is that, whereas all or nearly all the others who deal with the patient are concerned with rendering him some *particular* service (bodily, mental, spiritual, recreational, occupational, educational), our task is concerned with *whatever the patient may need* to further his recovery, either in one of the special departments of service just mentioned or in any other. In other words, it is a service to the *total personality* of the patient in so far as this service is needed to promote his health. This suggests that we might call it *personal service in the hospital,* a service devoted to the restoration of the patient's total personality. But, unfortunately, the term "personal service" has become associated with such occupations as those of the manicurist and the bootblack and cannot, I fear, be easily rescued.

Welfare work is in some ways a better term than any of those yet discussed, since surely we are concerned with the patient's welfare and with whatever may be necessary to maintain or secure it. But this word has now, especially in Germany, a very definite and fixed association with activities outside the hospital and not connected in any strict sense with illness. Moreover, we could say that the doctor and the nurse also work for the patient's *welfare* in the ordinary, nontechnical sense.

In view of all these difficulties I think we should come back to the word *social* as, on the whole, best characterizing the work which here concerns us. For many writers have rightly insisted that this work is essentially one of *linking* the patient to all available sources of help. This is the original meaning of the word *social—that which connects* or joins. Suppose we say that the purpose of social work in hospitals is to link the patient with all available sources of help: (*a*) in God, (*b*) in himself, (*c*) in the world around him. It is true, then, that this work is primarily and essentially a work of linkage, a *social* or intermediary work, or, as I like best to say, a work of *interpretation*—a term to the discussion of which I shall return later. After noting these advantages upon the side of etymology, we may also acknowledge that, for good or for evil, the word *social* has now taken very firm root in at least three of the four countries in which this work is extensively developed. Furthermore, it can be taken to emphasize another essential feature for its prosecution, namely, what we in America call "teamwork." Unless the work is social in the sense that many persons work together in close—yes, if possible, in affectionate—relations with one another, it will never be successful. Unless the patient himself, the doctor, the nurse, the social worker, and the manifold agencies of helpfulness outside the hospital can be linked together in helpful co-operation, we do not attain the objects for which we are striving. For reasons, then, connected with etymology, with usage, and with the form which the work actually takes when it is successful, I believe we should continue to call this work *social*.

The word *hospital* should always be a part of our title. For though similar work may be done in many other places, the peculiar traditions of hospital work, the peculiar complexity of the interrelations centering there, and the special knowledge needed by anyone who is to work there without giving rise to all sorts of trouble and without making herself a great nuisance differentiate her work both in the training required for it, the taste and character proper to it, and the results to be obtained by it.

IV. REASONS FOR THE RECENT ORIGIN
OF HOSPITAL SOCIAL WORK

The need of hospital social service is so basic and so obvious that when one has once perceived it one wonders why we have got along for so many years without it. It is not, I believe, that superior wisdom has only in our time appeared upon the earth, but rather for the following reasons.

1. A change in the conception of medical diagnosis and of medical treatment.

Although physicians have for centuries cherished the ideal of *getting to the bottom* of the patient's troubles, of avoiding superficiality and plunging as deep as they could toward the basic causes of his illness, yet they have been inclined, both by their temperament as a profession and by the nature of their training, to focus attention upon the *bodily* manifestations of disease and to ignore partially or wholly the intelligence, the emotions, and the will of the patient, together with the effects made upon him by his relationships to his family, his friends, his work, his recreation, his religion or lack of religion, and the other influences entering his life. There is nothing new in the recognition that a patient may suffer from disturbances of his stomach, his intestines, his heart, and other portions of his anatomy, all because of wounds of the spirit, fevers of the mind, moral degenerations, fatigue, sorrow, remorse, worry. There is nothing new, I say, in this knowledge. But even yet it has penetrated into the practice of only comparatively few physicians. Though our medical textbooks tell us all these facts, we forget them because our senses present us such impressive evidence of bodily disease and because, on the whole, our medical training centers our attention there and nowhere else.

This forgetfulness is especially characteristic of hospital work because there one sees the patient torn out of his natural setting and bereft often of considerable portions of his wits. Why should we be made vividly aware of the influence of his mind, his work, and his family life when very little evidence of any one of these appears at the bedside? It is strictly true to say that only a fragment of the patient's personality appears clearly at the hospital. He has left a large portion of himself at home or elsewhere. But his disease he brings with him. That we see. The rest we forget.

Especially is this true under the conditions of hurry which are unfortunately only too common in hospital work and, above all, in hospital outpatient departments or "polyclinics." We are prone enough under any conditions to neglect what is not before our eyes or on the surface, to ignore the psychological and social aspects of the patient's case. But we are more than ever in danger of making this blunder when we are in a hurry, when patients are seen in masses and in an atmosphere of distraction and confusion. The old-fashioned country physician, the general practitioner of the village, who saw his patients in their homes or at their work, who knew them, their families, their neighbors, who had been associated with them in all the neighborly offices of town life, was less likely to forget the man, less apt to focus blindly upon his disease. But such practitioners, I fear, are now growing rare; at any rate in hospital work it is impossible for the physician to enjoy such comprehensive understanding of his patients.

All this, as I have said, has long been true. But for various reasons it began to penetrate to the minds of those concerned in hospital work, that is, the doctors, nurses, and hospital superintendents, only a little more than thirty years ago. It was at about that time that we began to realize that only in a small minority of the patients who come to a hospital for treatment, especially of those seen as outpatients, could drugs or surgery produce any important improvement. In the great majority of cases the outpatient will not be better unless his hygienic conditions, the conditions of his work, diet, sleep, and his mental and emotional activities can be changed. But these changes in turn are often impossible unless his economic, domestic, or spiritual conditions can be improved. In my own case certainly it was the sense of my failure, of the uselessness of my work as a hospital physician, that led me to seek aid from social workers. The treatment needed by most of my patients could not be carried out without their help. But unless something could be done in the way of treatment it was hardly worth while to spend time and strength (as I was doing) on the niceties of diagnosis. To work hard in an outpatient clinic day after day with the sense that most of one's work is wholly useless because the patient cannot possibly get the treatment demanded by the diagnosis, must lead one either to careless and slipshod technique or to a demand for reform. So long as we could believe that we were doing all that could be done for the patient when we handed him a prescription for medicine or bandaged a varicose ulcer, one could take some satisfaction in one's work. But the advance of medical knowledge banished these beliefs and left us often quite hopeless.

2. Another change in our point of view was brought about by the development of campaigns against tuberculosis.

I have often thought and said that from the point of view of public health *tuberculosis was a blessing* because it taught us new ways of attacking disease, new aggressiveness, new hopefulness, and, above all, a new attitude toward our patients. This new attitude consisted in *taking the patient into partnership* in our campaign against his disease. We recognized in tuberculosis earlier than in other diseases that the disease cannot be effectively fought unless the patient himself understands it and does his part in the contest against it. In earlier years the doctor and the nurse were supposed to do everything, the patient almost nothing. That is, he was to do as he was told, to open his mouth and shut his eyes. It was not for him to presume that he could understand the complex mysteries of his disease, and even if he could, we arrogantly assumed that he was not capable of keeping his balance in the face of the ever present threat of death. That burden, we thought, must be borne by someone else. It was the doctor's business, or the nurse's, not the patient's. I cannot say that we physicians have as yet wholly conquered this fallacious idea, any more than we have conquered our stupid forgetfulness of the patient's mental and social life. There are still those who preach that the patient should not be told the truth about himself, so far as we know it, but should be treated like a child by others who know better than he does what is good for him and what he can bear. This autocratic and domineering attitude, though assumed often from excellent motives, has been made possible by a self-deception like that by which the ostrich was said to suppose himself concealed when he had hidden his head in the sand. The doctor has often been able to deceive himself into thinking that he can do all that needs to be done and think all that needs to be thought for his patient, even when everyone else except the doctor sees clearly how absurd this attitude is.

Modern public health work, beginning with the campaign against tuberculosis, has been centered about the conviction that the patient must understand all that we can teach him about his own troubles and about the ways to combat them. It is true that he may get to worrying about himself and his disease. That is a chance which we must take, and experience has shown that it does very much less harm than we used to suppose. The campaign against tuberculosis, begun in America largely by the laity, soon brought to light the fact that after the doctor has finished his expert work of diagnosis, there is relatively little as to the treatment of the disease which cannot be understood and carried out by intelligent laymen, among whom no one is so much concerned or so constantly in a position to do the right thing (if properly taught) as the patient himself. Ever since the beginning of the campaign against tuberculosis doctors have begun *to teach medicine to their patients*. At first this sounded revolutionary, and many physicians have not even yet begun it. But they are being compelled to move in this direction by the increased enlightenment of the patients themselves, who hear from each other what the more enlightened physicians have begun to do in the way of educating their patients medically. I know now many a diabetic patient who knows more about diabetes than the average physician. He has been forced to learn it for his own benefit and because it concerns himself more than it concerns anyone else in the world. So it is with venereal diseases, with many orthopedic troubles, nervous troubles, diseases of the heart—in fact, with almost all diseases which last more than a few days. Medical knowledge is becoming public property. It is no longer the exclusive possession of doctors and nurses, and on this rest our best hopes for the preventive activities of public health work in hospitals and elsewhere.

3. Just as that fortified citadel, the physician's exclusive possession of medical knowledge, has been broken down through public health work, so another closed fortress, the hospital, with its own peculiar standards and customs, has now been penetrated. Formerly the medical staffs were absolute monarchs there. The hospital superintendent, at any rate in America, was very much under the thumb of the physicians and surgeons of the hospital. His business was to give them a chance to carry out their work according to their own ideas. He owed no primary allegiance to the public. If people did not like hospital customs, they could go elsewhere. The physician and the surgeon were kings, each in his own sphere, and they wanted above all things not to be interfered with. Like the other reforms which I have described, the change whereby the hospital physician has become a servant of the public instead of an independent sovereign is still far from complete, especially in private hospitals and those without university connections. There is still often very little recognition of the fact that hospitals exist primarily to serve the public rather than the physicians who work there. But the process of enlightenment has begun, and one important evidence of it is the establishment of social service departments. For one of the chief functions of such a department is to connect the hospital with all the social forces and helpful agencies outside its walls.

I suppose that this has come about as part of a more general recognition of the connection between economic life and every other human interest. Hospitals exist still very largely for the treatment of the poor, and the connection between poverty and disease is now recognized better than ever before. But if we are concerned with the patient's economic life when we are trying to improve his health, we cannot escape the need to know something about his work and his home. And if we are concerned with the patient's mental, emotional, spiritual life whenever we are concerned with his disease, we cannot escape the need to know something about his social relationships both in his home and outside it, about his enjoyments and recreations, his habits, his fears, even his beliefs or his despairs about religion.

V. PRESENT FUNCTIONS OF HOSPITAL SOCIAL WORK

Wherever social work exists in hospitals, it is concerned with trying to accomplish the three things so well stated by Dr. Alter (*loc. cit.*) as *Vorsorge, Fürsorge,* and *Nachsorge*—prevention, hospital treatment, later treatment. It is also concerned I think, though in a minor degree, with diagnosis, in so far as a knowledge of the patient's social and mental life is essential to the understanding and evaluation of his symptoms.

But though these are the great tasks of social work in all hospitals, both in the outpatient department and in the wards, there are and ought to be the greatest differences in different countries and in different parts of the same country, depending upon the psychological and economic conditions of the time and place, and also upon the development (or lack of development) of social work outside the hospital. Whenever or wherever poverty is extreme, the task of social service will be concerned with attempts to improve the economic conditions of the patient, either directly, in case there are in the community no social organizations concerned with this work, or indirectly by co-operating with any that may exist. Where patients are excessively ignorant and uneducated, the task of educating them in a knowledge of their disease and of the methods of combating it, cannot be carried out extensively. On the other hand, with a relatively intelligent group of patients, hygienic education will constitute an important part of the social worker's task, always provided that she can depend upon accuracy in the diagnoses and prognoses given by the physician.

All her work for hygienic instruction and toward an adequate provision for the patient's future is useless or harmful if the diagnosis and prognosis furnished her by the physician are seriously inaccurate or are given her in a brief and largely unintelligible form, as is often the case. When medical diagnosis and prognosis are seriously inaccurate, or where the understandings between physician and social worker are not close and friendly, the worker often sees her plans fall to pieces like a house of cards.

At best she can attend to such economic necessities or such mental troubles as she independently discovers, but she can do relatively little to forward the patient's recovery by enlisting him and other allies as partners in a well-planned struggle against his disease. She can do relatively little also to guide his present and future life, since she does not possess the essential medical data of prognosis.

.   .   .   .

Another factor which helps determine what the social worker shall do within the hospital is the interest and intelligence (*a*) of the medical and surgical staff and (*b*) of the hospital management. If these gentlemen are not interested or not in sympathy with social work, all sorts of expedients have to be adopted to arouse them. Many a social worker is now doing in hospitals jobs which she knows are no part of her proper work, because she wants to be obliging and so, gradually, to win the interest of the staff and of the management. Thus we find social workers doing clerical work, arranging for the donors of blood when transfusions are needed, putting drops into the eyes of patients waiting for the oculist, carrying messages or escorting patients from one part of the hospital to another. Moreover, when social work is done by nurses, they are prone to relapse into assisting the physicians or the patient in ways proper rather to a nurse than to a social worker. I assume as a matter of course that in emergencies or times of special pressure the social worker or anyone else should do whatever seems most needed to help the institution through a crisis. Nothing is more contrary to the spirit of social work than the unwillingness of any worker to do, *in an emergency*, something obviously needed, though outside the field of her own special work. But in this as in any other field there is danger that exceptions and emergencies will become the rule, so that a person is permanently dislocated from her proper usefulness.

. . . .

If now I may add from my own experience of hospital social work, chiefly within a single hospital, some impressions as to what it does and ought to do, I should emphasize, first of all, the task of the social worker as an *interpreter*. The patient finds himself facing a new and often a terrible situation. To enter the hospital is often for him the most momentous event of his life, and he needs all the help that can be given him to understand it. When we say, then, that one of the most important tasks of the social worker is to cheer, encourage, and reassure the patient, to let him see that warmheartedness and good will are at the center of all the apparently impersonal and heartless technical procedures which he sees around him, we are saying that *the social worker must interpret the hospital to the patient*, must explain that "its bark is worse than its bite" and that, behind these apparently immovable faces, plans for the alleviation of his sufferings and for the reconstruction of his life are forming. Nurses and doctors, of course, should also do this work of interpretation, but they rarely remember to. Interpretation is therefore especially the business of the social worker who wants the patient to understand things as they really are and not as they seem, in order that his mind may not be terrified by fictions of his imagination.

Most of the people whom the patient sees moving about him seem to be frantically in a hurry and utterly unaware of any particular individual. It is therefore particularly important that the medical social worker should seem to be undistracted, at leisure, and wholly at the service of the patient so long as she is in his company. Because most of the doctors, nurses, and others whom the patient sees about him appear as wholly cool, unemotional beings, it is especially important that the social worker should express in a perfectly sincere and natural way some warmth of good feeling. She should be a person who can easily smile, who is naturally attracted to anybody in trouble, and who shows it. This can easily be distinguished from sentimentalism and from hypocrisy, and, of course, it is, above all, necessary that the worker should never pretend any feeling which she does not possess. Sincerity is desirable above all things in these trying times of the patient's life.

Because doctors and nurses so often speak in technical terms, unintelligible to the patient, and seem inexplicably reserved about matters that chiefly concern him, about the nature of his trouble and the future to be expected, it is especially the office of the social worker to explain in plain and truthful language all that the patient wants to know about his disease. She must be able to judge, through her unusual sympathy and sensitiveness, when patients want information for which they dare not ask and when they are quite content to remain in ignorance. When an operation, a special method of treatment, or a special technical procedure, such as a metabolism test, a lumbar puncture, an X-ray examination, a cystoscopy, is advised, it is generally for the social worker to explain what these things mean, how much and how little suffering they involve, how important they are.

Much more difficult but not less important is the task of the worker to explain as well as she can the answer to a question which takes the foremost place as a disturbing element in many patients' minds. I mean the question, "How does it happen that *I* am afflicted with this terrible illness? How can it be that in an orderly world such disaster can come to me?" Of course, the patient rarely, if ever, asks this question, but it is almost always in his mind, and, unless answered, it militates strongly against his recovery. The manner of the answer given by the social worker will depend, of course, upon her own religious, philosophic, or even political beliefs. If she has, as I think she always should have, a religious belief, she must attempt with Milton "to justify the ways of God to man," to explain the place of evil and suffering in the training and education of man's soul, and especially in a world where "we are members one of another." But even if religion means nothing to the worker she must still try to foster in the patient a contented or stoical attitude by giving him some idea of how his trouble has come about and what is likely to be its outcome. Her beliefs as to biology, economics, and hygiene will have here their place of usefulness.

Besides these difficult but all-important tasks of interpreting to the patient the hospital routine and the meaning of his illness, the social worker has the much simpler but still very important task of interpreting to the patient what the doctor has said as to the diagnosis and prognosis of his disease, and sometimes of interpreting the patient's more or less incoherent or scanty replies to the doctor himself. Especially in countries like America, where patients of many races and speaking many languages are assembled in a single hospital, the simpler problems of literal linguistic interpretation may be of great importance both in diagnosis and in treatment.

So far I have been describing the duties of the social worker as one who interprets the hospital world to the patient. But she has also the task of interpreting this hospital world and the manifold events which go on there to the patient's family or friends. Sometimes she has even to interpret the behavior of the patient, when he is apathetic, delirious, frightened, or hysterical, to members of his family who may not be accustomed to illness and its effect upon the mind.

Beyond the patient's immediate circle, his family or his friends, the social worker has to interpret to the social agencies outside the hospital or to other interested persons what it is that his illness means and what measures, financial, hygienic, psychological, are proper for its care. Not infrequently also she must interpret to the hospital physicians or to the hospital management conditions existing in the patient's home or community, which have a vital bearing upon his disease or upon its treatment. The doctor may be ready to send a cardiac patient home at once, but may change his mind when the social worker explains that the conditions in his home are such as to militate strongly against his recovery.

The intelligent social worker soon learns that in her task of explaining the patient's condition to persons outside the hospital, the actual diagnosis as it is written down in the medical record is often of very little value. Occasionally, of course, that diagnosis is one which should not be revealed without the patient's consent or to any but those who have a right to it from the point of view of public health. More often, however, the difficulty is of quite another nature. It is that the diagnosis itself reveals very little as to the real nature of the illness. For example, all that stands upon the medical record as a diagnosis may be the words, "Ulcer of the duodenum," a phrase which may be perfectly true and accurate so far as it goes. But in one patient this may mean only a slight inconvenience and in another a chronic and crippling disease. What the patient, his family, and those who are trying to help him after he leaves the hospital need most to know is that about which physicians are ordinarily most reticent, namely *the prognosis of this disease (a) in the average case and (b) in this particular individual.* Is he going to be partially or wholly disabled? Disabled for a week, a month, or a year? Disabled in his physical endurance or in his mental capacity and balance? None of this necessary information is ordinarily revealed in the diagnosis; and, as a rule, no prognosis and no statement of the kind, degree, and duration of disability is included in the medical record or in any statement that is vouchsafed by the physician. All this, therefore, the social worker must try to extract from the doctor, yet without annoying him or interfering unduly with his other duties. Then, after she has mastered all the knowledge that he can communicate to her, she must translate this into terms comprehensible to nonmedical persons.

It is quite clear that if the social worker is to succeed in the tasks which I have just been describing, she must know a good deal about the psychology of hospital physicians and hospital nurses, what they see and what they ignore, what they habitually express and what they ordinarily forget to express, what seems to them important and why, what will irritate or anger them, what is the right moment to engage their attention, how they may be induced to concentrate their minds upon a particular problem of importance to the patient but outside their ordinary medical routine. Further, the worker should come gradually to understand what the physician himself often knows little enough about, namely, in what matters he is really an expert and a leader; in what matters he is only an amateur; when his diagnostic or therapeutic knowledge approaches infallibility; when it must of necessity rest on much weaker foundations. Ideally, I suppose, it would be the part of the doctor himself to make this clear, but it is certain that he rarely does so, and perhaps it is expecting too much of him.

Another function of hospital social workers, of which almost all of them are aware but which most of them are tactful enough not to mention, is that of gradually teaching the doctors and nurses what they need to know regarding the social and psychological aspects of disease. I hope the time is long past when the hospital physician thought of himself as an omniscient autocrat, too wise to receive instruction from anyone on matters that concerned sick people. We physicians know well enough today that we must learn from the physicist much about X-rays, about light and other forms of radiant energy; that we must learn from the chemist much about our drugs, body-fluids, and about diet; that we must learn from the psychiatrist many things which intimately concern our patients within the field of mental life. Is it not abundantly clear that we have also much to learn from the social workers about the influence of domestic, industrial, psychological, economic, recreational, and religious factors which enter into and modify the course of our patients' maladies? We are very far from being omniscient in this or in any other field, and if we have true spirit of science and a decent portion of humility, we shall be always ready to welcome facts and interpretations concerning our patient's welfare from those in a position to furnish them to us. Physicians are usually ready to teach, and ought to teach, medical students, nurses, social workers, the family of the patient, the patient himself. But we should be equally ready to learn from any and all of these persons. Only so far and so fast as we do this, can hospital social work accomplish the objects for which it came into being. There is no sense and no justification for any doctor to treat a social worker as an ignorant subordinate. Subordinate she is and should be in all matters of direct medical technique, but not in her own proper sphere. Therefore, the doctor and social worker should meet in the wards and outpatient departments of hospitals as colleagues and consultants, each contributing his quota to the patient's welfare, each teaching the other what he needs to know.

Too often medical social work has been a virtual, though unacknowledged, failure because the hospital physician did not know enough about it to make use of it for the patient's benefit, just as in a good many of the more backward hospitals they do not know how properly to make use of the laboratories or even of the X-ray department, which therefore do not properly function in the hospital economy. Personally I think it is a mistake to introduce social work into any ward or outpatient clinic where the physicians are ignorant about it or indifferent to it. Their co-operation is a necessity. Without it social workers may do more harm than good.

Still more obvious is it that social work in the sense here described is impossible where the quality of medical diagnosis and treatment is not what it should be. Unless the social worker can trust the doctor's diagnosis and extract from him reasonably definite prognosis, she can make for the patient no plan that can be depended upon to produce good rather than evil results. At the Massachusetts General Hospital we have never attempted to introduce social workers into any medical or surgical ward or into any part of the outpatient department unless they were actually asked for by the physicians. Parts of our hospital therefore are virtually unsupplied with this kind of service, and I think should remain so until the physicians of these departments are sufficiently educated on the social side of medicine to do their part in the essentially co-operative efforts of medical social work. And even in the portions of a hospital where the physicians or surgeons ask for co-operation from social workers, what they can accomplish will be limited by the degree of close and intimate co-operation which they succeed in establishing with the physicians and nurses of that department. A formal, superficial contact will not do. Doctor and social worker must come to understand each other almost as the members of a family or of a string quartet or of an athletic team understand each other, instinctively, rapidly, accurately, confidently.

. . . .

VII. SELECTION OF PATIENTS AND LIMITATION OF INTAKE

In certain clinics the social worker is supposed to see every patient, and to do or get done whatever is most urgently needed. For special groups of patients, such as the tuberculous or the unmarried mothers, this is obviously the best arrangement. As soon as a diagnosis of tuberculosis or of pregnancy in an unmarried woman is made, the social worker is then brought into contact with the patient, the doctor's directions are explained, and the main responsibility for treatment is then transferred to the social worker. But in general medical and surgical clinics, especially in the larger hospitals, some process of selection is usually carried out. The social worker assumes responsibility, not for all patients but for those who are specially sent to her by the physicians, interns, or nurses connected with the clinic. In other cases she visits a hospital ward in which her co-operation has been asked by the physicians or surgeons in charge, and there assumes social responsibility not only for those directly referred to her but for any other cases which by reason of her special knowledge and experience she knows are particularly in need of her care. Thus cases of malignant disease or of chronic arthritis, when admitted to the wards of a hospital intended primarily for acute—that is, brief—diseases, should automatically fall into the province of the social worker because within a few days, or at most a few weeks, arrangements will have to be made for their care at home or for their transfer to other institutions.

Whichever of these methods we adopt, whether the social worker is given the opportunity to select patients for herself after coming in contact with all those in the clinic in which she works, or whether she confines herself to those specially referred to her by others, the main point always to be kept in mind and to be insisted upon by those in control of the social worker's activity is the *limitation of intake*. Social work in a hospital is never done. We never get to the end of it or do all that we see is needed and would like to do. We must make some selection. It is certainly reasonable, then, that the social worker should not take or allow others to force upon her a volume of work which leads inevitably to the habitual exhaustion of her energies or to superficiality in the attempt to accomplish an impossible task.

All this seems so clear as to need no argument, but it is nevertheless very difficult to enforce. We can set a limit to the number of new cases which any worker is allowed to take up during a given week or month or to the total number of cases "old and new" for which she is allowed to be responsible at any one time. But the difficulty with any such regulation is that one can never tell in advance whether a case will involve only a few hours' work or will extend over many days and weeks. Something can be done through the distinction later referred to between intensive cases and "short-service" cases. We can say that the worker shall not take more than a certain number of cases of each of these varieties within a certain period. Even with these precautions, however, it is very hard to prevent the worker from becoming overwhelmed both by the number of cases thrust upon her and by the especially fatiguing demands upon her sympathy involved in this sort of work. If she is sympathetic enough to respond properly to the patient's needs, it is difficult to prevent her becoming exhausted or discouraged by the bulk of human misery thrust upon her. If, on the other hand, she takes her work easily and is not troubled by it, she is apt to be or to become superficial and callous.

I believe, however, that these difficulties can be overcome by a proper supervision and scrutiny of records. From these the supervisor can form an estimate of the load carried by each worker, and if beyond this the supervisor is daily in touch with all the workers, she will be able to obtain an additional check on the judgments formed from study of the records. In any case one may say without fear of contradiction that if social work is to be kept at a high standard of usefulness, opportunity must be given to each worker to follow up a few cases with sufficient thoroughness to feel that in these she has done her best and has both learned and taught as much as she can. There must be time for each worker to study in this thorough way at least a small group of cases each month and each year that she continues in the work. All of us have to do a good deal of routine work which employs only a small fraction of our powers. But we all need the stimulus and the opportunity to do *now and then* our best, so that looking back after a lapse of months or years we can say that we have accomplished something.

.   .   .   .

IX. SPECIALTIES WITHIN MEDICAL SOCIAL WORK

I regard specialization both in social work and in all other professions as an evil, but a necessary evil. As no one can be a competent practitioner both of medicine and of surgery, so I take it there must always be the differentiation between social workers who are concerned primarily with the sick (hospital social workers, public health workers) and those who are attached to the regular welfare organizations (charity organiza-

tion workers, family welfare workers, etc.). Even this degree of specialization, however, seems to me in many respects undesirable. Certainly
the hospital social worker needs all the skill and experience in case work
that is the center of expertness in outside agencies. On the other hand,
sickness is so frequent a factor in *all* social work (outside hospitals as well
as within them) that no worker connected with a social agency outside
a hospital can carry on her task properly unless she has a considerable
familiarity with many kinds of sickness. Nevertheless, as I have said, I
think that degree of specialization which separates in some degree hospital workers from those outside is necessary.

There is a strong tendency at present to go beyond this and to train
special workers for psychiatric social work, for pediatric social work,
for orthopedic and neurological social work, etc. Especially where work
is done in an outpatient clinic, there is a strong tendency for one worker
to settle down in one special department, to become familiar with the
terms, traditions, and personnel of this department, and to make herself
almost indispensable there. When this happens, any proposition to move
the worker into another department, in order to broaden her acquaintance with other types of work, is apt to be resisted both by the worker
herself and by the physicians who have come to value her services.
Nevertheless, I think that, for the good of the worker herself, for the
maintenance of her interest, energy, and freshness of mind and so of the
fruitfulness of her work, this degree of specialization should be discouraged. For the same reason I am opposed to the organization of a
special class of workers, known as psychiatric social workers. Every social worker, outside a hospital as well as in it, deals primarily with the
mind and character of those within her care. She cannot know too
much about the mind, both in health and in disease. Any training, therefore, which is proper for a psychiatric social worker is equally proper
and necessary for all social workers, since this is the very heart of all
social work. To designate any special group of workers as "psychiatric"
tends to give the impression that other social workers do not need
psychiatric training and psychiatric knowledge. If the competence of
the psychiatric worker goes beyond what all social workers need, she is
apt to begin to practice psychiatry independently and without a physician's guidance. This I regard as undesirable. I think there is at least
as much reason for the separation of special pediatric social workers
as for those associated with nervous and mental diseases, and if once we
encourage this degree of specialism, we shall tend to still finer sub-
divisions until workers will be concentrating upon a single disease, such
as tuberculosis, diabetes, poliomyelitis, or syphilis. One sees the same undesirable tendencies within the field of medicine and of nursing. There
are physicians who devote themselves wholly to a single disease, and
nurses who feel themselves competent only to nurse tuberculous patients,
children, or maternity cases. The subject is too large for thorough discussion here, but I wish to record my opinion as opposed to this degree
of specialization either in medicine, in nursing, or in social work. In
all these fields the rule should be, "Specialize as much as you must but

as little as you can." The smaller and narrower the individual, the more he must specialize, but always with dangers both to himself and to those he serves.

.   .   .   .

XIV. THE FUTURE OF HOSPITAL SOCIAL WORK

1. The development or regressions of this work in the years to come will depend primarily, I think, on the sort of persons who are drawn into hospitals as physicians, nurses and social workers. Medical and social work can be standardized in a very limited degree. It can always be built up, extended, or pulled down by the character of those who go into it. In America the caliber of hospital superintendents is steadily improving, and their conception of the hospital as a public servant is clearing. This bodes well for the future of social work here.

2. Another favorable sign is the increasingly frequent connection of large hospitals with universities. The university spirit is one of devotion to the interests of man as a whole and therefore strengthens the hands of all who—like social workers—are thinking and working for the "mind, body and estate" of man and not for any of these elements alone.

3. At present an omen unfavorable to the best development of our work is the small salary of the worker. We cannot demand of her a long and expensive education and at the same time limit her salary to an amount on which few can save any money for the future or keep themselves properly alive to the sources of refreshment and cultivation around them.

4. I believe that a large remuneration to the trained hospital social worker should be paid by the hospital itself. But I hope that an additional source of income will gradually be open to her as her usefulness becomes more generally recognized—I mean paid service to well-to-do patients under the guidance of their physicians. For social work is needed by persons of all economic levels—not by the poor alone. In the wards of the Massachusetts General Hospital our social workers do almost as much for the well-to-do patients as for the poor. Obviously this must be so if *social* work is, as I have said, a work of establishing new and better *connections* between the patient and the proper sources of his strength, physical, mental, and moral. Rich people need this service when they are sick almost, if not quite, as much as poor people. Most physicians who are intelligent and disinterested perceive this need of social (i.e., connection-making) work for their well-to-do patients and try to do it themselves. They try to guide their patients into better hygienic habits, better habits of thought, emotion, and will, better occupations, recreations, and affections. If they felt competent they would try also to deepen and direct their patients' religious life.

But in all these fields the physician is usually untrained, an amateur. He needs "social" help as much in his private practice as in his hospital work, and occasionally, even now, he knows this and borrows some of the time of a hospital social worker for the benefit of his private patients. I hope to see this practice greatly extended. Time should then be allowed for it as it is now in the case of hospital radiologists, who serve hospital patients on salary from the hospital but are allowed also their own hours for private practice paid by the private patient.

.   .   .   .

7. As medical science and social-economic organization progress, many of the social worker's present tasks will be lightened. Even now, the bulk of her labors for the tuberculous has begun in the United States to diminish as that disease is gradually exterminated. Wherever the prevention or the cure of a disease is perfected (as in smallpox, malaria, diphtheria, typhoid fever, rickets, syphilis), there will be less burden for the social worker in hospitals. If, for example, the cure or prevention of hypertension should be discovered (which now seems not at all improbable), a large slice of hospital social work would become unnecessary. As institutional care for chronic disease is perfected, as old age is better provided for, as general education and common sense increase, as unemployment is diminished, social work will be relieved of heavy burdens. Whether new needs will spring up as fast as the old ones are abolished, only time can show.

Nothing is more characteristic of our age than the increase and improvement of the *means of communication* through locomotion, telephones, radio, newspapers, books, magazines, schools, colleges, and through associations, industrial, national, and international. The *socii* or bonds which join place to place and man to man are being multiplied and strengthened year by year. Surely we may believe that the profession which bends its strength to *social* work is now only at the dawn of its usefulness.

Indexes

Index of Subjects

Hospital social work—*continued*
specialization within, 267, 268, 269
use in private practice, 269, 270

Maternal and child health service, medical social work in; *see* Public medical care
Medical education
curriculum planning, 242, 243, 244, 245
preparation of teachers, 251
role of medical social worker in, 209–52
teaching social aspects of illness
attitudes of medical students, 212, 213, 214, 215, 216, 217, 218, 249–51
methods of case study, 212–14
methods of teaching, 246–48
training of interns, 219–20
ward rounds
content, 223–27
contribution to preparation of medical teachers, 235–36
evaluation by graduates, 229–34; 236–37
method, 221, 222
participants, 227, 228, 229
Medical practice, current issues in, 192, 193
Medical social work
definition of, 14, 15
functions of, 17–20

Prevention, role of medical social workers in, 12, 119, 120
Public assistance, medical social work in; *see* Public medical care
Public health, medical social work in; *see* Public medical care
Public medical care

case work demonstration in, 79–89
consultation and co-ordination, 73, 74, 95, 96, 97, 98, 106
crippled children's services, 59, 60, 61, 63, 64, 100, 101, 102, 103, 104, 105, 106, 107
determinations of incapacity 70, 71, 72, 73
differentiations between hospital and clinic practice, 76, 77
influence on medical social practice, 61, 62
maternal and child health services, 93, 94, 95
medical social worker's role in, 58, 59, 60, 61, 64, 65
need for, 53, 55, 56, 57, 64, 65
public assistance, 70, 71, 72, 73, 74, 76, 79, 80, 81, 82, 83, 84, 85, 86, 87, 88, 89
public health departments, 74, 75, 76, 90, 91, 92, 151–70
rehabilitation, 100, 101, 102, 103, 104, 105, 106
research, 77, 78
social needs of patients, 62, 63, 64, 92, 93, 94, 111, 112, 113
tuberculosis-control programs, 151–70

Research, social service department participation in, 12

Social action, role of medical social worker in, 117, 118
Social medicine, 5, 7, 8, 10, 133, 134

Tuberculosis control, medical social work in; see Public medical care

Index of Authors